AS USED ON THE FAMOUS NELSON MANDELA

MARK THOMAS

EBURY
PRESS

First published in Great Britain in 2006

7 9 10 8 6

Text © Mark Thomas 2006

Ebury Press, an imprint of Ebury Publishing.
Random House, 20 Vauxhall Bridge Road, London SW1V 2SA

Random House Australia (Pty) Limited
20 Alfred Street, Milsons Point, Sydney, New South Wales 2061, Australia

Random House New Zealand Limited
18 Poland Road, Glenfield, Auckland 10, New Zealand

Random House (Pty) Limited
Isle of Houghton, Corner of Boundary Road and Carse O'Gowrie,
Houghton, 2198, South Africa

Random House Publishers India Private Limited
301 World Trade Tower, Hotel Intercontinental Grand Complex,
Barakhamba Lane, New Delhi 110 001, India

The Random House Group Limited Reg. No. 954009

www.randomhouse.co.uk

A CIP catalogue record for this book is available from the British Library.

Cover design by Two Associates
Typeset by seagulls.net

Every effort has been made to trace and contact the copyright holders
of photographs featured in the book. If notified, the publisher will
rectify any errors or omissions in subsequent editions.

ISBN 9780091909215 (after Jan 2007)
ISBN 009190921X

Papers used by Ebury Press are natural, recyclable products
made from wood grown in sustainable forests.

Printed and bound in Great Britain by Mackays of Chatham Plc

Picture credits: p9, 181, 295 © Travis Beard; p19 © Chris Martin;
p55 © *The Throne of Weapons* is part of the British Museum's collection, and was created
at a Christian Aid-supported weapons amnesty project in Mozambique. Artist: Kester;
p77 © Duncan Barnes; p199 © Getty Images; p 223 © Sierra Leone Action Network
on Small Arms; p233, 238, 240 used courtesy of Channel 4/Vera Productions;
p315 © Robin Ballantyne, Omega Research Foundation; all other pictures © Mark Thomas

CONTENTS

A NOTE TO THE SKIM READER

You need to read the introduction ... sorry, I know intros are for students and book clubs, but you do need to do it. I know skim readers don't do intros, but a bit of concentration and effort now will pay dividends later. If it helps, console yourself with the fact that Victoria Beckham wouldn't even have got this far.

There is one other moment in the book when the skim reader will be tested to the limit. For one paragraph you will need to focus all your powers of attention and learning. To alert you to this paragraph, I have given it a special title: 'Ozzy's cocaine breastmilk'. I thought it might make it easier.

INTRODUCTION
HOW TO BE AN ARMS DEALER

To be an arms dealer, you need three basic things:

1. A contact list of people who want guns.
2. An ability to handle paperwork in a thorough manner.
3. The deductive logic of a good Cluedo player.

Admittedly, it helps if you have no belief in an afterlife or a God that wishes us to account for our actions. It seems you might also need one or more of the following, if you are a large arms company:

4. A series of 'commission agents' through which to pay bribes.
5. A vault in Switzerland to store a truckload of sensitive documents just beyond the legal reach of the UK.
6. Access to the British Prime Minister.

The contact list
The easiest way to make contact with people who want guns is to read Amnesty International's annual human rights report, see who comes out worse and then nip round to their embassy. These places often have picket lines of protestors outside, but you can always nip past the chants and candlelit vigils by saying you are going to hand in a letter of protest. Once in the front door, head for the Defence Attaché's office; they will probably have a list of the guns they want written out and waiting. Once you've got that, you can start to sort out the second chore, paperwork.

The paperwork

Quite a few export/import, customs and shipping forms do need to be done, but essentially there are only two really important documents you need to do an arms deal: a note from the person the guns are going to, and approval from the country the guns are going from.

The first of these is called an End User Certificate (EUC). This is the Willy Wonka Golden Ticket of the arms world. Without this bit of paper, officially you cannot buy and export a single thing that goes pop, bang or explodes with the intent of curtailing human life and movement. The EUC can be issued by a government, a government's armed forces or police and security forces. It gives the arms dealer permission to act on their behalf in the purchase of specified weapons, and comprises an undertaking that the arms will not be rerouted to another destination. This crucial document generally requires fewer bits of paper than you need to make a competent marijuana joint. You can get away with just one piece of paper for this.

The second important bit of paper is government approval; so if your guns are coming from the UK you will need a UK government licence. Britain will license most things: TVs, dogs, bingo halls, cars, bars. So it seems consistent and predictably British that the sale of devices that can decimate a small town, should be handled with a form and an official stamp. Britain has always seemed to function in this way. Looking back, I am shocked that William the Conqueror got those crossbows into the country without the proper import documentation. I'd put money on that he didn't declare them as weapons and snuck them through as agricultural parts.

The Export Control Organisation, working out of the Department of Trade and Industry, provides the licence, though if the deal is seen as problematic it can be referred to the Ministry of Defence, the Foreign and Commonwealth Office and the Department for International Development, all of whom will get a say in the matter. In practical terms, the final arbiter is the Prime Minister.*

Cluedo

If you want to kill Professor Plum in the library, you have to get the lead piping into the library. Either that or tell the CIA he is working for al Qaeda, sit back and watch as a pilotless drone plane bombs the entire game, taking out the library, local hospital and school and killing the Reverend Green, Colonel Mustard and a host of innocent civilians into the bargain.

Thus it is with the arms trade: a dealer must be able to move the weapons to where they are wanted. However, not all countries have the same rules, and it is a lot easier to export from some places than it is from others. For example, both India and the UK do not allow arms exports to embargoed destinations – countries with arms sanctions placed on them. But that does not mean the same thing. India recognises the United Nations (UN) arms embargoes and sanctions, while the UK recognises the UN, the European Union (EU) and the Organization for Security and Co-operation in Europe (OSCE) embargoes. So India can deal arms to Burma (which has an EU embargo), but Britain cannot.

On top of this, each country has its own personal list of places not to sell arms to: policy embargoes. India is unlikely to be selling much military equipment to countries like … oh, Pakistan, for instance. Britain, on the other hand, has traded with Pakistan. Or take Argentina as another quick-draw case: Britain will not sell Argentina anything that threatens the security of UK Overseas Territories in the South Atlantic (Falklands/Malvinas). Would

---

* In 2003 the UK exported $4,700 million worth of arms compared to the USA's $13,648 million. In 2004 the UK had slipped to fourth place in the list of arms exporters, behind the USA, Russia and France. Even so, the UK still managed to export $1,900 million.

India be upset if its companies won arms contracts to supply a version of the Exocet missile to Argentina? I doubt it.

As if there weren't enough loopholes already for the arms dealer to climb through, there is the fact that, for example, although Britain has an embargo on China, it is different from its embargo on Zimbabwe. Everything on the UK Military List is banned from going to Zimbabwe, but not all of it is banned from going to China. So even though there is an embargo on China, UK arms dealers can still export certain items of military equipment. For example, Rolls-Royce provide the engines for the Chinese JGH 7 combat aircraft, licensed and legally, despite the embargo.*

And there is still more complexity to come. Different countries regard different 'goods' as 'military goods'. Britain regards Bedford army trucks as military vehicles, and therefore military equipment. An Indian company, on the other hand, could simply paint the truck white and the vehicle would no longer be classified as a military truck. So India would not require a licence to sell the truck, and the UK would.

Once you apply these differences across the whole world, you can see that there really is plenty of room for arms dealers to work in. All the clever dealer has to do is work this out: where does my company need to operate from in order to buy guns from a country that will allow me to sell the guns to the people I want to sell them to? It is a matter of deduction. Prof Plum. Library. Lead piping.

Second note to skim readers: nearly there
Folk tend to think that the arms trade is just guns, the bits that go bang. However, only approximately 10 per cent of an army's equipment is weapons. The rest of the equipment contributes to the support and logistics of keeping an army in prime killing

---

* Hansard Quadripartite Select Committee, 25 April 2006.

order. What constitutes military equipment is itemised on the government's UK Military List 2004 and ranges from a Land-Rover jeep with tow hooks to navigational equipment, from certain types of handcuff to certain types of aircraft fuel, from parachutes to tin helmets, from plastic tubes with a military bent to a 24-volt battery. Not to mention the components of trucks, tanks, planes, missiles, radar, etc. So although some bits of military equipment might not look too bad at first sight, it is their usefulness in a full military context that is important. A seemingly mundane item can be a key component of a massacre.

In 2005 I met a Sudanese exile who had witnessed part of the genocide in Darfur, Sudan. On a summer afternoon we sat outside while he recounted the story. 'We heard lorries, vehicles coming in, people shouting, shooting indiscriminately. Some of the vehicles had machine guns mounted on, also shooting indiscriminately. Others had people on. On this spot, forty-nine killed.' He saw three villages attacked and described how the Sudanese government had given the Janjaweed military trucks to help them move around the region. 'It was actually an essential role for these trucks. They transported people from where they were to these villages ... They carry personnel, they carry ammunition ... they mount the machine guns on them.'

In his hand was an ID card, belonging to someone in the Sudanese army, dropped in the attacks, evidence of government collusion with the Janjaweed. 'The vehicles are a source of power. The villages are helpless. They are left to the Janjaweed. These vehicles are a source of power and flexibility. They enable the Janjaweed to attack anywhere in Darfur.' The trucks he saw were Bedfords – these are UK made, just like the green army lorries you might see going along the M4.

One final point

I would like to end this introduction on a personal note. My mother used to say that you shouldn't dish out what you can't handle when it comes back to you. My father used to tell me to 'take the tree from thine own eye first'. Friends tell me I should judge myself by the same rules I judge others. Considering that I am going to denounce the New Labour Cabinet as pimps for the arms companies, I think it only fair to heed this advice.

So, I'm Mark, I'm a fat dad with a failing mouthwash regime. I'm quicker to judge than to forgive, I'm not as smart or tough as I think I am. I'm adenoidal, I snore and I'm prone to sweat rashes in the summer. I'm self-obsessed to the point of making lists of my failings in public. My ability to make friends is matched only by my inability to keep them. I'm paradoxically work-obsessed and lazy. I am insecure, demanding, have an addictive personality, am inconsistent and I talk up a better person than I actually am. I have emotional Attention Deficit Disorder. Politically I am as strident as I am confused, not to mention being ideologically bipolar. I am also so opinionated that if you chop off my head, I will continue criticising you for two minutes despite being clinically dead.

Right, that's done and out of the way. Now the next 300 or so pages is my turn ...

PART ONE
AT THE HEART

1

AN ANSWER
WAITING TO HAPPEN

CHAPTER ONE

A chapter in which the tender-hearted reader is entreated to give a fuck. This chapter could be called 'Why you should care about the arms trade' – but it would sound a bit like a self-help book.

JEREMY, MICK AND MARK

It was self-loathing (on my part) and flattery (dished out by the producers) that led to me agreeing to appear on the Jeremy Vine Radio 2 programme. The show is essentially Middle England on air: a dash of music splashed into some 'topical debate', chat and a listener phone-in, or as I like to call it, the 'tut-athon'. I was led into the studio and sat in front of one of those BBC microphones that has a foam cover in a violent primary colour (it's like being asked to speak into a primate's angry penis). Behind the anglepoise mic is Jeremy Vine, a pleasant enough man.

'Have you been listening in on the show so far?' he asks during a record break.

'Yes.'

'Music's been a bit middle-of-the-road today. Think I'll play some Simply Red to liven it up.'

Which he duly does, and they duly don't. Leaving me with the notion that lunchtime Radio 2 is where Catholics go if they haven't been good enough to get into heaven.

But let's not rock the boat over the music. This is, after all, Jeremy Vine, the man the BBC have put into the 'clever but not too posh' category of broadcasting. Vine's tone on air is that of an elder brother gently boasting of his A-level results. I remind myself why I'm here. The aim is to be polite and put forward some arguments about the arms trade. Let's not get distracted by Mick Hucknall – this is lunchtime Radio 2, they are hardly likely to play 'Too Drunk To Fuck' by the Dead Kennedys. Not without a really messy divorce and a crack habit in the vicinity of the mixing desk.

The music fades; a light in the studio tells us we are on air. 'And with us in the studio is Mark Thomas, on the subject of the arms trade.'

That's my cue to start a gentle discourse on how we need to control the defence industry. Remember, be polite, Mark, and don't say 'fuck' unless Jeremy Vine says it first, and even then don't. I get a few minutes to speak about the issues, I might have even quipped that we should abolish the whole industry, Jeremy lobs in a couple of questions and we get ready to take some calls.

'What right,' shouts a middle-aged man with a London accent down a mobile, 'has he got to tell a British company what they can or can't do? What gives him the right? The right to boss a British company around? Who does he think he is?'

It's more Cockney primal scream than a question. A kind of Gestalt therapy for compulsive shellfish-eaters. Frankly, I suspect that no matter what I say, the caller will fume in agitation throughout the entirety of the next Simply Red song, which of course is the only way to listen to them.

But I have a stab at answering his question. 'In a democracy we have every right to tell companies what to do. That is what a democracy is – our voice, not the companies'. We have health and safety laws which force companies to comply with regulations, we don't leave it up to them to decide.'

At that point Jeremy jumps in and chats to the caller, and suddenly it's all over and I am led out of the studio past security, and I end up wandering down Regent Street thinking: What was the point of all of that? Why was I so polite to that man? Why do I go on these programmes? Some researcher phones up and says, 'It'll be a good opportunity to put your argument to the public.' And I believe them. I go into town and drink shite coffee in a green room with someone like the former Tory Party spin-doctor Amanda Platell, who is there to talk to someone like Steve Wright about something like the BAFTAS and why Iran should be bombed. If ever there was a licence to self-harm, this was it. I smile, nod, scald my lips on coffee and get shoved into the studio to end up with two minutes on air sandwiched between a Simply Red single and the political equivalent of Chas and Dave.

What I should have done is refuse to leave the studio until I had answered the question fully. If necessary, I should have taken the studio. I should have grabbed one of the obscenely coloured microphones, knocked Jeremy Vine unconscious with it, barricaded myself in, flipped the mics onto full broadcast and said: 'What gives me the right to boss an arms company around? I'll tell you what gives me the right, you Cockney Tory twat. There are six hundred and forty million guns out there.* Now I'll grant you that this is not a 100 per cent accurate figure, it is an approximation. So you can twist this figure any way you like. You can revise the number, question the empirical basis of it. You can say the figure is biased and cut it in half. You can even let an Enron accountant get to work on it, but the end result is always going to be bad. Six hundred and forty MILLION guns … though the technical term here is "small arms", which covers everything from a pistol to a machine gun and a grenade launcher. We have sold more guns than Elvis sold singles. How many of those guns fall into what the arms dealers call "the wrong hands"? One thousand? Thirty thousand? Not even close. There are over thirty thousand people killed by guns in America

* Figure is from Control Arms, a joint campaign by Oxfam, Amnesty International and the International Network on Small Arms (IANSA).

each year. OK, Abu Hamza might regard that figure as too low and that thought might even get some cynical reaction from the revolutionary paper-sellers. In fact, on a bad day, I might even concede that if they weren't so fat they might make for a smaller target, but each life in that statistic was a unique one, and they represent just a small fraction of the global figure. Across the world half a million people are killed with guns each year. That works out at almost one person every minute. Now there are two ways of looking at half a million dead people. You either say, "We have to stop this madness," or you say, "Fuck me, that is some business for the gun companies. Buy shares!" ... Incidentally, none of that half a million includes the hundreds of thousands of women and children raped at gunpoint in war zones, whose best hope is not to contract HIV and die. Nor does it include the souls caught in war unable to earn a living or grow crops, who starve and die. Or head to a refugee camp, and on the way they die. Or head to a refugee camp and get there, and then they die. And the lucky ones will live for long enough to queue for a food-aid truck, and if they are really lucky they will end up in the background of a picture in a Sunday colour supplement. If by some magic streak they are luckier still and the starving kid in the foreground is photogenic enough, pressure might be put on governments to keep the food trucks rolling in. Now, when your best chances of survival are reduced to 200 pixels of your face on the page opposite a fucking Audi advert, then, my friend, and only then, can you question what right I have to tell arms company what to do.

'OK, Sherlock, let's do some more deducing. That half a million killed each year, with pistols, rifles, grenades and the other bits collectively called "arms", come from all over the world. Child soldiers abducted in northern Uganda, trade union-ists butchered by paramilitaries in Colombia. There are fleeing civilians caught in the Congo, democracy protestors killed in West Papua, burnt villages and piles of corpses in Darfur. There are Kurds, Tibetans, Chechens, Palestinians, Somalis, Liberians, Nepalese, Uzbeks, Americans, Iraqis who help contribute to that half a million a year, but we are stupid— WHOA! What the—! ... Sorry there, BBC security's banging on the door here and to be truthful they caught me by surprise. I know that all of you listening will be mightily relieved that they can't get in and that the door is holding firm here ... and while I am addressing the situation in the studio, I'd better move Jeremy into the recovery position, so hold on for a moment ... there's dribble on his Paul Smith jacket but he's OK ...

'There we go ... The door is still holding so let's continue. Where were we? Oh yes. Let me quickly tell you how stupid we are. We are dumber than a Mormon at a wife-swapping party. We think the arms trade is something that happens "over there". The places where kids have flies hanging round their eyelids, out in Bob Geldof Land. So tell me – what exactly are those things that go bang outside nightclubs in our cities? If you live in London, Manchester or Nottingham, you probably live no more than 800 metres from the site of a gun crime. Nearest one to me is 500 metres. I pass it every time I take the children swimming. And where do you think the guns come from? They come from the well-established, law-abiding and respected companies that you so nobly defend. Companies whose reception walls are decorated with framed awards: Employer of the Year, Excellence in Health and Safety, Disability Awareness certificates; maybe they even have their mission statement up there for everyone to see. They are companies quoted on the stock exchange that support charities and sponsor the arts, companies with a gaggle of sirs and a recently retired politician on the board. Now you might think this hyperbole, so here's an example. How does a state-of-the-art sub-machine gun that is manufactured by only one company – who sell only to legitimate governments – and which is intended only for special security services, end up in the hands of a Dutch coke dealer? That is what happened in 1998 with FN Herstal from Belgium.* They make the P90 machine gun, useful in hostage situations, top of the range and described to me by one of the company reps as 'a Gucci item' – the designer label of the sub-machine gun world. They sell it to Jordan, where the then Crown Prince Abdullah flogs them on to a Swiss company called Brügger and Thomet, who let a Dutch gunsmith get hold of them, and in September 1999 a cocaine dealer is found to be holding four of these guns, the most advanced weapon of its kind.

'Listen up, caller. You phoned into this nice middle-of-the-road radio station, it's lunchtime, it's Radio 2, you've got a working-class London accent and you are upset that I'm trying to boss arms companies around. So from these facts I guess that you are reasonably conservative in your outlook and probably wouldn't like drug dealers charging around the place with machine guns. It is just a guess and I could be wrong. You could be a gangland drug baron who's concerned about the future of his industry. I don't know.

'I do know that this stuff has a horribly long shelf-life. Small arms – pistols, AK47s, carbines and munitions are the UHT of the weapons world ... I am going to have to be quick now because Jeremy is making some noises and sounds like he might be gaining consciousness and I don't want to have to hit him again with the dick mic. And to be honest I think the police have been called in because I can hear sirens and stern mumbles on the other side of the studio door ... Remember al Qaeda? Big at the start of the decade ... tried to bring down that El Al plane at Mombassa airport in Kenya in 2002 with ground-to-air missiles? Of course you do. Remember the amateur video footage taken on board, a whole planeload of people praying that they would

---

* UNIDIR report on Small Arms and Light Weapons Transfers, presented at Conference on Strengthening European Action on Non-Proliferation and Disarmament – How Can Community Instruments Contribute? 7 and 8 December 2005 – Brussels. Organised by UNIDIR, ISIS-Europe, and SIPRI.

not be blown out of the sky? Well, the missile launcher was a Soviet SA-7 made in 1978; the attack took place in November 2002. The missile launcher was twenty-four years old. The only reason the missile missed its target was that the person operating it made a mistake. Operator error – that is the only reason there were not hundreds of Jewish families lying dead on the tarmac. So, my friend, when you say it has nothing to do with us, let me tell you this stuff comes back and bites us in the arse every time.

'And we are so stupid we can't even be selfish properly. Who do you think pays for all of this? Some mad-dog dictator in central Africa with more gold braid than common sense and a couple of human heads in the palace fridge? Yeah, sure he buys the guns, but where does he get the loans from? The UK government underwrites millions in arms sales a year. So we pay for it. *We* do. Every time the repayments go tits up on a gun deal, we pay for it. Our tax money props up the arms trade and we still bleat, "It's good for the economy. It's good for the economy." Like you did just now. "What right has he got to tell a company what to do?" Listen properly here because I reckon, caller, I reckon from your accent and attitude and the fact that you have phoned in here, I reckon there is a fair chance you are or were self-employed. And I reckon that you reckon that a feller should be able to earn a crust without some do-gooder champing on his nadgers all the time. And if I am right, I want to ask you why you defend an industry that is subsidised by our money by just under £900 million a year? If it was anyone else sponging that kind of money, the *Sun* would have published their address and you'd be round there with a can of lead-free and box of Swan Vesta before you could say, "Sorry we thought he was a paedo."

'We pay for the arms companies to influence our government, bribe other governments and arm the world. And then we phone up radio stations and defend the arms companies for being good for the economy and creating jobs. We paid for the jobs. We bought our own jobs. How Mafia is that! And do you know what? When it comes to the arms trade, Britain is one of the better regulated countries on the planet – think how fucked the others have to be! And it doesn't have to be this way. An ethical foreign policy – just think what could have happened if it had been real. If New Labour had really meant it when they said it was important not just to be whiter than white but to be seen as being whiter than white. Do you know what New Labour are? They are the aspartame of politics: sugar-free but the same old shit in every other respect ... Bugger ... my wife is at the window with a megaphone and the children ... Shit shit shit ... apparently I have to think of my future before it is too late ... So I have to go now before they lob the tear gas in ... oh, before I do go, I have one further thing to say to you. This is the Jeremy Vine show, and this is "Something Got Me Started".'

That is what I wish I had said on Radio 2.

ARMS STATS

- ❏ 640 million small arms are at large in the world.
- ❏ 8 million new small arms are added each year.
- ❏ 1 person is killed every minute with small arms, that's half a million people a year. Three-quarters of those deaths are civilians, mainly women and children.
- ❏ 1,135 companies in 98 countries manufacture small arms, ammunition and components; the number has doubled in the last 40 years.
- ❏ There are estimated to be 300,000 child soldiers involved in conflicts.
- ❏ 60 per cent of small arms end up in the hands of criminal gangs, rebel groups and civilians.
- ❏ The UK is the 2nd biggest arms dealer in the world.

Source: Control Arms, BBC, Oxfam and Global Village websites

2

WE ARE THE NEW MASTERS NOW! NEW LABOUR 1997

CHAPTER TWO

A chapter in which New Labour offer hope of change, announce an ethical dimension at the heart of British foreign policy, and then get on with the job of arming mad-dog regimes. The author visits his first arms fair, talks to torturers, innocently expects the truth to set us all free and starts to see the influence BAE Systems has upon our democracy.

'WE ARE THE NEW MASTERS NOW.'

LORD SHAWCROSS, THE LABOUR GOVERNMENT'S ATTORNEY GENERAL*

The 3 May 1997, two days after New Labour was swept to power, and I was performing a stand-up show in a circus tent pitched in a Brighton park. Yep, life was good. I had started on the pub comedy-circuit in London in 1985, and had finally clawed my way up to a circus tent in Brighton. If my career strategy went to plan, I'd end up doing beer adverts and corporate gigs within the next ten years, then record a pilot show for a cable network, get some TV script-editing work with younger, better comics, make regular appearances as a guest on 'list and reality shows' – *Top One Hundred TV Shows about TV*, *Foreigners Make the Funniest Adverts!*, *Not Quite Grumpy Enough Old Men*, *John*

---

* 'We are the new masters now' was condensed by the press from the original Shawcross quote: 'We are the masters at the moment, and not only at the moment but for a very long time to come.'

Craven Presents Celebrity Cage Fight and *I'm a Wanker – Shoot Me!* By the time I start picking up live work on the sheltered-accommodation gig circuit I should be claiming my free bus pass. Call me cynical, but everyone needs a dream.

On that warm evening in Brighton, two days after New Labour's landslide, my opening line was: 'I hope you'll forgive a bit of self-indulgence, but I have waited eighteen years to say this. That Labour government – what a bunch of fucking bastards.' Needless to say the show was a triumph and I was carried around the tent on the audience's shoulders as they implored, 'Lead us, Mark. Lead us! You have opened our eyes with your wise wit and mocking charm! Hail, o truthsayer!' Fortunately I had to take the kids to swimming lessons and collect the cat from the vet the next day, otherwise I would probably still be King of Brighton.

The morning of 2 May had seen New Labour destroy the Conservative Party. The TV gushed epoch-defining pictures: the victor Blair striding through the crowds as dawn broke on the south bank of the Thames. Hours later the Blairs were apparently forced to abandon their official car and walk into Downing Street. Flags waved, people roared in exhilaration, the Blairs briefly grasped the outstretched hands of New Labour party workers posing as members of the general public in the throes of spontaneous delight, hailing the new champion. New Champion. New Britain. New Labour. It was as if every news team with a camera had decided to become Blair's personal Leni Riefenstahl, filming *Things Can Only Get Better – Triumph of the Will version*.

The spring morning seemed part of the iconography, a new dawn, a rebirth. The sun shone down from a clear blue sky, people chatted and joked with each other on the way to work. On that day people celebrated deliverance. More than anything else they had been delivered from the fate of another Tory government. A noticeable portion of the electorate didn't care so much that New Labour had won, what was important was making the Tories lose.

As long as the Conservatives suffered dire humiliation and disgrace of biblical proportions, they were happy. That was the gang I was in. Our gang would have cheered and probably prayed had we heard that Henley-on-Thames had been destroyed in a flood, killing all but for two members of every other political party, who had been safely stored on board an ark.

Like most people who have grown up on the left of British politics, I am stupidly optimistic, not about politicians but about people. Three people in an office in Lewisham refuse to change the photocopier ink and I think it is the beginning of a general strike. But the Tories' defeat saw a small and new hope enter my heart. A specific hope, a hope in the very people I despise – politicians – and I was not entirely comfortable with the experience. Nonetheless, hope appeared. I woke up and it was there, like a wart or thrush. Perhaps I had picked up second-hand optimism in elected representatives after coming into close contact with happy people that spring day and was suffering from passive trust. Or perhaps my hatred of the Tories diminished slightly in their defeat and into the vacuum rushed this small hope. It was based on a simple notion that had taken root in me: no matter what New Labour did, they couldn't possibly be as shite as the last lot. I didn't have many expectations of New Labour but I figured they were bound to get one or two things right, if only by accident.

In the final stages of its sick and infirm stewardship, the Conservative Party had been mired in sleaze: they had sex scandals (from Archer through to Stephen Milligan and his satsuma-and-stockings kinky stroke of death); they had arms scandals (from the Arms to Iraq and the Scott inquiry through to Jonathan Aitken's Ritz rendezvous with an arms dealer, which ended in a jail sentence); they had cash scandals (from cash-for-questions through to Mr Mohamed al-Fayed). Although the Tories appeared to be the pillars of the Establishment, church-going, *Times*-reading wearers of MCC ties, they were into cash, ho's an' guns! They were gangster rappers with OBEs. At one stage it was even rumoured that Tupac Shakur had been killed by Lord William Whitelaw, deputy leader of the Conservative Party, as a result of an ongoing beef about bitches, but I think I just made that up.

Elated at having finally defeated the Tories, Old Labour embraced Blair as their saviour. Not even the most ardent New Labour zealot actually expected Blair to be radical, but no one quite expected what was to follow. From Bernie Ecclestone's Formula One Fags to PFI schemes, the invasion and occupation of Iraq, and 'choice' in education, the feeling of betrayal would spread. For many in Old Labour the day Blair dies is the day that Judas will be found muttering in the depths of hell, 'I bet he comes and sits next to me.'

Old Labour supported Blair because he was a winner and for its troubles Old Labour was routinely abused. If New and Old Labour's relationship was domestic, the counsellors would have been called to the room with the two-way mirrors and anatomically correct dolls a long time ago.

Like any political party, the various tribal and ideological groupings within Labour celebrated the ascendancy of their allies and leaders, cherishing every single one of their own that gained a toehold on power. For the Left, the presence of people like Clare Short and Robin Cook in the Cabinet represented pragmatic compromise.

In the final spasms of the Tory government, Robin Cook had become known as New Labour's most ardent critic of the arms trade (although in fairness it was the likes of Ann Clwyd who did the donkey work on Britain's involvement with the torture trade and the issue of the gassing of Iraqi Kurds in Halabja). It was Cook who spearheaded Labour's media-saturated assault on the publication of the *Scott Report* on the Arms to Iraq scandal that engulfed the Conservative government. The Tories were old masters at rigging events and the Scott inquiry was no exception. Those accused of potential wrongdoing, namely William

Waldegrave, Lord Trefgarne and Alan Clark, were all given copies of the *Report* before publication. This gave them time to study it and prepare their defence. The Labour opposition led by Cook were allowed to see the *Report* only on the day of the Arms to Iraq debate in the Commons. The *Scott Report* is five volumes long. Cook was not allowed an individual copy; he had to visit a room specially designated for its viewing. He had only three hours to read and analyse the contents before heading into the chamber to take the Tory government to task over it. He wasn't even allowed to take a mobile phone into the room in case he sought outside help. Cook wrote later in his diaries, *The Point of Departure*, that after handing in his mobile phone to the Department of Trade and Industry, 'I discovered that they had laid out the *Scott Report* in a basement which had no reception for mobiles, just in case I smuggled one in.'

The traditional formula for a report such as Scott's is for the government to make a pronouncement on it and then the opposition to question it. Cook's lengthy but precise response listed the Tory government's arming of Saddam Hussein, its deception of the public and Parliament, its intimidation of the civil service and its willingness to see men go to jail rather than admit the truth. 'The *Report*,' Cook said, 'goes beyond the career of individual ministers or the reputation of some officials. It reveals the price that Britain pays for a culture of secrecy in government. The *Report* documents how ministers changed the guidelines [re arms to Iraq], but were more worried that Members of Parliament and the public might find out than they were about what Saddam Hussein might do with the weapons.' For some it was perhaps his finest hour, and it was a performance that certainly went down in the annals of Labour history.

We are the schoolmaster's son
In 1997 it was Cook who epitomised the spirit of change, photographed in the majestic Foreign and Commonwealth

Office, draped across a chair of such colonial splendour that it was easy to believe people had pleaded for their lives before it. Cook mused before the TV cameras that he had not done too badly for a science teacher's son. And indeed he hadn't. Though he did still manage to look like a science teacher's son, Cook was an ambitious MP. He had to be. He came from the Scottish Labour Party. He didn't have an option. At the coalface of Scottish Labour politics, MPs were either ambitious or resigned themselves to spitting venom from the deathbeds of their careers. Fortunately for Cook, he was also regarded as one of the most able minds in the Party.

On 12 May 1997, ten days into the New Labour government, Cook made his ethical foreign policy speech that came to define his time as Foreign Secretary, though not quite in the way he had intended. 'I am launching a New Mission Statement for the Foreign and Commonwealth Office,' he said, with a capitalised N on the word 'New', as was the fashion in those times. 'Our foreign policy must have an ethical dimension and must support the demands of other peoples for the democratic rights on which we insist for ourselves. The Labour government will put human rights at the heart of our foreign policy.' The press promptly abbreviated his speech to the 'ethical foreign policy', a phrase Cook insisted he never used. Frankly, he should have been grateful that the *Daily Mail* didn't splash the headline 'The Do-Gooders Charter! Now we have to be nice to foreigners – Official!' over their front page.

Launching an ethical foreign policy presupposes that the earlier policy was not ethical. And very broadly speaking, it wasn't. Historically, Britain traded slaves and had an empire, neither of which enterprise is known to have qualified for a Fairtrade logo. To the best of my knowledge not even the most cap-doffing historian has dared to describe the British Empire as an 'ethical empire', though there is bound to be one out there somewhere, just as there is bound to be a Conservative Party leader who doesn't look like a smug twat, if only we could be bothered to look.

What did it matter if the odd civil servant gave sniffy off-the-record press briefings rubbishing this 'ethical nonsense'? This merely made Cook look like more of a reformer than he turned out to be. The press plucked out the 'ethical dimension' but by and large managed to ignore the remainder of Cook's speech. A speech that was stunning in its unoriginality. Cook's New Mission Statement really didn't veer from the FCO's usual policy. 'The first goal of foreign policy is security for nations. Our security will remain based on the North Atlantic Alliance.' So not exactly a tilt to old Mother Russia in that statement. 'The prosperity of Britain is the next goal of our foreign policy. More people than ever before in Britain's long history as a trading nation depend on our exports to other countries or on investment from them into our own country.' So the first two priorities of Cook's new regime were security (with NATO and America) and trade, the sturdy fare of traditional foreign policy. The world is littered with foreign folk whom Britain has bombed, shot and captured, all in the cause of commerce and the flag. The main business of British foreign policy has always been business.

However, within Cook's famous speech there were promises of things to come. (There it is again! Hope! Hope in a politician.) He stressed the 'clear national interest in preventing proliferation [of arms] and promoting international control of conventional weapons. The Labour government will give a new momentum to arms control and disarmament.' This was new. It is nigh on impossible to envisage a Conservative Foreign Secretary making mission statements about controlling the arms trade, not without someone pointing a loaded gun to their head and kidnapping their family. As for imagining a Lib Dem Foreign Secretary and what they might ... oh frankly, it's a waste of time even attempting to finish this sentence.

Tess Kingham was one of the new intake of Labour MPs in 1997. Before walking through the stone arches of Parliament, she had worked for War On Want and Oxfam, sweating her way through the conflict zones in El Salvador and Nicaragua. Her job was tracking down survivors of atrocities and getting testimony out of them. She is not a person given to proselytising on the innate goodness of humankind. But like many of her colleagues, she saw Robin Cook as a real chance for change. Shortly after Cook's speech on ethics and foreign policy, Kingham told me she was invited to Cook's office, 'for drinks, about twenty of us … just to say this is the start of a new attitude to the world. You know, this is the start of some justice in the world. He gave a really inspiring little speech. It was great and he was just so upbeat and I actually think that he genuinely, genuinely believed at that point that [the policy] was a real force for good and he was doing something great. We toasted the ethical foreign policy. I phoned Mark [her husband] to say it was worth it, all the New Labour crap. It was worth it.'

Hindsight, dear hindsight, is the preferred viewfinder of quislings and cowards. Whenever a politician uses the phrase 'with the benefit of hindsight …' it is common knowledge that an enormous 'but' is lurking, ready to pounce with the finesse of a crack-addled mugger. Normally it is on these 'buts' that the justification for madness hangs. For Kingham the benefit of hindsight arrived much more quickly than she expected. After the heady days of toasting the new ethical policy with Cook, 'Very rapidly it changed,' she said. 'And it [had] come in right from the top. It wasn't about an ethical foreign policy, [it] was about the DTI and business, and don't you forget it, at the end of the day they call the tunes.' And call them they did.

'HI, WE'RE FROM McKINTOSH MORLEY AND YOU'VE GOT PROBLEMS WE CAN SOLVE!'

Back in the 1990s Channel 4 asked me to do a comedy series for them, and rather than fill it with sketches or take the piss out of gormless celebs, or walk on set to a house band every week, I decided to try to ambush politicians and corporations. Working with a small team I would film MPs like Elizabeth Peacock. Speaking at a Monday Club public meeting, she said she wanted young offenders to be thrashed live on the *National Lottery*. In front of the crowd I argued that if this policy was to deter younger people from crime, then logically it should take place earlier in the TV schedules and that the lashings should be conducted live on *Blue Peter*. She agreed.

On another occasion we invaded Jack Straw's constituency surgery with a band of folk who used cannabis for medical reasons, and ended up with one chap 'sparking up' in front of the then Home Secretary. Straw stormed out of the room and the police stormed in, but the toker had made his point: Straw's intransigent drug law criminalised a medically sick man. Some people liked the show, others didn't. But I just about managed to do what I wanted to do for seven series and at least I didn't end up touting sit-coms about the place, or even worse actually thinking I could act in one.

Like a lot of comics at that time, I was approached by Labour politicians and asked to write gags for their speeches. It was Robin Cook's people who approached me. A request I impolitely declined. Perhaps if I had taken them up on the offer I, too, would have been invited to raise a glass to Cook's brave new ethical world. Instead our encounters were somewhat more adversarial. Our meetings were few and I invariably ended up chasing him with a camera crew in tow, shouting questions at his disappearing head. While making a programme about Burma I met Cook in a car park, where a Buddhist monk offered to perform a ceremony of forgiveness for him. You couldn't call our relationship a close one. Though I did get close to some of the regimes he licensed arms sales to.

While preparing for a new TV series, Chris Martin* (a rakish

---

* Chris now works on some minor TV network and produces the work of some Australian chap called Pilger.

Scouse chap I used to work with) hatched a plan. Together we would apply to exhibit at the 1998 Defendory Arms Fair in Athens. An arms fair, we figured, was just a massive works outing for war criminals, chock-full of bastards, human rights abusers and their salesmen, black-hearted thugs in uniforms and soulless fiends in lounge suits peddling tools of violence – gun pimps and hooligans all. Should one of the bombs on display accidentally explode taking out the whole place, Satan would be rushed off his feet with the sudden intake. All the bastards would be there, mingling at the receptions and schmoozing at the presentations. All we had to do was offer them the one thing they didn't have: respectability. Arms dealers might be conversant in 99 per cent of the dark arts, but not the darkest art of all – public relations. So posing as PR advisors to the defence industry, our plan was to go to the arms fair offering media advice on how to counter allegations of human rights abuse.

Once inside we would run free on-the-spot training sessions. All we had to do was create a convincing impression of a PR company at the fair and persuade the visiting generals to try our free media-training session in which they would be filmed. Chris, armed with a bundle of Amnesty reports, would play the role of interviewer, and I would coach them on the different approaches they might take to the questions. We would include an option for them to tell the truth. They would spill their guts, we would film it, show it on the telly, save the world and get the girl. Simple. All we had to do was smile and lie, and not just little lies either – we had to lie like estate agents.

The fair was held in a massive and slightly run-down warehouse on the Athenian docks, the kind of setting where you expect Helen Mirren to be wandering around picking up tufts of hair with tweezers and putting them into evidence bags. The more professional and prepared arms dealers brought their own carpets to the event, which would emerge from mountains of bubble wrap for exhibition staff to fix in place with the dull thud of staple guns. Our company was called McKintosh Morley – a suitably pompous and nondescript name for a PR company. The McKintosh Morley stall, number 520, was on the first floor and consisted of a front desk and a section of easy-wipe, white plastic partition walls, creating an inner sanctum beyond the gaze of the public and organisers, in which to conduct our mock media-training sessions. The only attention-grabbing part of the stall was our two enormous posters. We were stuck far from the heart of the fair, on a dusty concrete patch by huge wood and iron doors through which sunlight poured into the fair. Despite being about as far away from the hub of the event as was humanly possible, we did have one advantage. The large industrial doors we found ourselves next to were the entrance through which all the official delegations came at the start of their tours. As they moved from the bright light of an Athens day into the darkness of the fair, the very first thing the delegates of military generals and ministers saw were our large white posters with black lettering: ARE YOU READY WHEN AMNESTY INTERNATIONAL COMES KNOCKING ON YOUR DOOR? And WHO'S WINNING THE WAR OF WORDS?

All the delegates came past stall 520, and most gave us a quizzical glance at the very least. A rather disgusted and slightly bewildered Sri Lankan officer spluttered, 'Are you Amnesty International?' as his military delegation walked in.

'No, we're here to help you against them,' replied Chris and I, giving our pitch all the motivated self-employed earnestness we could muster. Dressed in our weddings-and-court-appearance suits, wielding business cards, clutching clipboards and steeped in an aftershave that should have been outlawed under the Geneva Convention, we blended in remarkably well.

'Oh thank goodness for that,' he said. 'I was wondering what on earth Amnesty was doing here.'

'No, no, we're not Amnesty, but we could be, and the question you have to ask is are you ready for them when they come for you?' we said seriously. 'When Amnesty come round and accuse you of human rights violations, how are you going to handle it? Are you going to hope they go away? Because they won't, and they can do your country and your military a lot of harm.'

'Yes, indeed. So what is it you do?'

'We offer media training and advice on how to minimise the negative impact of the human rights industry. We teach crisis management, damage limitation, pre-crisis preparation, and we focus on training the trainers so that when we leave our work continues. We can't solve your problems with Amnesty but we can teach you how you can solve them.'

'I think we will see you tomorrow, maybe you can explain more,' he muttered, wandering away to shake out the shock.

'We can help you win the war of words,' we shout at his disappearing form.

Defendory International was organised by Mrs Dudu Car, a woman whose manner matched her name. She would walk into a room like she was expecting a man in coat-tails to announce her. Chris and I were granted a five-minute audience with Mrs Dudu Car on the day before the fair. We sat in the chairs indicated to us, which were low to the ground and left us holding our knees. Mrs Dudu Car paced around busily, glancing through folders and signing papers. 'We are very interested in you,' she said with a hard-to-place European accent. 'We have never had a PR company here before.' She handed some papers to her assistant, took a new batch and started flicking hurriedly through them. 'We will be very interested in how you get on. PR is absolutely vital.' She stopped and looked at us for the first time, her face wistful for a moment. 'If only you could get some good PR for the Serbs.' The idea hung in the silent air and then our audience was over.

As it happened the Serb delegation popped in to see us at stall 520, muttering that they had been stigmatised by the world. 'We are bloody Serbs. I wish you could help us but I fear we are beyond that,' one of them said sadly, before being led off. All the delegations continued to stream past the McKintosh Morley posters stuck up in our dusty corner. The Defence Minister for Zimbabwe busied by shouting out: 'Ah, you are the propaganda people!' with a huge grin on his face. 'You people cannot teach me anything – every year I get a better liar. Every year I get a better liar. Every year I get a better liar!' A crowd of cronies followed laughing.

The British Minister for the Armed Forces at the time was Doug Henderson. He breezed by and posed for a photo with us, shaking hands and cheerfully declaring: 'I hope you're winning lots of contracts for Britain.'

A major general from Indonesia

One day Chris and I arrive by our huge WHO'S WINNING THE WAR OF WORDS poster to find a shortish man waiting, wearing a nondescript sports jacket and carrying a brown leather man bag (think well-dressed East Asian gay jockey).

'Hi, Mark Thomas, Chris Martin, McKintosh Morley,' we chant in unison, while proffering hands to be shaken.

'I am Major General Widjojo.'

'From?'

'Indonesia,' he says, with a military smile that gives nothing away.

'Let me explain a little bit about ourselves.'

'I have heard about you, I know what you do.'

'Oh, that's good.'

'I am here for the free media training.'

Words come tumbling out of our mouths: 'media awareness programmes', 'deflecting the human rights industry', bucketfuls of words, some of them in the right order. Outwardly I am calm and businesslike, but inwardly I have turned into Hugh Grant and my mind is rushing around shouting, 'Fuck, fuck, fuck, fuck, fuck, fuck.' Indonesia! A major general from Indonesia! Man oh man, Indonesia is the dream nexus of human rights abuse, dictatorships, mass murder and the British arms industry. Half of me wants to run around the arms fair shouting, 'Scrub Seymour Hersh's name off the Pulitzer – we've got an Indonesian general!' I'm so happy I could cry.

Even the CIA describe the 1965 blood bath that took Major General Suharto to power as 'the worst mass murders of the second half of the twentieth century'.* High praise indeed from the CIA, and let's face it if you were going to have a Ruthless Fucker Competition it would be the CIA you called in as judges, them, Saddam Hussein, and possibly Jamie Oliver.

A quick glance at Indonesia's ignoble human rights scoreboard shows that between half a million and a million people were killed in Suharto's rise to power. And now – no effective democracy, mass human rights violations, 200,000 people killed in East Timor by Indonesian forces, 100,000 people killed in West Papua in an attempt to wipe out the independence movement (and that has to be a conservative figure). All of this, and the Indonesian military armed by the UK. You can understand why seeing a representative of this regime fills my heart with joy and anticipation.

Behind our white partition walls three chairs are laid out in our makeshift interview room. Two are on one side of a coffee table that is covered in small plastic toys, models of animals, action figures and cars. The third chair is opposite the other two, with a camera on a tripod standing over it. Major General Widjojo (pronounced 'Wid joe yo') sits on one side of the coffee table, I sit next to him, facing him in my chair, and Chris sits opposite. While the cameraman gets the equipment ready, I talk through how the training session will work.

'Firstly, Chris is going to interview you and ask questions about Indonesia's human rights situation using Amnesty reports. I want you to answer the questions as honestly as you can,

---

* John Pilger in the *New Statesman*, 13 March 2006

remembering to answer firmly. We will then see how you perform and suggest some changes and approaches you might want to take and try those out.'

'Good,' he says, shuffling into a comfortable position on the chair.

'As we go through this, some of the questions will get quite tough, as they would do in a normal interview situation, so to take out the sting or any emotional feelings that are stirred up, we work on a simple reward system. Every time you do well I will give you a toy.' I indicate the pile of farmyard trucks and model soldiers. 'Every time you do badly I will take one away. The objective is to get as many toys as you can.'

'Good.'

'Before we start, let's just do a little relaxation exercise to clear our minds.' I catch Chris looking away. 'Let's lift up our arms to the side,' I say, trying to sound like a relaxation tape.

Major General Widjojo lifts his arms.

'Let's breathe in deeply, wriggle our fingers and *stretch*. Very good. Let's do that one more time. Breathe in and arms up, wriggle your fingers and let's just pretend our arms and shoulders are waves – let the wave roll through your arms and out the other side. And again let the surf roll through you and let your arms become the tides and just sway with the tides.' I look at the major general from Indonesia, who to my surprise is being a wave.

It shouldn't come as a shock. Soldiers are very good at taking orders and acting on instructions. And so it dawns on me that if he trusts us, if he believes we have knowledge he wants to acquire, he might just feel comfortable enough to speak plainly. If so, then Chris's plan, developed on the back of a beer mat, might just work.

One other factor might just help our plan, and it is this: Major General Widjojo might be an army officer in a brutal regime that has invaded, occupied and slaughtered, he might be part of a military that has routinely bludgeoned, beaten and gouged its way into Amnesty reports, but Major General Widjojo probably regards himself as a moderniser. He is open to new ideas and ways of dealing with problems. He could well be looking for a way to improve his country's image with the international community without having to address the human rights issues that cause the image problem. He could be looking for a Third Way.

Major General Widjojo straightens his wiry frame in his chair, listening to my final instructions. 'Remember: keep eye contact, don't grip your knees with your hands, nice and clear answers. Chris is going to interview you and we shall see how you do.'

Chris looks up from the Amnesty files spread over his crossed legs. 'Are you ready?' He receives a nod. 'Then let's begin. Major General Widjojo, has your country tortured before?'

'No.'

Peering over his glasses, Chris enquires: 'Are you aware of the organisation Amnesty International?'

'Yes.' He tilts his head sideways as he answers.

'Are you aware of the reports that Amnesty International have produced concerning repression and torture in your country?'

'Yes.' He sighs with a sadness and resignation that is beautifully patronising to Amnesty. As a bogus media instructor I have to say that the major general has some natural talent in the interview situation. Not yet ready for Paxman, but certainly showing promise.

'Therefore, do you accept that, on the basis of Amnesty International's reports, there is torture in Indonesia?' Chris takes off his glasses and uses them to point at the major general.

'No,' he answers firmly.

'OK, excellent.' I jump in doing my best self-help-group facilitator voice. 'Now that is good – you gave good answers. You get a scuba man.' I slide the toy scuba man to him across the table. He nods and smiles. He knows he has done well, because now he has a scuba man in front of him. As the session progresses, Major General Widjojo accrues a Spiderman, a cow, a tractor and an octopus, though I later take the Spiderman from him for adopting an unfriendly body posture and not following instructions. He didn't show undue concern at the loss but I could tell he was hurting.

Throughout our time at the fair, all of our 'clients' expressed hostility towards Amnesty International and were happy to explain why. Major General Njoroge from Kenya had dropped in to see us on day one, a big man full of swagger and used to getting his own way. He said of Amnesty International: 'They do a good job but sometimes they are biased.'

'In what way are they biased?' asked Chris.

'In the way that perhaps they do not understand the cultural values of the situation or the environment. That seems problematic.'

When asked to explain further he said, 'Wife beating, for example. Some communities believe that a woman likes a little smacking ... to feel that she is wanted.' He warmed to his theme, ending our training session by saying, 'Wife beating is a way of expressing love.' So we were not surprised when Major General Widjojo from Indonesia took up the theme that Amnesty International does not understand 'cultural differences'. It is a common refrain from repressive regimes. As if torture was a tradition and if it was abolished there would be popular uproar in the streets.

Huddled in our plastic-walled interview room, I ask Major General Widjojo: 'You're saying that Amnesty fabricated these reports [of human rights abuse]?'

'Yes,' says an emphatic Major General Widjojo.

'OK. Hundreds of reports?'

'Yes.'

'OK. Now if you want to hold that line, OK, that's fine, but people will challenge it. People will challenge it and say, you can't make all of this up. They can't have fabricated it, look at these pictures –' motioning to a report – 'this man must be lying.'

'Yes,' he says, following the logic in a soldierly way, waiting to hear how he can solve his conundrum.

'So what I want you to do is think for a second: what would it be like if you said yes, on occasion we have.' Taking the role of confessor and counsellor I continue: 'Just think, how does that feel to you? What would happen if you said that? If you admitted that on some occasions, torture has happened?'

'Yes, I can do that,' he replies coolly.

'We're going to deal with the situation where you say: "Yes, torture does occur occasionally." Do you feel that is the truth, first of all?'

'Yes,' says the major general.

Inside the Hugh Grant voice is long dead. I am sitting alongside a man laden with plastic action figures who is admitting to the use of torture in his country. I am a comic. I earn my living telling jokes about politicians. This is new territory for me. How do I react? I do what anyone else in this situation would do. I take him through another quick relaxation-wave exercise.

With all the sincerity of the public relations industry, I coax: 'If that is the truth, I want you to say that, but what I want you to do is explain why it is necessary, in language that everyone can understand. OK?'

Chris restarts the training interview. 'Are you aware of Amnesty International reports?'

'Yes,' says the major general.

'Are you aware that they claim that torture and repression are widespread.'

'It's not widespread. We have to do it sometimes, but it is to protect the community.'

'Let's just clarify: so you do accept that your country does torture people and repress them?'

'We do some tortures.'

'How do you justify that?'

'It is to protect the security of the society. If not they will lose food, they will lose the freedom to move, and they will lose their freedom of expression. They will lose their freedom to educate their children.'

'So what you are saying to us, [Major] General Widjojo, is that you have to torture people so people can have drinking water?'

'Yes, and all the rights they have.'

By the end of the training session Major General Widjojo had a small pile of plastic toys. 'I look forward to your assessment of this morning's work,' he says, while chatting in front of the stall. 'Would you be able to prepare a programme to come to Jakarta for six weeks to teach the military media courses?'

'Of course we can look at that as a possibility.' Fuck. Hugh Grant has just re-emerged. Fuck. Fuckety fuck. Fuck. Fuck. Jakarta. Capital of Indonesia. Training the military for six weeks. Fuck.

Chris snaps into McKintosh Morley speak. 'Of course we can look at that. The most important thing here is to train the trainers, so when we leave you will be able to carry on the work.'

'Yes, exactly. I will think about this. We may be able to do that,' says the major general, toying with the idea. McKintosh Morley has obviously made an impression on him. Then he leans in to us, clutching his man bag conspiratorially, and says: 'I am a very big Manchester United fan.'

'Really?' says Chris, pointing at himself: 'Liverpool.'

'David Beckham, a great player. What do you think of Beckham?'

'Oh he is a great player, no doubt about that. What do you think of his wife, Victoria?' Chris continues with a smile.

'I like the Spice Girls very much. They are a great group. What about Geri, though?'

'Halliwell?'

'I do not think she will be as good without the Spice Girls,' opines the major general, and then he leaves with a departing handshake. 'I will see you later.'

The cameraman appears from behind the partition, with a workman-like smile. 'I've checked and we've got it all on tape.'

Chris is frowning and scuffing his shoes casually, deep in thought. He looks up with contempt all over his face. 'Typical,' he says. 'An Indonesian and he supports Man U. Man U supporters never come from Manchester.'

Talking to the taxman about poetry; talking to the gunman about moles

The hubbub and chatter at the heart of the fair is far louder than in our discreet little corner and the central aisles are lined with arms dealers. One hand casually in a trouser pocket they stand, pushing out their business cards. Shuffling their feet and their cards on a hot afternoon. Handing brochures to visitors, their faces show the tedium of barbarity. They could be selling anything from insurance to a nuclear weapon and they would still be hunched and listless, monotonously swaying from one foot to the other. Heck, you could give them a cure for cancer to sell and they would still shuffle out cards like it was a special offer for a cheeseburger.

For all of that they can still wipe on a smile in seconds at the merest whiff of a deal from some braid-wearing military yahoo. I arrive at an Iranian stall crammed with guns.

'Hi, Mark Thomas, McKintosh Morley.' I offer my hand, soaking up the rays from the newly plastered grin on the man opposite me. 'M16?' I ask, pointing at the machine gun.

'M16,' he confirms with a big bearded twinkle of forced joy.

'How much are they?'

'How many you want?' He shrugs nonchalantly, refusing to become too interested until he can see a deal.

'One.'

'Just one?'

'What I want is something for the pigeons. I've got a lot of problems with pigeons. They go to the top of the house. Would this be good for the pigeons?'

'I don't think so.' He pauses, gently affronted, smile still in place, unsure of what is going on. I beam back a smile that is so false you can see my considerable contempt bursting round the edges. If you want my unfettered opinion of these people, and let's face it there seems little point in reading this far if you don't – arms dealers are scum. No more, no less, plain old no-nonsense scum. And I just fancied fucking with them.

'Would that be a better pigeon gun?' I ask, pointing at something resembling a carbine.

'I think it is better, yes.'

'What's this one here?'

His smile is on a low gas setting but still on. 'This is a mortar.'

'That would be good for the moles. We've got a lot of problems with moles.'

Moles are apparently not a big problem in Iran, so I explain what a mole is and how much damage they can do to a well-kept lawn. And God bless him, he seemed genuinely shocked at the thought of brown hills of dirt appearing out of nowhere in the middle of the night. What reasonable chap wouldn't?

That afternoon I asked about a hundred and one different DIY-related questions. I asked a dealer how many people-carriers on a school run his anti-tank missiles would go through and what to do in the event of that happening. I chatted with a water-cannon seller about mounting one on an ice-cream van for queue-management purposes. I had about as much fun as you can have at an arms fair without taking in some beehives, a stick and a high-powered Supasoaker watergun filled with a sugar solution.

Back in London McKintosh Morley rides again

A couple of months after we arrived back home, the Indonesian Defence Attaché agrees to meet McKintosh Morley at the Indonesian embassy in London. His name is Colonel Halim Nawhe and he is the personification of diplomatic ennui: charming, well-mannered, with an air of boredom that has its own gravitational pull. Were Angelina Jolie to walk into his cramped office, strip naked and trim a rack of pork ribs St Louis-style on his desk he might raise an eyebrow in surprise, but it would only be one eyebrow. He is a cautious round man whose sports jacket long gave up the hope of ever being buttoned. He says little and listens a lot. He nods when coffee is served and gestures with a foppish hand for us to help ourselves.

'We are McKintosh Morley. We specialise in public relations for people and countries that have problems with their image abroad.'

The colonel meets our beaming confidence with a quiet gaze. He nods and occasionally sighs. We plough through our pitch and he stirs his coffee, continuously and pointlessly. The occasional tinkling of the metal spoon on the china accompanies our sales patter. He isn't dissolving his sugar any more – that was done long ago – he seems to be gently digging a tunnel through the bottom of his cup to escape another day. Faced with such a wall of indifference, Chris announces, 'Colonel, we wouldn't waste your time if we hadn't got encouragement from Jakarta.' The stirring stops.

'We have interest from Major General Widjojo.'

'Major General Widjojo!'

'We met him at Defendory—' but Chris's words are lost as the colonel jumps up out of his seat and plucks a framed photo from the shelves. 'Major General Widjojo is my friend. I know him very well.' He holds out the photo, which is a classic 'Look at me and my famous friend' pose. Widjojo stands trim and collected in the picture, and next to him is Colonel Halim

Nawhe, barely able to suppress a celebratory thumbs-up. But the framed photo is odder than a mere trophy shot. Every other person in the picture has been carefully cut out, leaving only Nawhe and Widjojo, and the outline of anonymous humans.

'You know Major General Widjojo?'

'We have sent him our report – you might want to phone him and ask him about us,' I say, feeling a faint waft of power come our way.

'I think what would be really helpful to you,' Chris adds, 'is if you came and saw the type of work that we do. Come and visit the office. Come round to the studio where we do our training – we'll run a free session for you and you can make a report back to Major General Widjojo.'

'I will think about this. Yes. Perhaps this would be a good idea.'

In a cab on the way home Chris gets out his mobile. 'I think he's going to do it,' he says, selecting a number.

'I think he will, too.'

'Do you hire office space?' he enquires crisply of someone at the other end of the line. Chris cups the receiver. 'I'm not quite sure what we should do with him once we get him into a studio, but he is going to come.'

And so he does.

Admit! Lie!

The colonel sits on a high chair on the TV studio floor, surrounded by a bank of cameras. He blinks and peers into the darkness that lies beyond the bright lights of the studio to where the red lights on top of the cameras glow. Round, small and perched on a stool that is too high for him, his toes only just reaching the rungs, he tugs at the side of his sports jacket, look-ing like a military Danny DeVito about to be interviewed on a late-night show. It has been an arduous day for the colonel – a tour of the McKintosh Morley office, hired days before and quickly decorated with files, computers, photos and a few friends pretending to be fellow PR folk. Then the poor colonel is driven to a discreet TV studio in London and after a tour of the facilities he now sits in the electric glare of the studio lights. To his left are a large white board and some marker pens. Sitting opposite him on the other side of the board are Chris and I, ready to take him through his first media training. It has been a while since we took Major General Widjojo through his paces at Defendory. Back then we had no idea what the major general might say, and today with the colonel it is no different. All we can do is try to set up a situation where he feels relaxed enough to talk.

'What we are going to do is take you through a preparation session and then try some practice interviews,' I tell the colonel. 'We set up three columns – ' I point to the white board – 'a middle column, neutral, and on the left an "admit" column. In the third column we have "lie".'

The aim is simple: put up the list of Indonesia's human rights abuses, see which ones the colonel believes should not be admitted to, and then see which ones he can admit to.

'Give me the items, Chris.'

Chris reads out a list of the human rights issues Indonesia has faced recently and I write them into the neutral column.

'OK, Hawk jets,' says Chris. These jets were sold to Indonesia by British Aerospace (now BAE Systems) and were used in East Timor, a country occupied by Indonesia on 7 December 1975. During the occupation, which lasted until the arrival of Australian peacekeeping forces in September 1999, a third of East Timor's population – 200,000 people – were killed.

'So, British military equipment.' Chris reads from the list and I write up each item in the neutral column. 'The shooting of people for raising the flag,' he continues, referring to West Papua, where independence demonstrators were killed for flying their flag. 'Shooting unarmed demonstrators.'

'The students, yeah.' I continue scribbling into the column.

'Disappearances. The army.'

'Yep.'

'Torture. And one more, the rape of the Chinese women.'

The central column on the white board is full, words in scrawled capitals starkly accusing – TORTURE, MILITARY EQUIPMENT, MURDER. Indeed, we only needed to add the phrase RID WORLD OF INFIDELS and we would have had Osama bin Laden's to-do list.

I look up at Colonel Halim Nawhe. 'Now, we had a client who had eight different charges against them, and if they had admitted to all of them, they would have been sunk. They didn't want to admit to any of them.' My tone is confiding. 'And we said to them, you have to admit to one or two. If you can admit to one or two, you can make a good impression, and then you can lie and deny.'

The colonel remains impassive.

'The public will think you are being open. But you'll be able to hide the worst things. Looking through this –' I motion to the white-board list – 'which are the most sensitive, in your opinion?'

The colonel studies the list, leaning into the board. 'The rape,' he says.

I double-check with him, like a game-show host making sure the contestant is happy with their answer before going for the big money prize. 'The rape of the Chinese [women]. Now, that's the most sensitive?'

He nods, referring to the orchestrated anti-Chinese mob violence in Indonesian cities in 1998, during which hundreds of Chinese women were raped, amidst widespread concern that the Indonesian army was involved.

'So we put this here, OK?' I draw an arrow from the word RAPE on the board to the LIE column. 'Whatever happens, you deny that. It doesn't matter if somebody comes up with the facts, you deny that. You deny it, you deny it.' I finish jabbing at the board with the marker pen. 'OK, what do you think is the next most sensitive?'

'Disappearances,' he says.

We continue putting human rights abuses into the LIE column, drawing lines on our flow chart of barbarity.

The colonel's selection of 'sensitive' issues is based on what would be most embarrassing to the Indonesian government. They are not, however, the issues most sensitive to the British government. Since the Scott inquiry into the Arms to Iraq scandal, increasing press and public attention has focused on British arms sales abroad and the inherent problems they bring. On the one hand, the UK government insist that they are acting responsibly by selling arms to legitimate governments, and on the other hand the simple fact is that the governments who buy arms have a nasty habit of using them. After all, a military commander is hardly likely to buy a howitzer cannon to look nice over the fireplace. The current reality is that flying bits of metal have an unerring ability to end up in civilians, democracy protestors and the like, who, if they are lucky enough to survive, spend the rest of their lives with small lead lumps stuck in their bodies, with 'Made in England' stamped on them.

So having sold Indonesia arms over the decades, Britain has had to defend those sales, which it does by insisting that 'good' British arms are not used on the populace of West Papua, Aceh, or on the streets of Jakarta. How do we know that UK weapons are not used in this fashion? 'Because,' say the UK government in plummy tones, 'we have assurances from the Indonesian authorities that the weapons will not be used in this way.' Let us pause for a moment to consider the level of wilful naivety required to sustain this fabrication. First, pick one of the following statements:

❑ 'Hi, I'm phoning to conduct some market research. This will just take a minute of your time.'
❑ 'And now on BBC 1, gripping period drama with Kate Winslet and Colin Firth.'
❑ 'Mum! I was just about to phone you.'
❑ 'Have you read Salman Rushdie's new book – it's brilliant!'

❏ 'Jeremy Clarkson has received an OBE for his services to
   entertainment.'

OK, now you have picked your statement, I want you to believe
it. Try defending it in public and keeping a straight face. Now
imagine the level of deceit employed when one of the world's
most profoundly barbaric regimes promises not to use UK
weapons on civilians, and the level of naivety involved when a
British diplomat believes them.

The diplomat has to believe that Indonesia's military forces
have two arsenals run side by side. One arsenal with a big sign
above the door saying, 'British guns – parades and peacekeeping
use only.' The other doorway says, 'Non-British arms – general
purpose.' So every army squadron leader that comes into the
armoury to requisition would have to be quizzed by the quartermaster. 'What are you up to tonight?' he says, standing there in
a brown overall with pens in the top pocket.

'We're going to abduct, torture and "disappear" some teachers and civil rights lawyers.'

At which the quartermaster shouts down a corridor to an unseen
assistant: 'Keith! It's torture and abduction. Put the British guns
away and get the bad guns out ... that's right, the French ones.'

I turn to the colonel in the studio and with all the sincerity I
can muster say to him, 'This is between you and me in this room,
we have confidentiality here. It doesn't go any further.'

'It doesn't,' he affirms, looking round the room and into the
darkness where the camera operators are filming.

'OK, which one do you think you can put into this column
here?' I say, pointing to the ADMIT column.

'Maybe, this is UK equipment.'

'So we will say the UK equipment is used in East Timor?'

'Yeah,' says the colonel.

'Let us try that in the interview situation. Chris will ask you
the questions. Chris.'

Chris turns to face the colonel, clipboard at the ready. 'You know, of course, that Britain sells Indonesia military equipment?'

'Yes, I know.'

'Is that military equipment used in East Timor?'

'We use some. But it is old equipment ... for example, Saladin and Saracen [tanks],' says the colonel, trying to soften the blow of his admission by insisting that the tanks are old and therefore their use is more acceptable. He seems to suggest that the Indonesians were giving unarmed East Timorese civilians a sporting chance by not sending in the new tanks. The colonel is not entirely comfortable and it's not due just to the overly high chair and tight jacket. He is admitting to something the Indonesian military and government have denied. 'You promise me, this is only between us.' He looks back out at the tiny red camera lights filming from the darkness.

'Of course this is confidential,' I lie.

USE OF UK EQUIPMENT ON INDONESIAN AND EAST TIMORESE CIVILIANS BY INDONESIAN MILITARY

Confessions like Colonel Halim Nawhe's are unusual. However, the tales of UK weapons being (mis)used are unedifying in their predictability. They turn up as regularly as a Dan Brown novel in an Oxfam shop.

All military equipment listed here is UK produced and exported up to December 2005.

❏ 1994 – Jose Ramos-Horta, now Foreign Minister of independent East Timor, claims Hawk aircraft (sold by British Aerospace/BAE Systems) have been used regularly in East Timor since 1983.

❏ 1994 – Hawk aircraft rocket attacks on an East Timorese village.

❏ 1995 – UK journalists see Hawks over East Timorese capital Dili.

❏ 1996 (April) – Scorpion armoured personnel carriers used to assault students from the Islamic University of Indonesia in South

Sulawesi. Students were protesting against military brutality and increased bus fares. Three students killed; many more injured.

- ❏ 1996 (June) – Tactica water cannon used against demonstrators in Bandung. CS chemicals used.
- ❏ 1996 (June and July) – Tactica water cannon used against demonstrators in Jakarta.
- ❏ 1996 (August) – Tactica armoured personnel carriers used to quell riots ignited by military-backed takeover of the Indonesian Democratic Party HQ.
- ❏ 1998 (March) – Water cannon deployed against students in Surakarta.
- ❏ 1998 (April) – Water cannon spray what appeared to be the contents of septic tanks on university students in Surabaya – many report vomiting and fainting attacks.
- ❏ 1998 – Regular use of Scorpion armoured vehicles and water cannon in putting down peaceful protests against the rule of President Suharto and his successor, President Habibie. 12 May: four students killed at Trisakti University, Jakarta. 13 November (Black Friday): more than a dozen people killed in Jakarta.
- ❏ 1999 (February) – Tactica water cannon used on striking workers demonstrating for higher wages.
- ❏ 1999 (July) – Hawk aircraft deployed in Dili at the start of registration for the independence ballot.
- ❏ 2000 (July) – Saladin tanks used in Ambon.
- ❏ 2000 (September to October) – Hawks used in Wamena and Central Highlands of West Papua.
- ❏ 2000 (December) – Saladin tanks used in Ambon, again.
- ❏ 2002 – Stormer armoured personnel carriers used in Aceh.
- ❏ 2003 and subsequently – Hawks and armoured vehicles deployed in martial law offensive in Aceh.
- ❏ 2005 – Water cannon used in West Papua to break up independence demonstrations. Kim Howells, junior Foreign

Minister, considered this to be 'a more appropriate response to public disorder than some of the methods employed by the police in the past'. Considering the previous response was to shoot demonstrators, it is hardly a ringing endorsement. Note the way Kim Howells calls demonstrations 'public disorder'.

Source: TAPOL (Indonesian Human Rights Campaign) and exchange of letters with Kim Howells

MARK THOMAS CAUSES RADICAL SHAKE-UP IN GOVERNMENT

When I was four years old, I stood in the pulpit of the Thomas Memorial Church of the Nazarene in Clapham Junction, looking out over the light-coloured wooden lectern, which held a huge soft-backed black Bible, at the white Wesleyan walls and the congregation in black suits and best overcoats. I was reading a poem. The pastor, a spry old man who smelt of soap and always had just-scrubbed pink skin, had said, 'If you want people to spread the word, you have to start them young.' That's what I was doing in the pulpit, starting young, getting ready to spread the word. Reciting 'Has Anyone Seen My Mouse?' by AA Milne in the Church of the Nazarene was my first ever gig. It wasn't a storming show but Wesleyans are a tough crowd. Frankly, Milne's material wasn't right either. Maybe it would have worked had Eeyore been possessed by demons and cast off a cliff, but essentially the Hundred Acre Wood lacked a sense of apocalypse that churchgoers would respond to.

And though I lost my faith when I was six, found it again when I was ten and lost it for ever a week later, I still can't walk into a church without wanting to climb into the pulpit. I imagine a return to the memories of certainty, that holds if people are presented with the truth – they will act upon it.

After Channel 4 broadcast the programme with Major General Widjojo and Colonel Halim Nawhe in 1999, I sat back and waited for the low rumbling noise of the winds of change. Something had to change in the government's dealings with Indonesia and the arms trade. Labour had 419 MPs – surely one of them must have been watching the telly and caught the show. And if they had, they would have thought: Shit, we ain't got it right at all – them Indonesians are wrong 'uns. Then rushed to Number Ten the next morning to tell Blair. There was bound to be some double-checking, maybe even a bit of shouting from Whitehall, but something would definitely happen. And it did.

In 1997 Derek Fatchett, the Minister of State for the Foreign and Commonwealth Office under Robin Cook, wrote to Ann Clwyd, 'The Indonesian authorities have provided assurances that British-supplied military equipment would not be used in East Timor.'

After Channel 4 broadcast the programme that showed Colonel Halim Nawhe talking of Saracens and Saladins being used in East Timor, the government changed its standard response to enquiries on the subject. Indonesia provided the UK government with assurances that British-supplied equipment '*will* not be used in East Timor'. The ethical foreign policy changed the tense of a verb.

MAN DON'T GIVE A FUCK

The dressing room to the Comedy Store has white walls and an occasionally working coffee machine. A large pipe runs across the ceiling and if you look straight upwards you can see the thick glass grid that is set in the pavement above. Comics sit and chatter, moan about the running order, write out lists of gags on small bits of paper, slip the paper into the top pocket of their suits and slag off other comics. It's all part of the preparation for a show.

Simon Bligh is on the bill tonight, a lanky but fit man with the frame of a karate teacher. He sits next to a cork noticeboard covered in postcards and photos, and tells the story of doing a benefit show for Britain's largest arms manufacturer, British Aerospace, now BAE Systems. A well-known children's charity, phoned and asked if he would perform a fundraising comedy night for them.

'I said yeah, no problem,' says Simon in his Liverpool accent. 'Anyway on the day of the gig they move the venue. This woman phones and says, "We've had to change the venue." And I thought this is a bit odd but, you know, she gives me this new address in Aldershot. So I think fucking hell. But you know, you do it, don't you?' So he drove down there and it was only when he got to the venue that he realised it was a British Aerospace night to raise money for cancer. 'They had a fucking big banner on the wall: British fucking Aerospace.'

'What did you do?' I look on flabbergasted.

'I did the gig. No point in not doing it.' Being a sensible and caring chap and not wishing to cause offence, Simon wandered onstage and with wit and charm announced: 'You lot are a bunch of bastards. You make arms. You make stuff that kills kids.' Before continuing with his act.

'When I got offstage this manager for British Aerospace, the wanker who hands over the big cardboard charity cheque with British Aerospace all over it, this manager comes over to me and he is fucking furious, he goes: "You'll never work for British Aerospace again." I said, "I'm not fucking working for you now. I'm doing a benefit gig and I don't give a fuck." But he carries on: "You will never work for British Aerospace again." I said, "I don't give a fuck." And still he is going on: "I will make sure you never work for British Aerospace again."'

Simon was perplexed at this repetition. But it might be explained by the fact that BAE Systems is the most politically connected company in Britain. They have the 'key to the garden door' of Number Ten, they influence government decisions, reverse ministers' rulings, chat to MI5 and 6. They receive millions in subsidies each year and an annual clutch of knighthoods. They are the real 'dimension' at the heart of British foreign policy. They are central to government decision-making. They are too big and powerful for anyone to ignore. If a comic doesn't show the appropriate respect, it must be because they didn't hear the threat correctly. So let's say it until they do. 'You will never work for British Aerospace again.'

Cocky Cook Robin and the disappearing Hawks of East Timor

Back in May 1994, a certain Robin Cook MP was not impressed with the Tories' love of flogging British Aerospace (BAE Systems) Hawk jets to Indonesia. Indeed Cook harried the then Tory Trade Minister, Richard Needham, in Parliament. 'The minister will appreciate the fact that this [East Timor] is a major humanitarian issue,' said Cook. 'He [the minister] will be aware that Hawk aircraft have been observed on bombing runs in East Timor in most years since 1984.' Cook ended by demanding what assurances the Tories had that the Hawks that Needham approved the previous year would not be used in the same way. 'Can he guarantee that we can believe those assurances?'

Given Cook's passion on this subject, it was appropriate that the first test of his ethical foreign policy was over British Aerospace Hawk jets to Indonesia. It was in August 1997, a mere three months after the birth of his ethical policy. The Tory government, in its final death spasm, had granted licences for sixteen Hawk aircraft and fifty Scorpion armoured vehicles to go to Indonesia. The jets were worth about £160 million and the tanks from Alvis (now part of BAE Systems) were worth about £100 million. Cook faced a decision whether to revoke the licences or to allow them to stand. The media and activists expected Cook to revoke them. After all, what was the point of electing a new government if they could not change things?

Cook took the option to support the deal, stating that cancelling it would create legal difficulties – despite the fact that the Export of Goods (Control) Order 1994 states: 'A licence granted by the Secretary of State … may be varied or revoked by the Secretary of State at any time', giving him the legal right to cancel the licences. Cook could have stopped the deal. Instead he allowed the sale of the very aircraft, to the very regime, he himself had condemned.

BAE Systems were, and still are, the heart of British foreign policy when it comes to arms sales and politics. If Cook's attempt to transplant them and replace them with an ethical dimension was genuine, then he must have underestimated the company's political strength. It didn't matter if the decision on the Hawks was made by Cook or Number Ten, British Aerospace had their way. Three months after toasting the ethical foreign policy, Cook had been publicly bitch-slapped by the arms trade. And this was just the start. New Labour felt the need to further justify its actions and so in October 1997 the government said that having studied the evidence available, they were confident that Hawk jets had not been used in East Timor,* thereby siding with the Conservative government who had said anyone accusing Indonesia of using UK military equipment in East Timor was a paedo liberal Argie Trot fondler.

So it must have come as a bit of a shock to New Labour's sushi-sucking apologists for barbarity when one of Indonesia's top military officials admitted in 1999 – after our programme had gone out** – that the Hawks Britain had sold were used in East Timor. But only a bit of a shock. General Wiranto, the most senior figure in the army, admitted that Hawks had flown over

---

* Or in counterinsurgency roles in Indonesia.

** This is a fine example of coincidence.

East Timor in 1999. Days later, the Indonesian ambassador admitted that Hawk flights had provided general security in East Timor. Despite this admission, the Foreign and Commonwealth Office, in a letter to the Campaign Against the Arms Trade in 2001, still insisted there is 'no evidence' of Hawk jets or military equipment 'of any sort' being used for external aggression or internal oppression. More than that, the government had assurances, no less, from the Indonesian authorities that 'in no circumstances' would the UK-produced equipment be used against civilians.

BAE bitch-slapped Cook real good.

A BRIEF RECAP ON THE DISAPPEARING HAWKS OF EAST TIMOR

- ❏ 1994 – Cook says there is evidence of Hawks being used in East Timor by Indonesia.
- ❏ 1997 – Cook allows Hawks to be sold to Indonesia.
- ❏ 1997 – New Labour government says no evidence of Hawks being used in East Timor by Indonesia.
- ❏ 1999 – Indonesia admit to using Hawks in East Timor.
- ❏ 2001 – New Labour government says no evidence that Hawks have been used in East Timor by Indonesia.

THE BAD, THE UGLY
AND THE ILLEGAL

CHAPTER THREE

A chapter in which the author sets up another front company, this time for the purposes of exploring the effectiveness of arms controls and how to buy guns for Zimbabwe. The author accidentally uncovers a gunrunner, nearly becomes an agent for an arms company and discovers that God is working for at least one of the arms companies. BAE Systems have a small walk-on part in this chapter.

WINDOW-SHOPPING FOR SUB-MACHINE GUNS

It's spring 2002. From six storeys up looking down onto Piccadilly Circus, human faces are indistinguishable. From six storeys up, the only things that come into focus are billboard adverts. All I can see are slogans. Peering down at the current of shoppers I can hardly tell men from women. I definitely couldn't say if any of the flow of people wore glasses, or if they had one eye or two, or even if they had a guide dog. But I can tell you that *Queen the Musical* is on at the Dominion and that someone whose photo is worth slapping onto a bus is wearing Gap. I'm looking out of the window of the newly hired offices of Clifford Martin Associates, my new arms company. Clifford Martin, six floors up and opposite Tower Records in Regent Street. I could go home since work is finished for the day, but the view is one of London's greatest. The communal meeting room is all mine for another half an hour, when an internet start-up firm has it booked until 5.30 p.m. This is the rock and roll reality of hired office space. Clifford Martin Associates is a fiction, and the internet company by its very nature will either have a share price of a cool billion or have gone bust by the time it gets to use the meeting room.

Office life has its own rhythm, which is another way of saying it is dull. Once the emails and faxes have been sent, all you can do is wait for the replies. So I'm leaning on an arched window, looking down at herds of people streaming by Eros. Tourists and drunks are hanging out at the fountain of love, which incidentally isn't working. Most people barely notice the drunks and the fact that the fountain of love is broken. The view might be great but a man could get maudlin gazing down from this height, especially with blunt metaphors around. I remind myself I am an arms dealer and arms dealers don't get maudlin. They don't get doubts. They get rich.

Multinational arms manufacturers are wealthy creatures, suckled on the fatty milk of government defence contracts. They are hugely secretive entities too; they have contacts with prime ministers, armies, dealers and agents, not to mention security services all over the world. So it takes a special kind of arrogance to believe that they can be targeted in a sting run by a comedian armed with a fancy address, an email and a mobile. And there are only two ways to acquire this supreme arrogance. Either spend ten years of your life working the late-night Comedy Store shows at 2.00 a.m. in the morning, getting pissed groups of accountants from Penge to laugh. Or spend ten generations inbreeding with close family relatives, stick a title in front of your name and turn up at the House of Lords.

It is a simple fact that arms companies rarely volunteer information. Just as no sane person would willingly talk to the media about their activities, so no sane arms company will either, placing such an activity on a par with snogging lepers. However, the companies will talk to arms dealers. They have to. They couldn't do business if they didn't. Which is why journalists go to excessive measures, like setting up front companies in order to find out what they are up to. Fortunately, Channel 4 was picking up the tab for this one.

The first time I called up an arms company, the conversation went something like this:

Mark: Hello, is that the arms company?

Arms Company: Yes, it is.

Mark: Oh hello, I am an arms dealer.

Arms Company: Yes, of course you are, why else would you be phoning us?

Mark: Oh yes, of course. Well, I'd like to buy some guns, please.

Arms Company: Yes, of course you would. What type?

Mark: Machine guns.

Arms Company: MP5s?

Mark: Yes please.

Arms Company: How many?

Mark: Two hundred.

Arms Company: Ammunition?

Mark: Oh, that would be lovely.

Arms Company: Can I supersize you?

Mark: Of course you can.

Arms Company: You could order our special offer, the Happy Cache. That's gun, ammo, magazine and cleaning kit. Plus it comes with a free Disney action figure.

OK, I'm making some of this up, but you get the picture. Arms companies will talk to you if they think you are on their side. Trust and empathy are not things that can be quickly engendered in a sudden phone call from a journalist, but with my new company in place I could merrily phone any arms manufacturer in the world posing as an arms dealer. If you want to talk to an arms dealer, become an arms dealer. You can form a registered company quite easily at Companies House. From there, get a phone, an office, an email address and some business cards. Of all the things required to set up a company, it was the business cards that took the longest time to sort out.

The machine-gun taste challenge

In May 2000 the UK government placed a long overdue arms embargo on Zimbabwe. For those of you wondering why this was done, the Cluedo answer is: President Mugabe in the Democratic Republic of Congo with 10,000 to 13,000 troops. For a snapshot of the internal situation in Zimbabwe you could try: state torturers in the jail with anything they can get their hands on. The bottom line was no UK arms could go to Zimbabwe. In fact, by 2002 no European countries could export guns to Mugabe either, as the EU declared an arms embargo in February that year.

However, in spite of the arms embargo, the UK had no laws to stop a dealer brokering arms, acting as a middleman and sending the arms direct from one country to another without them touching UK soil. So if a dealer knew the law, they knew how to circumvent it. How do I know this? Because an arms dealer could find a way to sell sulphur to Satan, so Zimbabwe wouldn't be a problem. And secondly, because Clifford Martin made some calls.

Heckler & Koch: Is it a gun? Is it a comedy double act?

Heckler & Koch is a German gun manufacturer. They make one of the most successful sub-machine guns in the world: the MP5.

At the time I was setting up Clifford Martin Associates, the German company was owned by Royal Ordnance, which in turn was owned by BAE Systems (formerly British Aerospace).* Heckler & Koch extended the chain of supply by licensing the manufacture of the guns to Pakistan, Iran and Turkey, among other places. According to a sales rep from the Pakistan Ordnance Factory (POF), in 1983 the company got a licence from H & K to make MP5s. As you might have expected, H & K did not grant these licences as an act of charity. Generally speaking, there is little altruism in the arms trade; spreading the gift of machine guns is done at a price. H & K must have been handsomely paid for the licences.

As a German company, after February 2002 H & K were subject to the EU arms embargo on Zimbabwe. Put simply, they can't export to Mugabe. But what of the companies who pay H & K to produce MP5s under licence? Could they sell to Zimbabwe? Clifford Martin Associates decided to find out.

It takes a week or so but the faxes and emails are eventually replied to and I get an answer to the question. Unsurprisingly, the answer is yes. The cheapest machine gun on offer turned out to be from Iran, from the state-owned arms company, Defence Industries Organization (DIO). They would provide 200 units of their licensed version of the MP5 (a 9mm T9 sub-machine gun with retractable butt stock) for US $300 each. The quotation came on letterheaded paper, which bore the words, 'In the name of God'. All that statement needed was an exclamation mark at the end of it to make it entirely appropriate.

Religious devotion does not automatically spring to mind when conjuring images of arms dealers. One can easily imagine arms dealers shoving briefcases stuffed full of dollars into the

---

* Later in 2002 Royal Ordnance sold their subsidiary company Heckler & Koch, which was bought by private investor buyout. H & K history – http://www. heckler-koch.de.

boots of sports cars; it is less easy to envisage them packing crates of machine guns and then finding a quiet corner of the factory in which to face east and pray. However, given that the arms industry is basically about taking life, it is nice to know that some arms dealers are concerned about what happens afterwards, though I doubt if many buyers look at a quote from DIO and say, 'We should buy these guns. These guns are holy.'

Looking at this all from a *What Gun?* consumer angle, the Iranians offer a good price, but maybe too cheap. There is also one other factor I can't quite dismiss. While I know it is wrong to judge one group of people by the actions of a few, I can't quite shake the notion that if Middle Eastern arms production is so brilliant, why does the region have such a reliance on suicide bombers?

The Turkish state-owned arms manufacturer, MKEK, would deliver the consignment to any Turkish port for free, but the price was a lot more expensive at $850 per MP5 sub-machine gun. Life might be cheap, but guns are expensive. Then the POF offered MP5 sub-machine guns at $550 each. The question was: would POF supply the guns for Zimbabwe? Mr Khawar Nawaz, their export director, had some concerns when I mentioned the Z-word.

'Mr Clifford [my *nom de guerre*], I have a small question to ask you, can I?' he whispered almost conspiratorially.

'Yes.'

'Is it the Zimbabwean government buying it?' said Mr Nawaz. His voice was grave and heavy with significance. He sounded as if he might be about to turn down my request.

'It is for the security forces,' I innocently respond.

'I just hope it's not to any of the rebel groups – you've got to be very careful,' said Mr Nawaz.

For those with more than a passing knowledge of Zimbabwe, his comments would seem strange, as there are no armed rebel groups in Zimbabwe.

'When I said they are security forces, these guys are very close to Mugabe,' I said.

And at that he cheered up and became exceedingly helpful. 'We only export to countries that are not on the UN banned list ... If your end user certificate says UK, then stuff will be exported to the UK, but if you want us to send it directly to Zimbabwe, then with your reference, we have absolutely no objection whatsoever.'

Zimbabwe is not subject to a UN embargo, and POF would be quite happy to help me broker guns into Zimbabwe. They even quoted an approximate air-freight charge to get them to Harare (it's only $3,500 for the 200 guns – one way of course). So despite an EU arms embargo, European arms dealers have a whole host of ways of getting guns into Zimbabwe without breaking the law, a method that benefited Heckler & Koch, via the licence and potential upgrades. And a supply chain that came back to the UK. This much I expected. What happened next I did not.

PROMOTIONAL MATERIALS

Clifford Martin Associates got on very well with POF's director of exports in Pakistan, Mr Nawaz. Sometimes I would travel to the office early so I could phone him at a decent time in Pakistan, catching the first tube trains in the morning, trudging from the underground stations into a cold and damp central London and imagining him sitting with scented tea and air conditioning to keep the heat down.

Mr Nawaz is chatty, charming and prone to odd bouts of 1950s vernacular. He tells me if I need any help I should 'tinkle' him. When I ask him for information about other clients, he shrieks like a camp banshee: 'Sanctity, oh sanctity!' Imagine Kenneth Williams playing Julius Caesar in a Pakistani accent ('Infamy! Infamy! They've all got it in for me!'). He playfully keeps mum and doesn't budge on client confidentiality. But for all of his wailing of 'Sanctity, oh sanctity', Mr Nawaz is quite the talker.

'We're producing it [the MP5] under licence with Heckler & Koch in Germany,' he says, and going into the sales pitch adds that the prices are 'rock bottom'. 'One thing I forgot to offer you is that if you buy a substantial quantity, let's say 1,000 or so, each machine gun comes with a fibreglass carrying case, which is a beautiful carrying case ... they cost me 82 dollars per piece, but as I said if the quantity is large then we give.'

A free bag with a gun if I buy over 1,000! At that ratio we should get a Smart car with every tank.

Mr Nawaz chats away, warning me about the dangers of personal greed in the arms industry. 'Please do not put too much of a mark-up ... Please do not, as one of our customers in the UK lost a very nice lucrative offer as he became a little selfish and added a lot of mark-up on it.'

'Who was that, because I think I might know that person?' I enquire.

'Oh, sanctity, sanctity, ha ha ha,' he giggles. I almost find it endearing.

Then from out of nowhere Mr Nawaz says, 'We're looking for people who can promote our products.' This is an entirely normal thing for him to say, but for some reason I am suddenly curious.

'If you think you've got contacts and you think you'll be strong there [Zimbabwe], we'd be pleased to give you an authorisation in the future.' Mr Nawaz has just asked me to become one of their agents, an authorised dealership for the Pakistan Ordnance Factory in Zimbabwe. Hell yes, I've arrived! A few phone calls and some faxes and I'm about to become a bona fide arms dealer.

In keeping with being offered a chance to become one of their sales agents, I went to visit the Defence Attaché's office at the Pakistan embassy in London for a chat. POF are a state-owned company and the Pakistan embassy is listed as its London office. It is in Lowndes Square in Knightsbridge, round the corner from Harrods and a short stroll from Hyde Park. In the middle of the square is a park for residents only, surrounded by iron railings and with a locked gate. The blocks of flats look 1950s, the kind of penthouse pads where politicians had affairs with starlets and were blackmailed by the Krays. A flat here would sell for £2 million and the estate agent wouldn't even have to bother with a smile to get it.

The embassy has half a dozen steps to its black front door, framed by two columns and a first-floor balcony with stone balustrades. Building work is being done and the whole place is covered in a light green mesh that hangs from the scaffolding. Inside I was led up some cramped stairs into a cramped office and invited to sit in a cramped chair by a suitably small man, who no doubt found the whole place quite spacious. He worked for the Defence Attaché's office and he served coffee from municipal cups and saucers. The meeting was as short as my new friend. His conversation was short too, though his pauses were long. It was soon time to go. As I got ready to leave, he handed me a copy of the POF sales catalogue. On the front cover were their name, logo and slogan: 'Provide Force to the Forces'.

'Thank you, this will be very helpful,' I said, and politely started to flick through it. 'This is very good,' I continued, when suddenly I notice in the middle of the brochure a picture of a round white disc. My flicking stops and my eyeballs pop. I can't quite believe what I am looking at. I try not to look surprised, but it is not every day that a man in a foreign embassy gives you sales material for landmines. I'm sure that's what it is. That small white disc can't be anything else: it is an anti-personnel landmine.

Smiling at my host, I'm caught between two desires. One of them is to get out of my chair and slap the midget across the face.

I want to slap that little fucker until he cries. Slap him for being a dirty filthy arms-dealing fucker, slap him for offering landmines like they were nothing more than a range of office equipment.

The conflicting desire is to dance gaily around the room with streamers shouting, 'We've got you now, you bastard!' Hurrah! Landmines! What a palaver! I not only want to slap him, I want to kiss his cheeks and say, 'Thank you for being a bastard – you've confirmed my prejudices and made my day!'

I do neither. I leave and, standing in the square out of sight of the embassy by the locked gates of the residents-only park, I double-check. There are not one but two types of anti-personnel mine on offer. The second is labelled 'MINE A.P. SHRAPNEL'. The picture shows what looks like a workman's metal box mounted on two sets of metal V-shaped legs. Embossed on the front are the words: 'FRONT TOWARDS ENEMY'. I might not appreciate the weapon but I do appreciate sensible labelling. It might be an indiscriminate, explosive device that sends shards of metal flying through flesh, but there is no need to be lax about workers' health and safety.

The Ottawa Convention banning the manufacture, transfer, use and stockpiling of AP mines was signed in December 1997, by Clare Short for Britain.* Pakistan is one of the nations that has not signed up to the treaty, but even so, flogging AP landmines off the back of an embassy? It's a tad Trotter Trading meets the Janjaweed, hardly the image of the suave cosmopolitan diplomatic service. You wouldn't expect the host of an embassy black-tie function to be clutching a flute of champagne while surreptitiously opening their jacket and hissing, 'Over here, guvnor.' Especially as the AP mine is a genuine weapon of mass destruction, responsible for the killing and maiming of tens of thousands of civilians.

---

* 154 countries have signed up to Ottawa, 150 of whom have ratified it, as of March 2006 – leaving 40 countries unsigned. http://www.icbl.org/treaty.

I call Mr Nawaz about the mines, but he says it is 'a very old brochure' and it turns out that POF 'don't do AP mines at all'. Which is odd, because in December 1999, sixteen months before my trip to the embassy, POF had been caught offering AP landmines to undercover reporters in London. You'd have thought the Pakistan embassy and POF would get their act together, if only for appearances' sake. As a basic minimum precaution, they shouldn't hand out landmine promo' catalogues to comedians pretending to be arms dealers at their embassy.

ON SWISS HOLES AND FINNISH PICKLES – HANGIN' WITH THE GUNRUNNERS

Switzerland is not in the European Union. I'm aware that this is old news – so is John Lennon getting shot – but people still find it shocking. The significance of Switzerland not being a member of the European Union is this: does an EU arms embargo apply to Swiss arms manufacturers? Once again Clifford Martin Associates bravely emailed where others fear to email and sent a note to the Swiss arms dealers Brügger and Thomet. Can they help us get sub-machine guns to some dodgy destinations? The Swiss response is swift: 'Thanks for calling. Love to help. No can do at the mo'. *Que sera sera*, innit. Always next time. Yadda yadda. Best wishes B and T ...' OK I might have changed some of the words from the original but that was the essence of their communiqué. So Brügger and Thomet were forgotten about.

Until, out of the blue, an email arrives: weeks later, unsolicited and unexpected, a handful of words from Brügger and Thomet hurled across cyberspace. The note is short, sharp and to the point. 'Please note that your request will be handled by our agent Finnrappel Oy in Helsinki. Please find attached company details.' Not wanting to appear rude, I decided to get in contact with their agent in Finland.

Finnrappel Oy

It transpires Mr Olli Salo runs Finnrappel Oy, a gun and outdoor shop in Helsinki, Finland. Olli will sell MP5 sub-machine guns for $1,160 each. Which is not cheap. They are easily the most expensive MP5 sub-machine guns to be offered so far. Why so expensive? Has Naomi Campbell accessorised with one? Well, there is a reason they might seem a bit on the pricey side: Olli is a gunrunner, and gunrunners do tend to charge over the odds. Brügger and Thomet had just put us in touch with an arms smuggler.

Olli will get the MP5 sub-machine guns to Zimbabwe (and Algeria too as it turns out*) from Finland. Thus breaking the EU arms embargo. Guns to Mugabe from the EU should be illegal. But when I call Olli to confirm the destination is Zimbabwe, he says:

'No problem.'

'No problem to Zimbabwe?'

'No, no, no … Only North Korea, Iran and Iraq is out of the question.'

Just to make double sure I ask again: 'So if I wanted to move some MP5s to Zimbabwe, that wouldn't be a problem?'

'No, no, no.'

'Olli.'

'Yeah?'

'You're a life-saver,' I say.

'I know,' he says laughing.

Like many gunrunners, Olli doesn't care too much for paperwork. In fact, he only needs one piece of paper to do the deal. That's right, folks, just one piece of paper. This might not sound like much of an issue, but bear in mind you need one official bit

---

* Clifford Martin Associates originally asked about moving guns to Algeria, which although it has no EU embargo is still a place that's a tad lively on the human rights abuse front. We included Zimbabwe as the destination for the weapons as discussions progressed.

of paperwork just to watch TV, and these are guns. Olli says he doesn't need any of the really important bits of paper either, not a Golden Ticket – an End User Certificate – nor does he require a government licence to export arms. How can he do such a deal legally? He can't.

23 April 2002. Olli and I are on the phone discussing machine guns to Zimbabwe and Algeria.

'We don't need any licences here,' he says.

Somewhat taken aback, I stammer: 'That is fantastic. If we don't need any licence that's absolutely brilliant.'

'All you need is an import permit from the country of destination. That's the only paper we want.'

'That's fantastic,' I blurt out.

'Apart from money.'

If I was doing this deal for real, then the only thing Zimbabwe would need to break the arms embargo and get the weapons is to apply to itself for an import licence. I imagine Groucho Marx explaining the situation: so Robert Mugabe has to ask Robert Mugabe for an import licence, and no one in Zimbabwe turns down Robert Mugabe, not even Robert Mugabe. In these circumstances I think it highly likely that the import licence would be found.

Olli's smuggling route is uncovered in a series of phone calls over the next three days.

Day one: 24 April

The guns are from Heckler & Koch and coming out of Germany and into Switzerland.

'Officially, we are the only ones dealing with you,' Olli says.

'It is definitely Swiss kit?' I ask, referring to the machine guns.

'Officially Swiss, but it's unofficially made in Germany.'

'It comes from Germany?'

'Of course, it comes from the H & K factory ... I mean obviously ... but they can't say that.'

Day two: 25 April

The relationship between the Swiss arms dealers, Brügger and Thomet, and Finland's Olli Salo is further explained. Mr Thomet of the Swiss company knows that Clifford Martin Associates have asked Olli for a quote for 225 Heckler & Koch MP5 machine guns. Mr Thomet would know that, as Olli is going to buy the guns from him.

'He's our agent for many parts of the world, with stuff like this, and the fact that the regulations we have there [Finland] is very liberal, and it's working very smooth.' At least that's what Mr Thomet says.

Day three, a busy one: 26 April

Olli sends an email explaining: 'MP5 parts are made in Germany and assembled by hand in Switzerland.' Later on the phone he says: 'It [the guns] has to come from outside the European Union. If it comes from Germany we need an export licence but when it comes from outside it doesn't. That's the trick.' So the gun parts come out of Germany to Switzerland. The guns are assembled in Switzerland and imported into Finland. But how do they then get to Zimbabwe?

So I phone Olli once again.

MT: The client is absolutely insistent that they know step by step what's happening with the package, with the guns, on each stage of the journey ... they're very pleased that it's Heckler & Koch and it's coming out of the factory.

OS: Yes.

MT: I've said to them it's coming out of the factory in parts and that it's on an export licence into Switzerland.

OS: Yes.

MT: The Swiss assemble it with Brügger and Thomet.

OS: Yes.

MT: And that gets exported on an export licence to Finland.

OS: Yes.

MT: Um, and they're saying what happens to the guns once they're in Finland?

OS: They're transported from here ... That's our problem ... You don't [want to] know it.

MT: Are you sort of saying, OK, once it's Finland we're going to change the label and basically say ...

OS: Yes, yes, of course, yes, yes. All the labels are changed. We don't open the packet.

MT: OK, so you're changing it from import to transhipment?

OS: Yeah.

So this is how the great gunrunner intends to beat the EU sanctions. He is going to sneak into a warehouse and change the labels. Skulking like a schoolboy thief, he is going to put some new stickers on some crates. The mechanics of barbarity are stunningly mundane. No midnight runs across borders or high-powered speedboats. Just lurking in a bonded warehouse with a false set of labels. There is no dark romance, no amoral enigma; there is no mystery or suspense-cling to his petty thuggery. Olli Salo, the gunrunner, has all the dangerous allure of a shoplifter in a gardening centre.

Off the back of a lorry
We are frequently urged by the authorities to report crime. We are offered cash rewards for informing on everyone from drug dealers to people signing on and working at the same time. We are told it is our duty to prevent antisocial behaviour. Olli Salo was prepared to break EU sanctions and get guns to Zimbabwe,

and you'd have to go a long way to get more antisocial than that. The chain of supply involved not just Finnrappel Oy but Brügger and Thomet, Heckler & Koch, Royal Ordnance and BAE Systems. So it only seemed fair to dob them in.

With cameras blazing, I put down the phone after speaking to Olli about changing the labels and went back to my desk. On the desk is an angle-poise lamp and a Newton's cradle executive toy. The desk, in turn, stands on a faded piece of carpet, and has a pot plant stuck next to it. The carpet sits on the floor of a flatbed lorry, which is currently being driven around London. Clifford Martin Associates' entire operation is on the back of a travelling truck and is best described as a *really* open-plan office.

I was determined that the government should not only know of the tangled arms mess it had allowed to happen but should also be seen to be told. As the lorry picks up speed leaving the traffic lights, my paperwork starts to fly up and I grab it before it becomes litter. We chunter along following the Thames out of Victoria, come up from the Embankment along the cutesy streets beyond Parliament and Westminster Abbey that house the think-tanks and societies for this and that, then turn the corner into Victoria Street and park the lorry half on the pavement outside the Department of Trade and Industry. The DTI reception is a large glass box bolted onto the front of an office complex.

One of the security guards is coming over; he is a good bloke. I've demonstrated at the DTI so often that we all know each other and get on quite well. He is a very big bald man with a stubbly goatee and a large smile. He looks like a Teletubby on steroids.

'Who you after today, Mark?' he shouts up.

'Do you reckon you could get the minister to open the office window?' I call down at the benign face of the security staff.

'What?'

'Would reception phone up the minister and say: "Open your window, there is an important message for you?"'

The big feller smiles. 'You can ask 'em, Mark.'

'Is it turned up nice and loud?' I say to the techies.

The lorry, as well as housing my mobile office complete with easy chair and pot plant, has two large stacks of loudspeakers balanced at each end of the flatbed. This time the authorities are not just going to know what went on, they are going to listen to me confront Olli live as it happens. The techies give me the thumbs-up and I phone Olli back, ready to broadcast our conversation to the entire street. I'm about to put gunrunner Olli Salo on some serious speaker phone. With this volume there is no way the DTI can say they were not informed.

Olli's phone rings and he is in. I quickly explain the situation to him: the truck, the DTI, the recording of the phone call. On learning all of this Olli naturally says, 'No way,' in direct contradiction to what he said only minutes before.

'You said to me that you would get the guns from Finland—' I start to remind him before he interrupts.

'It was a lie.'

'But you were explaining how you were going to get H & K MP5 sub-machine guns—'

'We can't do that.'

'You've explained to me on numerous occasions that you can and you've given us paperwork providing a quote for it.'

'Don't believe everything you hear.'

'You're retracting everything – is that correct?'

'Er, no.'

'So you're standing by everything.'

'No, it's a joke.'

'OK, Olli, so you're saying it's a joke, yet you were explaining to me how—'

'We can't do that.'

'So why did you say to me that you could?'

'For money. I'll say anything for money.'

Olli's escapades were picked up by the press in Finland and became quite a story over there. Finland became one of the first EU countries to introduce brokering laws controlling fixers and middlemen for arms deals. Did my part in Olli's story have anything to do with Finland's decision to change the law? If it did, it was absolutely minimal. The British government followed suit and introduced brokerage laws in 2004. That too had nothing whatsoever to do with me.

Shortly after the programme was broadcast in 2002, BAE Systems and Royal Ordnance sold Heckler & Koch. I am not privy to the inner workings of BAE Systems, but I just don't see them calling an emergency meeting at two o clock in the morning, sitting round the boardroom saying, 'Thomas has made another telly programme showing us in a bad light! We have to sell Heckler & Koch!' All I have managed to achieve is some embarrassment and discomfort to some arms dealers and the government, which is not a bad thing. Considering I earn my living from causing embarrassment, this is not a bad thing at all. But there has to be more to it than that.

Nick

Sitting outside a coffee shop on Waterloo station after the programme has been broadcast, I chat to my friend Nick Hildyard, who works for the Corner House, a human rights and environmental NGO. Nick is fiftyish, skinny, posh, with a receding hairline and swept-back, mousy, flyaway hair. He is all baggy cords and worn jumpers, roll-ups and rucksacks full of reports. He dresses like his local Oxfam shop had a sudden surge of lecturers in Bob Dylan poetry pass away and leave their wardrobes to charity.

'Embarrass the fuckers, man,' he says, drawing on a roll-up so thin it shouldn't qualify for a health warning. 'Embarrass them.'

Nick has been involved in campaigning for human rights all

over the world. He has been detained in more than one continent and has taken on multinationals, governments and dictatorships. Sometimes he wins, too.

'So a few executives go a bit red-faced for a day or two. It
doesn't exactly change much,' I cheerily denounce myself and my
failings, like an old Maoist before a purge.

'It all helps. Every bit helps. It encourages others, it shows
the companies to be vulnerable to the truth, and making a few
execs embarrassed for a few days is better than them having an
easy ride of it.'

Here is what Brügger and Thomet said when they were
approached for a statement about their role in all this. 'Brügger
and Thomet has never issued any quotation for delivery of its
materials to the countries in question nor to the best of our
knowledge has any of our representatives … we reserve the right
to bring this matter to our attorneys,' they said. Which is almost
true – no one sent a quote out with 'Guns for Zimbabwe' on it.
If, on the other hand, they are trying to claim that their 'agent'
and 'office in Finland' didn't quote for the guns knowing they
were to go to Zimbabwe, then they are liars. Great big fat Swiss
chocolate-hoarding liars!

Here is another quick story about the dodgy Swiss bastards.

BRÜGGER AND THOMET'S ROLE IN THE SUPPLY CHAIN THAT LED TO THE ARMING OF DUTCH COKE DEALERS

As referred to in Chapter One. Belgian arms manufacturers FN Herstal make the top-of-the-range P90 sub-machine gun, described as 'a Gucci item' in the world of sub-machine guns. In 1998 they agree to sell 200 guns to the Jordanian Special Forces, who protect the royal family. Before the guns even leave Belgium, $153,000 is paid by Swiss arms dealers Brügger and Thomet to the then Crown Prince Abdullah bin Al-Hussein (now king) of the Jordanian royal family to buy the P90 machine guns. This happens despite the Jordanians having made assurances that the guns will not be re-exported. The guns stay in Jordan for two days, then head out to Switzerland and are re-exported to the Netherlands for conversion by JFY, Postbus 1033, Maarssen. Twenty of the guns remain in the Netherlands. In September 1999 four of these state-of-the-art guns are found in weapons' caches belonging to Mr Kok, a coke dealer.

Source: UNIDIR report on Small Arms and Light Weapons Transfers

4

DESERT STORM

CHAPTER FOUR

*A chapter in which Mr Robin Cook starts to
make a habit of defending arms companies, arms
Morocco against Western Sahara, and then practises
the noble art of telling porkies. Meanwhile, the humble
author finds himself in a paradoxical situation in the
middle of the desert, unable to reconcile a country's
right to defend itself with the inevitable glorification
of violence, and takes a message with a Western
Sahrawi to the board of BAE Systems.*

BAE SYSTEMS – THE ANNUAL GENERAL MEETING, MAY 2001

The Queen Elizabeth II Conference Centre is but a vigorously pitched spit away from Parliament Square. It is exactly the type of building that Prince Charles hates but probably wouldn't object to quite so much were it ever to be renamed the King Charles III Conference Centre. It is a large cement block with all the charm of a gentrified inner-city sports hall. The cobble-stoned low wall at the front makes for an awkward but popular perch in the summer, as office workers and tourists collect sunlight and eat sandwiches out of triangles of plastic, unaware that the wart of concrete behind them plays host to some of the biggest corporations in Britain. Today it houses the BAE Systems annual general meeting. The conference centre is conveniently situated opposite Westminster Abbey and the Methodist Hall, should any of the board of directors get the inclination to beg for forgiveness before going to lunch.

The AGM is a chance for the shareholders to question the board and for the chairman to apportion praise and blame for successes and failures. Opponents of the arms trade, for the price of a single share in the company, can gain entrance to the event as a shareholder and sit within heckling distance of their foes. This entertainment is normally cheaper than cinema tickets, you get tea and coffee laid on, and although you will be thrown out for excessive shouting, you have to work fairly hard actually to get arrested inside the meeting. As most of the AGMs are held around spring, activists and anti-corporate campaigners have an 'AGM season', which traditionally starts around May Day. It's all a matter of different strokes for different folks. For some it is the sound of the first cuckoo that heralds spring; for others it is the sound of a breaking McDonald's shop-front window.

Outside the BAE Systems AGM, by the Methodist Hall, a mixed bag of protestors has gathered: Quakers, peaceniks, anti-corporate campaigners, liberals, nuns, Campaign Against the Arms Trade members and supporters, concerned vicars and a few foreigners whose homes have been reduced to rubble by military forces kitted out by BAE. The event has a relaxed feel to it as people on the protest wander off into the meeting for half an hour or so, ask their question and then come out to report to the others what is going on. They pick up a banner, rejoin the picket and then it is someone else's turn to head into the meeting.

Today is a suit day for me and I wait by the steel barriers as an old friend ambles over.

'All right?' sighs Em cheerfully, her scruffy black hair bobbing hello. She wears a big grin and old khaki trousers, which is one of the great ironies of the anti-war movement. The will to destroy all elements of the arms trade is genuine, but without army surplus most peaceniks would be walking around entirely naked. A couple of drops of blood stand out on Em's vegan-white face; her

T-shirt, which is so old you could carbon-date it, is covered in blood.

'You decided to start eating meat again?' I quip.

'I've just been doing the die-in,' she laughs, jerking a thumb back in the direction of the conference centre and trying to contain the adrenalin excitement that accompanies her forced eviction. The blood is fake and if you look closely at the T-shirt you can see old stains from previous 'die-ins'. The die-in is a popular tool of choice for anti-arms-trade activists. One group of folk run into the 'target' – an arms company's head office or an MP's constituency surgery – cover themselves with fake blood, then lie on the ground in improbable positions to signify violent death. They remain immobile for as long as possible, until the police pick them up, drag them off (still feigning death) and arrest them. The protestors then spend the rest of the day trying to sleep in a police cell. The more experienced protestor might take a book to the die-in that they can read later in custody. The second group of campaigners will be handing out leaflets over the 'bodies', shouting slogans on the megaphone, phoning the local press, organising legal representation and keeping friends and relatives of the arrested informed. For those doing the dying part of a die-in, there isn't a lot to do by comparison. It is a job for the lazier activist – the term 'inactivist' might be more accurate.

'How did it go?' I ask Em.

'Not bad, not bad. Stopped the meeting while security moved us out, but we had a load of webbing which linked us all up, so it took a while to sort that out. Carried me out through the lift.' She smiles, dragging on a roll-up only marginally thinner than herself.

'You going in? Silly question, you're in the suit.'

'I'm waiting for a friend; we're going in together.'

'Who's that, then?'

'Breica Lehbib. Polisario. Western Sahara.'

'Oh right … Who?'

'The Polisario Front, the liberation movement for the Western Sahrawis. Hence the suit. Third World liberation movements love a good suit.'

'Shame that's a shit one, then.'

I tug the cuffs of my Marks & Spencer special in mock indignation as a giant puppet of the grim reaper appears behind Em. The reaper is decked in a long black cowl. Red and white missiles strapped to his back protrude from behind the grinning papier-mâché skull. The whole thing must stand nine, maybe ten feet tall. The contraption fits on the wearer's shoulders, who can see out of the puppet through black gauze sewn into Death's robes, thus hiding the wearer's face, which is roughly the height of Death's stomach. All this is topped off with two giant hands operated by long poles, each hand clutching a missile.

'All right, Em? Mark?' says Death in a northern accent.

'Not bad, just done the die-in.'

'Been in yet, Mark?

'Waiting for a mate.'

'It's bloody hot in this thing and I'm dying for a fag,' says Death.

At this moment a police officer approaches Death. 'Can you move off the road and onto the pavement, please,' he orders.

Em turns to face the officer. 'That's the grim reaper you're moving on there,' she says grinning.

'You're obstructing the flow of traffic,' continues the impassive PC, motioning with both arms for Death to move. 'It's for your safety as well, please, not just everyone else's. I'd rather not have you hit by a car, if you don't mind, so will you move behind the barrier, please?'

I have a fleeting vision of a London cabbie leaning back to tell his fare, 'Guess 'o I knocked over vis morning. Go on, hav' a guess. Only Death hisself, won' it.'

Death hobbles onto the kerb and gets behind the metal barrier, before someone starts up on the megaphone distortedly chanting: 'Stop the merchants of death! Stop the arms trade!' A little while later I spot Death having a crafty cigarette through the black gauze. It looks like the grim reaper is smoking through his belly button.

Getting inside

Although they work together on these events, the police try not to mingle with the private security guards. I suppose the officers have a sense of 'there but for the grace of God ...' The private security game features a lot of clip-on ties (never a sign of over-achievement), worn with a bullish lack of charm that reeks of low pay and crap training videos. They are all bad haircuts and thousand-yard stares that peter out after fifty. By comparison, the PCs swagger confidently around the front of the building, with an air of undefined purpose. Occasionally the police saunter across to the protestors corralled behind matt-silver barriers, amble past and look on from a discreet distance. Though they quickly get out of the way when the police Forward Intelligence Team turns up to photograph and video the protestors. This is par for the course, if you will forgive a golfing expression, and invariably results in someone from the protestors' side of the metal barrier shouting: 'If you want to catch the real criminals, they are inside!'

To get into the AGM, demonstrators, like the investing shareholders, have to go though the glass doors, past the metal detectors, endure a brisk body frisk, leave their mobile phones in a grey tray at the cloakroom counter and then move into the care of the next level of security. Anyone suspected of being a demon-strator is accompanied down the short corridor to the lifts, into which all the security staff bundle alongside the demonstrators. The lift is smaller than an actor's IQ and as the ratio of security to protestors is roughly one to one, it is a short but extremely cramped journey upwards. Should the lift judder suddenly to a halt there is a fifty-fifty chance of intimacy occurring. Once out of the lift more guards keep a watchful eye on the protestors as they gather in the main hall.

Amid the high ceilings and bad corporate works of art, the minimum-waged are serving filter coffee and passing out plates with biscuits on doilies. It is here that the more sartorially minded protestors (wearing jackets that were purchased at shops other than Oxfam) try to mingle with the genuine shareholders, attempting to engage them in moral discussion. Opening with pleasant small talk, the exchanges go along these lines:

'Biscuits are lovely again this year.'

'Yes, they are, though they always put on a good spread, don't you find?' says an elderly lady, saucer in hand and annual report tucked under her arm.

'Oh yes. Do you come each year?'

'We try to, but my husband Derrick doesn't like driving in London.'

'Are you happy that the company are helping to kill babies in Iraq?'

It is the kind of moment Patricia Routledge would relish in an Alan Bennett monologue. You can almost hear her clipped voice: 'Well, I reported him straight away to the security guards but they didn't do anything, despite him having a large rucksack and unwashed hair … He was right about the biscuits though, they were very nice.'

The meeting
Inside the meeting room, investment-fund managers sit in clusters surveying the familiar surroundings. They are all Savile Row torsos and train-spotter faces. Clutching briefcases that cost more than a foreign holiday, the investors have a curious demeanour. They know all the right people and regard the rest of the crowd with polite disdain, so they manage to look connected and detached at the same time. This rare quality they share with Buddhist monks and Pete Doherty. Though Pete might have

cheated on the chanting and incense and taken a quicker route to happy vacancy.

The ordinary shareholders, the smaller individual investors, are mainly retired folk and pensioners. The women in the room look like they smell of dried lavender, but actually don't. The men look like they smell of car leather, and do. Their collective noun is a surrey of shareholders. People with proper jobs don't waste their valuable time off work at shareholders' meetings.

To the shareholders, the protestors are equally baffling and contemptible. A mixture of do-gooders and anarchists who are either on the dole or, worse still, subsidised by Ken Livingstone and whatever acronym he is in charge of these days. They are troublemakers with a political naivety born of redbrick universities, who don't understand the world nor value those who create the wealth that pays for their social security.

'I wouldn't mind so much but BAE Systems supplies the British armed forces who fought for the very freedoms they are now hell-bent on abusing by covering themselves in red paint and lying on the ground.'

'It's not paint they want to cover themselves with but soap and water.'

'If they really cared about these people in Third World countries, then why are they here spoiling a meeting and not there helping starving children?'

'Because they don't care about them, they just want to cause disruption.'

For the protestors the event is a piece of theatre, a spectacle. To the board, the AGM is a corporate performance with compliance rituals. To the shareholders it is a ruddy pantomime. And to the fund managers it is a day out of the office.

The board

The raised panel behind which the directors of BAE Systems sit is a plinth in an olive concrete colour. It rises slanting from the floor to tower over the meeting, like a Kremlin balcony. It looks like it could withstand a small bomb blast. The men behind it look like they would sell you one. They sit under a BAE Systems banner and no longer appear as individuals. They are 'the board'. Nonetheless, the odd human trait still manages to emerge ... if you regard dandruff as a sign of humanity.

Maybe they would come across differently if they put pictures of their children on the podium. Or started the meeting by saying, 'Before we get going I must just tell you what my five-year-old said at the breakfast table ...' Or if the chief executive said, 'Kenneth is going to present the accounts, but first, Kenneth, do the Crazy Frog noise, go on. It's great, Ken's impression is.' But I doubt it. Arms dealers are judged not by who they are but by what they sell and to whom. There are even people in this meeting room and outside on the demo whose communities and families face destruction from the board's product range. Not because they have done anything wrong, other than want democracy or their land back. The fate of these communities is irrelevant to the company. So the communities face military might and political indifference. I am sitting next to a representative from one of those communities.

Amid the shareholders of middle England, who sit flicking through the company report or gazing off into the middle distance, is my friend Breica Lehbib. He is nervous and clutches a tightly rolled-up company report in his hands. Breica is the London representative of the Polisario, the Western Sahrawi people's organisation. They are not a rich group; his suit looks like it was inherited from a previous organiser. It's two sizes too big and threatens to engulf him as he sits with his bum on the edge of the seat, hunched over, legs apart. With his Arab skin and fidgeting manner, he looks like he is waiting outside a courtroom to hear if he will be deported. 'I think this is a good initiative,' he mutters in an Arab-inflected drawl. 'This is good that we get the message to these people.'

Breica and Western Sahara

Breica is from Western Sahara, which sits beneath Morocco and opposite the Canary Islands, caught between a kingdom and a nightclub. The Canary Islands have not posed too much of a problem for the Western Sahrawis. Occasionally the sea breeze, when blowing in the right direction, wafts in the strains of 'Hi Ho Silver Lining' from Alfie's Irish Bar on Tenerife, but nothing much besides. The royalist Moroccans, on the other hand, have not been quite so demure. They invaded Western Sahara in 1975, occupying the top two-thirds of the country. Mauritania, the country to the south of Western Sahara, saw the Sahrawis' plight and, in the spirit of communal concern, promptly invaded the remaining third of the country. All of which should have put Western Sahara in the frame for a guest appearance on ITV's *Neighbours From Hell* series. I believe the Sahrawis were passed over when the show's producers found someone in Sussex with an interesting hedge dispute. As you might have guessed, not a huge amount of press coverage has ensued.

The invasion came with the usual barbarism, with Morocco napalming fleeing civilians as they crossed the desert, some on foot and some by truck, to the sanctuary of Algeria. From there the Western Sahrawis launched a bloody guerrilla-style war on both occupying forces, resulting in the withdrawal of Mauritania in 1979, leaving the Sahrawis with the bottom third of their country liberated. The war continued with Morocco until 1991, when a ceasefire commenced and the United Nations moved in and set about organising a referendum on independence from Morocco. How successful was this referendum organised by the mighty UN? Need you ask?

So far, fifteen years after their arrival, the UN has not even been able to get a decision on who is eligible to vote in the referendum. As there aren't a huge amount of natural resources in Western Sahara – some phosphate mines and fishing rights off the coast – there is virtually no reason for the Coalition of the Willing to do anything but poke their heads round the tent flaps once in a while and say, 'We are doing everything we can't ... sorry, can. Everything we can! Yes, that's what we are doing.' Before wandering off to ignore another conflict in another part of the world. So the Western Sahrawis have patiently waited in their refugee camps in Algeria. A quarter of a million people have lived in these camps in the desert for over thirty years. Were they squatters in Lambeth council houses, ownership would have reverted to them by now.

Meanwhile, as Morocco stalls any chance of election, six things happen:

Morocco builds a huge military wall across the desert on the edge of the occupied land of the Sahrawis. It is called a 'berm'. It is 1,500 miles long and crosses the entire territory.

Grassroots pressure within the refugee camps in Algeria calls for a return to the armed struggle against Morocco. Polisario state that they may be forced to go back to war.

Morocco starts arming itself to prepare for any renewal of the conflict.

Britain sells arms to Morocco. But somehow you knew that already.

So do Spain, France and Switzerland (neutral, my arse ...).

The Sahrawis in the occupied territory start an intifada – an uprising.

A HELPFUL MP?

Months before I sat with Breica in the BAE Systems meeting, I received a phone call from an MP. I have a fear of meeting politicians. Especially the obnoxious ones who want to privatise breathing or shove children up chimneys to pay for their school fees. My fear is that I will like them. Half the time the most reactionary demagogue turns out to be charming, self-deprecating and witty in the flesh. It is a strange paradox that an MP (let us assume it is a male one) could be sharing a pot of tea, displaying the genteel urbanity of Oscar Wilde, then put down his napkin, say, 'I wonder if you would excuse me for a moment, I have to go into the Chamber,' stroll gaily onto the floor of the House of Commons, scream 'Hang council tenants!' for ten minutes without pause, then, when the flecks of spittle start to dry on the necks of the MPs sitting in front of him, he will leave the Chamber, straightening cuffs and collar, to return in time for cucumber sandwiches, continuing as if he had not left. 'Have you seen the National's production of *Peer Gynt*? Very moving, I nearly cried.' It's a form of political Tourette's syndrome.

Fortunately, the phone call was from Tess Kingham, perhaps the only MP I could call a friend. She was elected in 1997 and served on the International Development Select Committee, as well as the Quadripartite Committee that oversees arms licensing. During her term as an MP, Tess had twins, which didn't enamour her to some of her colleagues of the willy-waggling brigade, who didn't know whether to shudder with shock or pleasure at the thought of a woman breastfeeding in Parliament.

It is winter 2000 and Kingham has asked me to meet her in Portcullis House, the bourgeois shopping mall that some MPs inhabit opposite Parliament. It is an odd place with a lot of glass, a couple of fountains and those thin-looking palm trees that for some reason like to be planted in pebbles. She is waiting at the entrance and escorts me through the corridors of wooden panels that smell of new carpets and home improvement programmes. We make small talk. How are the kids? What are you up to? How is it going on the International Development Select Committee? Inside her office she declares: 'Do you know, I am getting more and more forgetful as I get older. I keep leaving government documents lying around on my desk. I am just going to the loo, I'll be about thirty minutes.' With that she gets up, moves some papers on her desk and departs. Leaving me in silence, alone in an MP's office with a set of documents that are about to reveal just how duplicitous Robin Cook could be.

The document detailed the licensing of a deal between Royal Ordnance (a BAE Systems subsidiary) and the Moroccans to refurbish guns, which later turn out to be 105mm howitzer cannons and placed right in the heart of a potential conflict zone. The howitzers are situated on the 1,500-mile military wall that divides the Sahrawis and the territory occupied by the Moroccans. Should the stalled peace process collapse back into war, the Sahrawis would be facing these guns. New Labour, the ethical arms dealers, were equipping Morocco's occupation, in contravention of their own publicly stated foreign policy and the EU Code of Conduct on arms sales.

Derek Fatchett, then Foreign Office Minister, spelt out New Labour's policy on Western Sahara in 1998. He said: 'As you know, we support the UN in their efforts to achieve a resolution of the dispute through a free and fair referendum. We would not be able to reconcile this objective with supporting one side or the other, be it via the export of arms or through some other channel.'* Yet a year later New Labour were most definitely arming one side, and the side they were arming was the invading one at that.

The EU Code of Conduct on Arms Exports, signed in June 1998 by Britain, clearly sets out guidelines on arms sales. Criterion Four says: 'Member states will not issue an export licence if there is a clear risk that the intended recipient would use the proposed export aggressively against another country or to assert by force a territorial claim.'

Does Morocco assert its territorial claim over Western Sahara with force? Of course it does! How else can it? Assert it by exploiting internationally accepted conventions of social conduct, perhaps? Does Morocco get up really early, sneak out and put a

---

* A letter to the Western Sahara Campaign, 7 September 1998.

beach towel on the entire country of Western Sahara while the Western Sahrawis lie awake thinking, Damn, they've bagsied us again? No, it doesn't. Morocco's occupation is made with military might, and now with New Labour's help, who are breaking the very EU code they signed up to.

What a Cook-up!

Parliamentary select committees are composed of MPs from all parties and are designed to hold ministers and government policy to account. The committees can call ministers to answer questions, take expert testimony, take oral and written evidence and publish regular reports on government policy. Most of the select committee hearings are held in public. Anyone can wander in, take a seat and watch the spectacle of ministers and civil servants being questioned by MPs. The minister faces the committee and sits just in front of the first row of the public seats, so the public are inches away from ministers and the back of their necks. The committee hearings are predominantly filmed for TV news. So should anyone wish to sit behind a minister, facing the questioning MPs, wearing a T-shirt with the word LIAR on it, they could do so. While on this point, I merely note that although you do have to go through searches and metal detectors to get into Parliament, you could probably smuggle in a glove puppet, which could in theory appear at a minister's shoulder, musing and cogitating on the proceedings. When Alastair Campbell appeared at the Foreign Affairs Committee to discuss 'sexing up' the Iraq dossier, I would have paid a small fortune to see Matthew Corbett produce a yellow bear puppet at his shoulder saying, 'What's that, Sooty? A cover-up, you say!'

Generally speaking, not many folk bother popping in to observe this process of scrutiny. Most sane people don't take time off work to go along to hear the minister for local government get a grilling over changes in the database provision for the electoral register. And those that do should probably face up to the fact that they need a proper hobby, like measuring bricks or collecting flies, or anything other than sudoku. (Sudoku is nothing but the *Puzzler* of the middle classes.)

However, the private sessions for select committees contain confidential and possibly classified information. They are held behind closed doors away from the NGOs, campaigners, journalists and school trips of politics A-level students.

It is 30 January 2001, and Robin Cook takes his seat before a routine select committee. The public seats are crammed with his advisors and civil servants, an entourage of Elton John-sized enormity, each armed with lever-arch files and briefing notes. They

TIMETABLE FOR THE DEAL

❏ August 1998: Derek Fatchett, Minister of State with responsibility for the Middle East and North Africa, judges Royal Ordnance's licence application to refurbish thirty 105mm howitzer cannons and export six new 105mm howitzers cannons to Morocco to be at odds with Criterion Four of EU Code of Conduct.

❏ 28 August 1998: DTI inform the company of the refusal.

❏ September 1998: Royal Ordnance appeal the decision.

❏ December 1998: Derek Fatchett still opposes licence of the deal.

❏ June/July 1999: New minister who replaced Fatchett approves part of the deal.

❏ 12 July 1999: DTI inform Royal Ordnance that they can have a licence for the refurbishment of the thirty guns but not to supply six new ones.

❏ 30 January 2001: Cook drops a bollock in the committee and blabs the story in public.

Who was the new minister who approved the licence for Royal Ordnance?

Geoff Hoon, no less ... the ex MoD minister who led Britain so successfully into Iraq.

shuffle into their seats, leaving room for only a handful of campaigners. With a twist of his neck, a nod of his head and a flourish of his cuffs, Cook takes his green leather seat before them.

It is towards the end of the session that Cook is asked a general question about military equipment sold to Morocco, and he starts talking in public about 'the refurbishment of guns' and how the original arms deal was 'for the supply of fresh guns and then we rejected that'. A Mexican wave of panic surfs the line of servants. Cook is giving details of a deal which it later emerges was meant strictly for the private session with the MPs. Cook, the very man who will be criticised for the deal, is revealing it to the world. It appears that he simply forgot he wasn't to mention the details in the public session. Sitting in front of his civil servants and advisors, he cannot see their faces. He can't see the exchanged glances of confusion nor the hunched, rapid rechecking of notes. He cannot see the bureaucrats currently re-enacting Edvard Munch's *The Scream*.

WESTERN SAHARA: PLANE OF FOG

A charter plane is being hired by trade unionists and lefty types in Spain to fly into Algeria to visit the Sahrawi refugee camps, at the invitation of the Polisario Front. The invite is to celebrate twenty-five years of government in exile. Having a party to mark the passing years in exile is a little strange. Surely the point is to move through the exile phase as quickly as possible, get your country back and have a party marking that occasion. Celebrating the length of time that you have not achieved your objective seems ... well, it seems oddly British. It is almost Colonel Blimp territory: 'Well, chaps, we have failed, but by God we've stuck at our failure and not given in to success.'

The elderly plane is packed with solidarity activists, a handful of journalists and Tam Tiernan from the Scottish Fire

Brigade Union. Tam breaks the stereotype of Scottish trade unionists by spending most of the flight incredulous at the knowledge that he is going to spend a week in a desert refuge camp, with no bar. The plane rattles down the runway, creaking of plastic and the sound of overhead lockers rattling open. The revving jets wheeze and gasp skywards. Faster it moves until we all tilt back, cheering as we leave the ground, and virtually the entirety of the trade union movement on board promptly light up. So now the plane, which I am convinced has asthma, is full of chain-smoking Spanish lefties, a handful of coughing BBC reporters in linen trousers and a man shouting above the grinding noise of flight, 'Nay fuckin' bar! Not fuckin' one bar! Ah must be mad. Ah must be.' The flight lasts five hours, which in trade-unionist time is about a pack and a half of cigarettes. They smoke as if it were a human right to do so and they are working for the betterment of mankind.

The bloodletting from the military assault on militant Islamists and an internal conflict that cost 150,000 lives probably plays a significant part in Algeria's failure to establish itself on the European tourist itinerary. Algeria might not welcome package tours in their droves but they did welcome the fleeing Western Sahrawis in 1976, letting them set up refugee camps and providing varying degrees of assistance. Algeria's help has enabled a quarter of a million people to stay together as a nation in desert exile.

Thus we descend to the Algerian city of Tindouf. The airport is a small and barren place where the tumbleweed long ago gave up and moved on to a more interesting location. There are so few visitors to Tindouf that the airport doesn't have a taxi rank. It barely has a car park, and the duty-free is a wooden kiosk selling cups of coffee and Lucky Strikes singly. We land, passports are stamped, the local mosquitoes are informed of the fresh meat and somewhere behind me I hear Tam groan.

It is the Sahrawis who collect us at the airport. The drivers, khaki-clad, wearing headscarves and nonchalantly nursing machine guns, lounge confidently against the parked jeeps, catching the last heat of the sunset.

'What type of gun is that? It looks like an AK47,' I gauchely enquire, peering at the banana-shaped magazine, trying to appear knowledgeable.

'These, for your protection. You must not leave camp. You are safe with us. By yourself, no,' says Brahim Mokhtar, a lightly bearded translator swathed in a camouflage jacket.

'Tindouf is dangerous for you. Yes? But with us, no problem.'

And with that our bags are unceremoniously chucked into the Land-Rover. With only slightly more dignity than our luggage, a group of us, including my friend and cameraman Duncan, scramble into the jeep, which hurtles away from Tindouf, headlights full on, into the encroaching darkness of the desert. It is four hours since we left the confines of the plane. We are tired, dirty, and already one of the non-smoking BBC reporters is experiencing nicotine withdrawal for the first time in his life. Brahim sits in the front with the driver and a chap with a gun between his legs, offering a commentary throughout the journey.

'An hour and a half. Maybe more to get to the camp. You are all staying with a Sahrawi family in their tents tonight.'

The BBC groan. I think they were expecting better accommodation, and they certainly don't relish the thought of sharing a tent with others while they try to broadcast from a satellite phone.

'We are pleased you are here. We need all international support to get a free and fair referendum for our country. We need support.'

'You need tarmac,' mutters a grumbling voice under his breath, which is quite possibly mine, as once again the jeep hits a rut of piles-inducing intensity.

'First solidarity, then liberation, then tarmac!' declares Brahim.

Article 51

Article 51 of the UN charter states that every country has a right to self-defence, which also happens to be one of the most frequently used arguments to justify the arms trade. Indeed the very term 'Defence Industry' echoes this noble notion of repelling an invader. This is entirely understandable. Few captains of commerce would feel comfortable sitting down to a dinner party and making small talk along the lines of: 'What do I do? I work in the Attack Industry; spent some time prior to that in the Ministry of Obliteration, in the Annihilation Sector, now I'm back at Attack. And you? … Oh really? That sounds fascinating. What's it like working for Antisocial Services?'

The fact is that people do have a legal right to self-defence, enshrined by the UN. Practically it might not mean much. I doubt, for example, that Ho Chi Minh ever said, 'Before we lift a finger against the imperialist US pig-dog invaders, does anyone know a good lawyer?' But it is there, it should be there, and frankly even if Article 51 didn't exist the right to self-defence still would. It is perhaps one of the most fundamental tenets of natural justice: that we have a right to life and a right to defend that life.

A brief gander at the Gandhian perspective

It is stating the obvious to say that dialogue is better than conflict, peace is better than war, and in tests nine out of ten consumers said they preferred breathing. It is just as obvious to say that in some circumstances a violent reaction to a violent situation is justified. The practice and principles of peaceful non-cooperation simply can't be applied that often in brutal conflicts. Non-violent resistance as a tactic works by eliciting shame in your attacker and respect for the dignity of the attacked. Which doesn't tend to work if a pilot is dropping napalm on you. Burning to death with your human dignity intact is still burning to death. Either way it is doubtful that a pilot thousands of feet above your charred but well-mannered corpse is going to have his moral expectations confounded by your willingness to be barbecued.

The Western Sahrawis have used their rights under Article 51. They fought a bloody war to regain their land, got a third of it back and since then have endured a fruitless peace process.

'Unless we have a free and fair referendum, we have to go back to war,' shrugs Brahim.

'But that is going to result in your friends and family and possibly you being killed.'

'Yes. It is very sad. But what can we do?'

'You have no hope of winning against the Moroccans.'

'It will be another guerrilla war. We are very good guerrilla fighters. We capture the Moroccans' own weapons and use them against them.'

'The point is, it seems to me, that you are just saying you are going to go back to war to try to move the peace process forward, you're not actually going to return to war.'

'There is pressure in the camps to go to war. From the people. The leadership cannot control it for ever.'

So Article 51 remains an option that is depressingly justified.

Reeking of permanence

Daylight reveals that we are on the edge of the camp. In front of us is open desert and a few camels; behind us 70,000 people live. Each family has a traditional square nomadic tent for the winter and a mud-brick hut for the summer. Sometimes there are two small walls connecting the sides of the hut with the sides of the tent, creating a little yard in the middle. This camp Laayoune,* named after a city in their occupied homeland, is twenty-five years old.

---

* Some Sahrawis refuse to call it by its Moroccan name and use the Spanish name El Ayoun.

As the morning sun rises I look on this city slowly coming to life and think: a refugee camp shouldn't be like this. It should by its very nature be temporary. Its life should be shorter than that of an average boy band, not longer than the solo career of David Bowie. A refugee camp should spring up as a result of a flood or drought or war; people flee to it, they get food and medicine, life normalises, problems are solved, people return or move on to new lives and then the Red Cross packs the gear up ready for the next one. That's how a refugee camp works. Refugee camps should not get their own fucking postcodes! Refugee camps should not get more tourists than the nearest city with an airport! This one has its own schools, a hospital, a courthouse, a council building and its own jail. On the outskirts it even has a parade ground and wooden grandstand for civic occasions and prize-giving cere-monies. This place looks like it could be twinned with Newport!

These thoughts should be tempered with the information that mornings are never the best time of day for me.

Desert parade

After bread, tea and honey, Brahim sets off at a jaunty pace through the alleyways of tents and huts to the parade ground. The sun is warming the night air away, though there is still a chill as we tramp through dusty corridors of canvas and mud. The gentle sting of wood smoke calmly announces breakfast to the awakening families. The early morning stillness accentuates the fluttering of the Western Sahara flags that fly from every tent. Brahim's pace through the camp is only momentarily slowed as he stops to greet friends, casually air-kissing their cheeks, mutter-ing '*Saleem aleikum*' and moving on before his final question to them has left his mouth. The BBC have forged ahead of us, eager to interview the President of Western Sahara. I amble unprofes-sionally, talking to Nati, the eldest son of the family playing host to us. He is twenty-four, has a degree, wears a fading Disneyland T-shirt and has decided to accompany us to the parade ground where nearly 100,000 people will gather to celebrate the twenty-fifth birthday of government in exile.

As we near the parade ground the crowd gets larger. UN American peacekeeping forces mingle, in their pressed uniforms. Polisario officials in olive-green direct the throngs of women and children in their Sunday-best dresses and headscarves. Thousands line the parade ground, one long line of women, corralling kids, dispensing drinks from old water bottles and organising seats for the grandmothers and the odd elderly grandfather.

In the middle of the line of people stretched across this patch of desert is the wooden grandstand, now filling up with dignitaries taking their places on the benches. They wear sports jackets, headscarves and the look of bored diplomats. Occasionally they exchange words with the person sitting next to them, but their primary purpose seems to be preparing themselves for the arse-numbing four hours of speeches and marching soldiers ahead of them. The only two people who seem cheerful at this prospect are the Cuban ambassador, to whom four hours is light relief compared to Fidel's speeches, and Tam Tiernan, whose skinny Glaswegian face beams out a smile and who waves a thumbs-up as we pass.

'Come,' says Brahim, who has reappeared. 'Come, you must talk to the women.' He leads us along the parade ground to the thousands behind the ropes. As we approach, the women ululate and shout.

'"Victory to Polisario," they are saying,' translates Brahim.

The women clap and cheer each other and take turns to punch the air with clenched fists and proclaim their slogans.

'Long live the Polisario. Long live Western Sahara,' smiles a translating Brahim.

The noise of the crowd rises as Duncan approaches with the camera. The women call to us, beckoning us to film their protests and predictions of victory. One woman, however, angrily wags her finger as she cries out to us.

'What did she say?'

'"Long live Polisario,"' says Brahim, suspiciously quieter.

'Do you think she said that?' I whisper to Duncan.

'Nah, she said something he didn't want us to hear,' he mutters out of the corner of his mouth.

'What? Along the lines of "Death to the Moroccans"?'

'Could be, could be worse.'

'Hang our enemies with their own entrails?'

'More likely to be: "You're fatter than you look on the telly, Mark."'

'Here, look, point your camera.' Brahim motions to the Sahrawi army band standing before the podium. A wave of a hand and a tune stabs the air. I don't recognise it, but it manages to be both atonal and pompous at the same time. The kind of noise Shostakovich would have produced had he lived in Trumpton and been forced to write marching music. Odds on the noise they are making is their national anthem. It stands in stark contrast to the ululating women, who are now quietly sharing out little plastic Western Sahara flags among the kids to wave when their brothers and fathers march past. Though for some of them their family won't be marching past, but they will remember that once they did.

The speeches ring through an old tannoy system. Photographs are taken, hands shaken, poses struck and finally the parade begins. The best troops march first, past the formal podium, along the desert strip with cheering crowds waving plastic flags, until the gathering just peters out, the marching men lose step and break off before any formal command can be given. They hurry to hug children and wave at friends. Some of the younger soldiers have proud smiles that say, 'Mummy, did you see me out there?'

'Machine guns,' says Brahim, who is determined to give a running commentary.

More brigades or battalions pass, their uniforms becoming bit by bit more dishevelled.

'Mortars,' says Brahim, as a truck with mortars on the back goes by. There is something strangely moving about the pride in which these men and women hold this battered old equipment.

'Missiles,' points out Brahim, as that truck draws level. Brahim is trying to inject some technological competency and pride into the occasion, though the missiles themselves look like they came from a 1970s film set involving Mini Mooks and an ugly villain mysteriously surrounded by women in bikinis. If these missiles were ever launched and took to the air, the Sahrawis would surely scream in shock at their commanders: 'You didn't tell us you had a live one!'

Some of the trucks have got four different makes of tyre on them. Some of the rifles have no straps; some machine guns have no magazines.

'Much of this we capture from Morocco.'

Much of this won't be missed by the Moroccans, though it might be by the *Antiques Roadshow*. It takes an hour of slightly decrepit trucks and marching men with untied bootlaces before the crowd get their favourites: the camel riders. Charging down the parade ground from out of the desert, headscarves trailing in the wind, they make a thundering noise.

'Camels,' I say to Brahim, before he can say it to me.

The parade meanders to a finish, as meandering to a halt would give it a degree of military precision it simply doesn't have. The crowds begin to wander off, soldiers put their arms round their wives and kids try to grab hold of the guns before they are collected up. The UN return to their jeeps, one of which has its bonnet up with jump leads spilling out.

'This is like the peace process,' Brahim laughs. 'Broken and not going anywhere.'

The UN soldier replies defensively: 'Easily fixed, don't you worry.' But he is talking about the jeep, not the peace.

Brahim is in a good mood. 'You are happy? You have all the filming you want?'

'Great, thanks.'

'You are happy, I am happy.' And he strolls through the crowd, merrily translating as we walk and chat to Sahrawis in the departing melee.

'Do you want to go back to war?' I ask mothers with armfuls of children.

'We have no option. If the peace process will not deliver a free and fair referendum we have no choice,' the veiled voices say.

Two young women, sisters, calmly tell us: 'It is better to fight than die out here in the desert.'

'But a return to war will mean you could lose your family.'

'What else can we do?'

An old woman to whom I ask the question answers with one word. We turn to Brahim for the translation. Without a flicker of doubt and with the speed of a racing commentator, Brahim begins: 'She says she agrees with the Polisario decision to work within the UN framework for a free and fair referendum for independence. But the Moroccans must abide by the process, using the Spanish census to establish voting eligibility and—'

'She only said one word!' we splutter, laughing. 'She didn't say all that.'

'Yes, but she is tired. She did not want to give you the full answer. I am only clarifying her thoughts for her. I am only saying what she really believes. Come. Eat ...' gesturing to the building where the dignitaries are gathering.

'Do the camels really have a military use?' I change the subject.

'They are just for show. We use the camels for meat.'

'What does *that* taste like?' I enquire, probably giving away my vegetarian inclination of nineteen years.

Brahim pauses, strokes his beard with a quizzical furrow on his forehead. 'Er ... a little bit like giraffe. Have you ever had giraffe?'

'No ...'

'I had giraffe in a restaurant in Nairobi. The Carnivore. You get game meat there. I said I wanted giraffe, crocodile and elephant. But they did not have elephant, so I had zebra.'

'Zebra! What does that taste like?'

'Er …' His eyebrows softly rise as his answers dawns. 'Have you ever had gazelle?'

Nati's question and the camel

Incidentally, if camel meat is anything to go by, giraffe should taste just fine. After nineteen meat-free years, it is camel meat that breaks me. Sitting in the tent that is bedroom, bathroom, office and living room, Nati's family transform our canvas home into a dining room for the evening meal. The kids shuffle the cushions on the floor into the lines of a three-sided square that faces the doorway, creating 'top table' effect for the guests. Nati brings in the battered metal tray on old wooden legs that he normally uses to prepare the tea. He places it in the centre of the tent to give the camel meat pride of place before it is served. Outside the children are excited and are making the kind of noises that say, 'Can I have the leftovers? Please. Pleeeeease.' Their mother makes the kind of noises that say, 'Stop it. These are for our guests.'

Then she walks into the tent smiling, holding a tray of steaming camel.

'Camel,' says Brahim. 'Because you are here the family have been given camel by the camp committee. This is very good. For the children this is special. They will have camel too.'

'Do they get camel often?' enquires Duncan, trying to sound as if this is a question one would normally ask in the circumstances.

'No no no. This will be the only time this year. Very excited. They are very excited.'

Nati smiles, awaiting confirmation of our enjoyment. If he were in a Piccadilly gentlemen's club he would be handing over a crystal glass, leaning back into a leather chair and muttering through his jowls, 'Is there anything finer than a fifty-seven claret?' But he's not. He is a refugee handing over camel kebabs, which is the best meal they are going to get all year.

We chew, nod and do exaggerated smiling back to Nati.

Duncan leans over and whispers: 'You OK? You're doing really well.'

I whisper back: 'It's fucking delicious.'

Later Nati makes Sahrawi tea, a dark green sweet drink that is decanted from one glass to another until it has a froth on it. It takes an age to prepare, but no one is going anywhere fast around here.

Milka is Nati's four-year-old sister. She has charged in through the doorway of the tent and then stood upright and stock still, announcing her presence with wide eyes and a huge grin. Everyone laughs. This is her cue to skip over to us with a notebook and pencil.

'Should we bring the family a gift?' I had asked back in London.

'Pencils and paper,' Brahim had replied. 'Not sweets. They must not see our guests in solidarity just as a means of getting sweets. They must not become reliant on aid. That thinking will not help them. What we need from the international community is justice.'

So pencils and paper it was. 'She is asking for you to write your name,' says Nati, as a pencil and notebook are thrust into my hand. Milka snuggles unselfconsciously against my arm and after we have drawn some pictures together she curls up on my lap, desperately sleepy but too curious to go to bed. It is the perfect setting for Nati's next question.

Some of the poorest people on earth have just fed us; the best meal of the year is shared with strangers from a foreign land. They share their family life and home, and the raggedy kids do what kids do best, play and endear themselves. Only when this setting is complete does Nati lean over his tired sister and in a quiet voice ask, 'Tell me, Mark, why does your government want to help my enemies kill me?'

Back home if someone had called New Labour 'my government', I would have snapped back: 'It's not *my* government. If it was *my* government I would be in the Foreign Office at the weekends using the phone for overseas calls.'

I had never really thought of any government as mine. I always thought they were 'the' government. On the other hand, I am their 'citizen', which is an altogether nicer way of looking at the arrangement. It also confers upon me the right to shout, scream, protest, meddle, demand answers and insist on change. In fact, as the government want to promote active citizenship, it is not only my right to interfere with the way they are running things, it is my duty – the thought of which is quite cheering.

Nati's question, though, demands an answer. 'Money.' I decide on the honest option. 'Money and politics. BAE Systems has a lot of influence on the government.' If you judge a company's power by the number of government decisions in its favour, then we have to conclude that BAE is about as powerful as they come. 'They want the contract for the guns. The British government was bound to give in to them.'

'Hmmm. But your government can come here and see how we live. Why do they not help us?'

'Because they want to keep things sweet with Morocco, as an ally in the region and as a trading partner.'

'But it is our land. For a long time we have suffered.'

'You're not a voter issue.'

'I don't understand.'

'They don't care about you, Nati.'

'But you? You have seen. You can tell them.'

'The government?'

'Your government, yes. Tell them.'

I imagine walking through Heathrow airport, talking on the mobile. 'Mr Cook? ... Mark Thomas here. Registered voter, thought I'd give you a call. Couldn't speak earlier, was in the desert with the Sahrawis, terrible signal, kept cutting out ... Now this howitzer business, it really isn't on … OK, I'll leave it with you … Might see you if you're in the office on Saturday – I'm nipping in to make a phone call.'

'You must tell them.' The words are spoken softly, with neither the distress nor the urgency they deserve. They are whispered calmly, and the moment threatens to become an epiphany, but tiredness is the winner. Two tiny arms reach up to Nati, the signal that Milka wants to go to bed. Our conversation is at an end and she is asleep on Nati's shoulder before he gets through the doorway.

Curled up warm in the sleeping bag, just another dozing body in this nation state of tents, I wonder what our itinerary is for tomorrow. For the Sahrawis, tomorrow won't be that much different from today. Another day in the desert, concentrated on the task of staying alive and sticking together.

Fridge magnets in Auschwitz

The jeep jolts further into the desert the following afternoon, clinging to the rough track that is barely discernible to the human eye. From out of the windows the desert looks as if a child drew it, just a long strip of yellow and a big strip of blue. For creationists the desert was God's lazy day, a knackered omnipresent being mumbling, 'I've spent ages on the rainforest eco-systems, bust a gut on the Arctic tundra, bollocks to this. This place gets sand and sun. If anything lives good luck to it, I need a beer … Fuck it, I haven't invented hops yet.'

A small group of us are taking a cultural break to visit the Sahrawis' museum. Penny from the BBC, Duncan and a freelance journalist called Karen Thomas.

'They've got just about everything else out here, why not a museum?' shouts Duncan over the roar of the jeep. 'They probably have an opera house somewhere.'

'I bet they have a gift shop,' I shout back.

'With liberation-struggle tea towels and bad fudge,' he

replies, but the noise of the journey makes conversation difficult and I settle into pondering why the National Trust in Britain sells gardening gloves in castles. Who visits a historic site of a massacre and wants to buy gardening equipment? Maybe all historic sites do that. Maybe Auschwitz has a gift shop. I wonder if they have fridge magnets at Auschwitz. Or worse still, gardening gloves. And if they don't, how long before they do? It is impossible to calculate exactly when the most potent monuments of atrocity and barbarism will lose their iconic status, but they do, as the memory of each massacre or genocide dies with the generations who witnessed them.

The Sahrawi museum is a brick fort in the middle of nowhere. It's as if the French Foreign Legion got halfway through and said: 'What on earth is the point of this? Come on, let's go home and face the music.' The walls stand fifteen feet high; it's a brick box with no roof and a wooden doorway. There is no gift shop. There is a guard-cum-curator who nods at Brahim as we dismount the Toyota, gathering cameras and sunhats.

The museum feels even bigger for the lack of a roof, as the wind manages to cut across open ground within the brick square. Covering the entire area are unusable munitions, guns and cannons captured from the Moroccans. In one corner howitzers point to the sky. Naturally there is a British one, old and battered, from another era. Among the arranged avenues of weaponry, a plain of landmines stretches out, a crop of lily-like discs. The makers are mainly Italian. Row upon row of mines, each one defused, so Brahim says, by Sahrawi guerrillas. Piles of rifles are propped up in triangles, like black witches' hats, all evenly spaced out. We crunch across the dusty museum past big belt-feed machine guns squatting on the sand next to old missiles, shells, casings. Wreckage from aircraft moves gently in the breeze, bits of engines, a tail fin, parts of the wing, gouged metal casings leaking wires flung from the belly of an unknown craft.

A busload of Sahrawi schoolchildren is ushered into the

museum by a teacher, here to see the history of their conflict in metal and plastic. Giggling, the girls in headscarves huddle in groups, glad to be out of the classroom and pointing at the exhibits. Somebody playfully grabs something that belongs to someone else. They shriek loudly but quickly cup their mouths when the teacher looks at them. Suppressing laughter when the teacher turns away again.

In the middle of this open-air museum stands an armoured personnel carrier. Centre stage in the geometric display of redundant weapons. The carrier's back door opens at a tug on its metal handle, grating slightly, and light pours in through the door to reveal its contents. Old, dark wooden crates. Masses of rectangular boxes, ammunition cases, piled carelessly, almost ransacked, filling the whole innards of the vehicle. Each crate overflows with photographs. Spilling out, piled in mounds, covering the metal floor. Thousands and thousands of photos, tiny passport photos, wallet-sized family shots. Pictures of young men posing in uniform in bars, of children smiling, fathers holding youngsters up to the camera, mums and kids, parties, formal group shoots of soldiers taken in a studio. They stand in front of backdrops, some of palm trees, some with camels or a city skyline; elderly parents kissing during a celebration, wedding photos, sports days, receiving trophies, kids in their best clothes, hair brushed and parted. Piles of them tumbling through my fingers as I scoop them up, images falling from my hands, cascading from the crates as I shift them to see if they contain anything else but these photos. All of them, every crate full of photos. Fistfuls of falling pictures, babies, drunken embraces, sports teams, bridesmaids.

Duncan says, 'This is really weird.'

Penny from the BBC team says, 'Oh my God.' Penny realised quicker than anyone else what we were looking at. These pictures have been taken from dead men, taken from their wallets and pockets. Snatched from corpses and stored in an armoured coffin. These are dead men's photos. These are scalps. They took the last scrap of intimacy from the breathless, the pictures of their loved ones taken into battle, and turned them into tawdry victory bunting. They have celebrated their enemies' death, with scalps.

Brahim has wandered over. 'After the war,' he says with gravitas, 'we will hand these photos back to the Moroccan authorities, so they know what has happened to their people.'

'This is awful.'

'We do not hate these people. It was not their fault they have been forced to fight. We do not want to fight them. What can we do? They have taken our country.'

'What do the children think of this?' I ask.

'They will laugh, they will see this as a defeat for their enemy. We have killed their enemies, and this makes them feel proud. They are children. But when they grow older they will understand. We do not hate these people.'

Stopping on the journey back, we stand a few metres from the jeep, stretching our legs. Penny from the BBC kicks some stones, arms crossed and head down.

'You OK?'

'I'm sad,' she says, 'and angry.'

'At the Sahrawis?'

'Yes. I just thought they were noble, I suppose. But that back there was horrible. Horrible. I suppose I always thought that here was one group of people who were right to struggle, who were so brave and resilient and right to fight. But I just found that ... that truck sickening.'

'It doesn't change the fact that they are right to struggle, does it?' My question is naive, trying to shore up the faith I have placed in the Sahrawi cause. In my eyes these people are heroes, surviving in the desert, staying together as a nation, betrayed by the UN and fighting a war of attrition with Morocco. Wrapped up in my admiration for them, I have turned the Sahrawis into something they are not: a PR version of a liberation movement, and in that version I stupidly expected a war without corpses. A war that could be won on the front of a T-shirt with a good slogan. But it really doesn't matter how justified a cause is, or how downtrodden, wretched and oppressed the people are in whose name the cause exists: taking a human life is a brutal act. I had forgotten that. The Sahrawi right to defend themselves is also their right to kill.

Penny from the BBC answers: 'No,' she says factually. 'I don't suppose it does alter the cause. I just thought they were better than that.'

A deal for howitzers on Morocco's military wall arms an aggressor in an unequal fight, but if war starts the Sahrawis, from what I have seen, would not back down. It will be a fight that neither the arms dealers, nor the civil servants, nor the government will witness. They will not see the next handful of photos slung into the back of a truck. They will not see the Sahrawi families waving plastic flags at parades of poorly equipped soldiers, they will not know of the brothers and fathers who march past as ghosts. They will have moved on. They will be working on another contract. If I cannot see the board of directors at BAE Systems as anything other than two-dimensional humans, it is perhaps because their absence from the carnage deprives them of that final third dimension. They have absented themselves from responsibility.

BACK AT BAE

Centre stage and slightly in front of the rest of the board stands Sir Dick Evans, his hands gripping the sides of the podium. Another man at that podium might have looked like a tank commander in his turret. Not Sir Dick Evans. He looks like what he is: a knighted salesman. He is a confident, successful arms manufacturer, a legal Harry Lime, peering at the ants below. Bull-necked, with cropped hair and a short moustache, he chairs the proceedings in a masterful manner, part comedian, part head-master. He has to, what with Quakers cropping up, small share-holders quibbling about remunerations, people falling on the floor in front of him covered in fake blood, all that and a legal requirement to vote and approve accountants and appointments. No wonder he ordered a boisterous anarchist to be thrown out on hearing the words, 'I've got a question for you, Captain Pugwash.'

A gentleman with a folded raincoat over one arm and waving an underlined copy of the company report in his other hand is asking a question. Sir Dick Evans respectfully directs the gentle-man to various pages in the report, to tables and appendices. Mid-flow, a young activist with a good line in baggy sweaters stands up. His name is Gabriel and he has managed to smuggle a large false nose past security. He fixes the nose to his face by pulling its elastic string over his head and stands in front of the podium bearing Sir Dick Evans. This bold skinny Pinocchio turns to face the crowd with a grin and starts pointing first at his long nose, then at Sir Dick Evans.

'Will you please return to your seat, sir,' says Sir Dick Evans. Security around the room flexes itself in preparation, the suited men stand legs apart, arms hunched like gunslingers, ready for action. Puckish Gabriel defies the request and, cheered on by protestors, prances first one way and then another, ignoring shouts of 'Sit down!' from other shareholders, while pointing at Sir Dick Evans and the nose with increasingly exaggerated gestures.

'If you don't take your seat, I shall have to have you removed from the meeting.'

Gabriel returns to his seat in the front row and promptly stands on it, now nearly at eye level with Sir Dick Evans, still pointing, with the look of a pantomime clown.

'Please take your seat.'

'I have taken my seat,' he says with mock indignation.

'Could you please remove this gentleman?' Sir Dick Evans orders.

The security move in but Gabriel is now springing over the rows of chairs, dancing in between the tutting mass of the surrey of shareholders. The guards are slowed down by the possibility of accidentally putting an elbow or worse in a pensioner's face, and Gabriel looks at his pursuers in wide-eyed mock horror, clutching his face with his hands. Inevitably his clowning is short-lived. He is cornered, caught and carried with a security guard on each limb out of the room, to protestors' applause and shouts of 'More!' and 'Encore!'

Sir Dick Evans pauses and points with a stub of a finger, picking a questioner seemingly at random from the raised hands on the floor. A chap in a suit, possibly an employee with the company that provided the sound equipment, brings the roving cordless microphone into the audience for the speaker. He hovers at a respectable distance, ready to retrieve the mic once the shareholder has finished speaking. This questioner is a nun. She explains her work in conflict zones and the impact of weapons in conflicts. She firmly asks Sir Dick to try to find a way for BAE Systems to make less harmful products and introduce more socially useful items. He answers politely. She is a nun, after all, so he's hardly likely to tell her to fuck off. If I were in his place I too would answer politely, but I would also be thinking: we make fighter planes, and you seriously want me to turn this company to producing table-tennis bats and seed sorters. Get a life, love. Tsk tsk tsk. Stroll on lunchtime.

Sir Dick, though, talks of how many Airbuses BAE makes and fleets of civilian aircraft. He finishes, scans the room, picks and points to another questioner. A woman takes the mic and nervously says, 'I am opposed to the arms trade,' pausing just long enough for Sir Dick Evans to quip, 'Well, may I suggest then that you don't buy shares in arms companies. That *is* what we are, you know.' The surrey love this, tittering lightly and whispering comments to each other.

And so it goes. Sir Dick listens, answers, picks and points.

Until I realise he is pointing at Breica. It is Breica's turn to speak. He is the only Arab to address them, and the normal background hubbub of the meeting has stopped. I wonder briefly why we are here. Is this moment a chance to prick the conscience of a company? No. It is debatable whether human beings have souls, it is impossible for corporations to have them. If it turns out that multinational legal and financial trading entities do possess a conscience, then we can only conclude that God is a globaliser, the cross is a brand logo and entry into heaven will be means-tested. Companies have distinct legal duties, obligations, remits and procedures. All of which are geared towards the creation of profit, with a few public safeguards tacked on. The essential ingredient for a conscience is a sense of shame, and the nearest any corporation has to a sense of shame is their publicity depart-ment. These departments react to adverse stories only when they feel the company's image is in danger.

There is little danger of embarrassing the corporate entity either. There have been so many bad stories about BAE Systems that the company has turned into the Millwall FC of the corpo-rate world. The *Guardian* front pages can scream all the allega-tions of bribery and corruption they like, BAE Systems' response is to stand there singing, to the tune of 'We Are Sailing', 'No one likes us, we don't care!' You would have to catch every member of the board sacrificing kids in pentangles before any embarrass-ment was felt by BAE. And even then, what would embarrass BAE more would be a story that their executives were using another arms company's products to do the sacrificing.

Breica and I are not really part of the entertainment. Many protestors have perfected the fine art of turning an ordinary event into a spectacle. Take one AGM, simply add protestors staging die-ins, throw in some jibes, jokes and general disrespect for the board and presto, political panto! This might have a purpose in convincing the shareholders that their esteemed company is held in contempt for its actions. But it is not ours.

Who knows if what Breica has to say might touch some humanity in a shareholder or two? This kind of thing has happened in the past, but not often. Occasionally one or two of them have been shocked by the company's actions, though what they did about it I don't know.

No, the reason Breica is here is altogether more elemental than any of this. It is simply his chance to represent the Sahrawis, to appear before the crowd as a human being instead of a statistic or a target.

Not surprisingly, Breica's hands shake a little when he takes the mic. Here he is, miles from the home he has been driven out of, standing before the men who armed the country that drove him out. If this isn't standing in the belly of the beast, then it is certainly somewhere in its alimentary region. 'My name,' he begins, looking at the floor, 'is Breica Lehbib. I represent the Polisario here in London.' His thick Arab accent leaves the room silent. I am positive half the people here are the Home Counties type who have never had a kebab in their life. On principle. They are from a rarified white enclosure that as a rule has difficulty with foreign words. Just to pronounce 'onion bhaji' correctly would be a step forward; names like 'Thabo Mbeki' are steered well clear of. On hearing Breica's accent, half have switched off. They look on with the mannered disdain of those who have learnt to endure boredom with ease.

'It is my job to tell the people of Britain what has happened to my country, to tell the people here how we live and that we seek justice, and I say to myself, well, I can't be very good at my job because you do not know how we are suffering. If I was better at my job, then you would not have sold these weapons, the 105-millimetres, to Morocco. I am sorry I have not done my job well enough, so please allow me to try to do it better. Please let me tell you about Western Sahara, my country, so next time you will know and not make this mistake again.' It is a beautiful conceit. Who is to blame when one of the largest arms multinationals in the world sells arms to Morocco? A poor man in a cheap suit who spends half his life in a tent. His logic, that had the company known the situation they would not have sold the arms, is simple and poetic. What you have done has no defence but ignorance, so let me enlighten you, he seems to say. Breica lifts his head up to face the crowd and smiles at them. The surrey look on. They know he is a foreigner who comes from ... well, somewhere. And that 'somewhere' is having a hard time of it, or he wouldn't be here. So he speaks to blank stares and silence. 'All we want is a free and fair referendum, to decide the fate of our own country.' He finishes after five minutes, which is the longest I have ever seen anyone speak at an AGM. 'All we want is justice. Thank you.' And he hands back the mic.

'Thank you,' says Sir Dick Evans, slightly glazed. 'Er, you, madam.' He has picked and pointed and moved on.

Q: HOW DID ROBIN COOK GET AWAY WITH IT? A: HE DIDN'T TELL THE TRUTH

Cook said that in between Derek Fatchett refusing the deal and Geoff Hoon approving it, 'the United Nations in Western Sahara and in New York confirmed the refurbishment was within the terms of the ceasefire agreement and they were willing to supervise the refurbishment'.

Kim Howells, FCO junior minister, said on a *Newsnight* programme,* 'I know very well about the process that resulted in refurbishment of some guns in Morocco and I understand that it had permission from the UN in New York.'

The UN Department of Peace-Keeping Operations (DPKO), to which Cook and Howells referred, cannot give permission for arms deals to go ahead

---

* *Newsnight* programme was broadcast on 8 March 2001.

and they certainly do not supervise them either. David Wimhurst of the UN DPKO, referring to the howitzer deal, said: 'It's not a question of us giving permission or approval, it's not something we can do ... There was no question of permission being sought or given.'

Carne Ross is a 39-year-old ex-career diplomat who was fast-streamed straight out of university into the civil service. Ross told me he knew of the deal. 'I was head of the Middle East section of the UK mission to the UN in New York and I supervised a couple of other diplomats, one of whose primary responsibility was covering the Western Sahara in the UN Security Council. ... The issue [of the howitzers] was basically raised with us by the UN, by the Department of Peace-Keeping Operations, who were concerned that there should not be any export of weapons to the zone of conflict.'

So had the deal been cleared by the UN?

'It was a fairly generous way of describing it,' says Carne Ross. 'The UN had raised concerns and we [the UK] had given them assurances in return. The UN did not raise further concerns about it. That is not the same as clearing it. You have to remember that the UK is an enormously important, powerful country at the UN, it is a permanent five member [of the Security Council], it is one of the biggest supporters of the UN and the current Secretary General. It is not wise for UN members and staff to belabour countries such as ours, even if they have serious concerns. I detected in my conversations with DPKO and others that this was quite a profound worry on their part, but there were limits to how far they could press the case.'

(Ross insists he respected Robin Cook very much, so his criticism does not come lightly. Both Cook and Ross resigned from their jobs over the government's deception in the lead-up to the invasion of Iraq.)

5

CODES ARE MADE TO BE BROKEN

CHAPTER FIVE

*A chapter in which the government sets out
rules for arms licences and then promptly ignores
them, attempting to send arms off to three
conflict zones and one dictatorship, and to make
a sale of overpriced equipment to one of the poorest
nations around. BAE Systems is the beneficiary
of each breach of the rules.*

THE CODE OF CONDUCT

New Labour introduced a set of rules they were to follow when considering arms licences. This code of conduct was grandly named the Code of Conduct, and on 11 June 1998 all EU members adopted it with the even more important-sounding title of the European Code of Conduct on Arms Exports. Like many events of this type, a huge amount of work had been put into the creation of the code by NGOs and campaigners, although a begrudging tilt of the head deserves to be cocked in the government's direction. Britain held the EU presidency at the time and was seen as a cheerleader for the code's adoption.

The code's rules, which governments are to follow, are fairly simple and sensible ones: don't sell to regimes who are going to use the weapons for internal oppression or external aggression – is essentially the gist of it. Thus, having signed up to the Code of Conduct to restrict arms sales, would New Labour start refusing export licences to the biggest arms dealers in the country? Simple answer: no. And how would they get round the code? Again, simple. They broke it.

The EU Code of Conduct on arms sales has been broken more times than a Premier League footballer's marriage vows. However, as the code is not legally binding, it can be ignored without breaking the law. Unfortunately, the cops are not going to burst into a smoky backroom full of ministers and civil servants somewhere in the DTI screaming, 'Ethics Police! Freeze! Put the licences on the table and your hands in the air!' But what a civilised thought that scenario is. The Ethics Police Squad …

The code has other problems: governments need only *consider* the rules when deciding on arms licences, rather than adhere to the rules. If this caveat were to apply to common law, a burglar would be at liberty to rob someone's home as long as he asked himself, 'I wonder if this is a positive contribution to society? Ah well, that's that considered, best get on with the dump in the knicker drawer.'

The code's other problem is that the government is given two major get-out clauses. Firstly, all the rules can be completely ignored if it is in the UK's national economic interests to do so. Again, if this was applied to common law, a burglar would be entitled to nick someone's valuables as long as he said, 'I want some money,' before going into their house. The second get-out is that the government can ignore the code if it is in the interests of national security. Using the analogy of the burglar for the last time: if the burglar was asked by the police, 'Why did you break into this house?', he would only need to say, 'Because a bloke in the pub called me a wanker,' and he would be free.

Here are some of the known examples of New Labour breaking the code.

INDIA AND A SHORT SHARP SHOCK

'I never once knew of Number Ten come up with any decision that would be incommoding to British Aerospace [BAE Systems].' Robin Cook, former Foreign Secretary, 2003.

Clare Short MP, studiously outspoken and with a bad sense of timing when it comes to resigning, appears on the other side of the glass wall that separates waiting visitors from MPs in Portcullis House. Draped in her trademark neck scarf, this one black with some silvery bits, she waits for the door to open before leading the brief distance to her office. Clare Short was in Cabinet as Minister for International Development, so she got to witness a thing or two.

In 2002 it looked like India and Pakistan would go to war. Troops headed for the front, the massing of armies began in earnest, front-page headlines fretted and for several days the collective consciousness of the world reeled at the prospect of war. Normally, the collective consciousness of the world wouldn't get involved in a war between India and Pakistan, but both nations are nuclear states and in possession of the wherewithal to reduce each other to dust. Dust with a half-life of a hundred thousand years admittedly, but dust nonetheless. The prospect of the planet's first ever nuclear war and simultaneous live CNN coverage with up-to-the-minute results, strikes and mushroom-cloud count was obviously too tempting for the collective consciousness of the world to miss.

'There was nearly a war that would most likely have gone nuclear,' says Short, sitting in her office. This fact obviously focused the mind of the Prime Minister, who back in 2002 stepped into the breach to play the role of peacemaker. 'We can have a calming influence,' said Tony Blair. He flew to India to promote peace and flog arms for BAE Systems. That's right, folks – as the two sides started to slide down the road to war, Britain responded in its traditional manner and set about a series of high-profile lobbying visits to India in order to sell £1 billion worth of Hawk jets. With all the moral dignity of loan sharks waiting outside a Gamblers' Anonymous meeting, ministers traipsed to India. Geoff Hoon, John Prescott and Jack Straw all piled in to help flog sixty-six BAE Systems ground-attack and trainer aircraft.

So while half of Britain's democratically elected Cabinet were out working for BAE Systems, Clare Short was dealing with the fact that 'a lot of very serious nuclear war-planning experts thought there was a high likelihood of a nuclear exchange'. As Short's department had staff working in the region, she was faced with the problem of what to do with them. 'We pulled all our staff out of the region on pure protection and our local staff we paid to get out of the danger zone,' recalled Short back in her office. Her face concentrates, narrowing her eyes, like she is trying to focus in on the memory.

'I had experts mapping where the fallout would be and where I had to move the staff from.'

Peering at her, I asked: 'What was the range of the fallout?'

'I had to take the staff out of Bangladesh and out of Sri Lanka because, you know, if there's going to be a war and then a nuclear exchange and it really is a serious threat, then you can't just leave your staff there.'

Let's recap. India and Pakistan are on the verge of a war that could go nuclear, a government department is evacuating its staff the length and breadth of the region on the basis of predicted nuclear fallout, and John Prescott and the rest of the British government are trying to arm one side with aircraft that could be used to attack the other side. But this is not quite the end of the story. It gets worse.

Tory MP Tony Baldry questioned the government, asking if: 'the Jaguar combat aircraft supplied directly from the UK to India and produced under licence in India is capable and will be modified to become capable of carrying nuclear payloads?' It was a simple enough question: could planes previously supplied to India by the UK, the Jaguar, deliver a nuclear bomb? The answer was essentially yes, it could. 'Any aircraft capable of delivering a bomb is capable of modification to enable it to deliver a nuclear weapon.'

So what UK arms company sold the Jaguar planes capable of delivering a nuclear payload to India? Some readers might wish to take preparations at this point, before the company name is revealed. You might wish to surround yourself with cushions and mattresses to absorb the impact of your body hitting the ground when you fall off your chair with shock at the mention of the arms company's name. The company name is ... BAE Systems. I know, I know. It is about as shocking as finding a coke dealer's number in an ad man's mobile phone. However, according to the Stockholm Peace Institute, the deal with India was worth some 126 Jaguar planes and there were plans to upgrade the planes with Israeli help. These planes could be used to deliver a nuclear payload.

So the final recap shows the New Labour government trying to sell arms in a conflict region, during heightened tensions, which threatened to go nuclear, and as if that wasn't quite enough, Britain had already provided India with the means of delivering its nuclear payload. All of this was happening at the same time as UK civil servants and local staff were being evacuated from the potential nuclear fallout. It almost seems churlish to point out that the deal broke the EU Code of Conduct, but it did. Remember Criterion Four, which forbids export: 'if there is a clear risk that the intended recipient would use the proposed export aggressively against another country or to assert by force a territorial claim'.

Gun pimps and Cabinet whores

Half the British Cabinet have ended up as pimps for BAE Systems. I understand that this is an unpleasant description. Especially if you try to envisage Jack Straw as the Man, strutting in a tracksuit with wrists shaking gold chunks, while Geoff Hoon and John Prescott hang off his arms in five-inch stilettos and ruby-red lipstick, each with a dirty whisper that says: 'Is that a missile in yer pocket or are yer jus' pleased t'see me?'

However, pimping is what half the Cabinet did, and indeed still does.

According to Short, the British attempt to get the Indians to buy the Hawk jets had been going on for some fifteen years and 'every British minister who visits India is briefed to propose and push the billion pounds' worth of Hawks'.

'Did anyone ask you to do that?' I enquire.

With a wave of her hand, Short dismisses the notion that she might have obeyed an instruction of this sort. 'It used to get into my briefing, these kinds of things, but I never did it. I'm not doing it.'

According to Short, every minister who makes a foreign trip has three briefings: one from their department detailing the purpose of their trip, a second from the Foreign and Commonwealth Office explaining the political situation in the country the minister is to visit, and a third briefing, talking points, from Downing Street, things to mention and plug, like arms deals. Every time there is an arms deal in the air it is a minister's duty to talk it up, no matter what the purpose of the trip. They could be visiting victims of the tsunami or having a meeting about carbon emissions, and somewhere on their to-do list scrawled in biro are the words – 'Big up the guns'.

Trying to deliver a puff piece for the arms industry must be quite difficult if the primary purpose of your visit is to develop projects to combat malaria. Picture the poor minister standing in a hospital in sub-Saharan Africa, faced with row upon row of suffering children lying in packed wards on barely habitable beds as a heavy fan laboriously chugs through hot air overhead. The minister then turns to their African counterpart and cheerfully quips, 'You know what would bring those mosquitoes down!'

So next time a minister makes a trip to India, Indonesia, Colombia, Saudi Arabia, why not drop them a line to ask what arms sales they pitched in their informal moments? You might even send a pledge card to ministers to try to get them to break the habit. You could even ask your MP to sign up to it, even if they are not a minister, just on the off-chance that they may be one day. Photocopy this coupon and send it to your MP, write them a note to go with it and include an SAE for them to return it to you.

ARMS TRADE PLEDGE CARD

Selling weapons is not a dignified way for a minister/junior minister (delete as appropriate) to behave, it fuels conflict, burdens countries with debt, helps undemocratic states remain undemocratic and contributes to human rights abuse. So I have decided to ignore what is expected of me by HMG. If I ever make departmental visits to foreign countries, I will not promote the sale of arms. I acknowledge that my political life is shorter than the shelf-life of most weapons, but longer than the life expectancy of those facing them.

I (name) ....
want someone to live after my political career is dead.

Constituency...

Signed ....

Date ....

If you succeed in getting an MP to sign this, please send a copy to me c/o the publishers.

BAE SYSTEMS SELLS OVERPRICED
PIECE OF SHIT TO TANZANIA

In 2001 the New Labour government was faced with yet another dilemma: should they or shouldn't they licence a deal for BAE Systems to sell a military air-traffic control system to Tanzania, worth £28 million. Tanzania is poor, and if they were about to spend £28 million, well, that money had better be well spent. So let's play Sherlock. Will Tanzania, a desperately poor country (with a GDP of £170 per person per year), spend its money well? Or, will Tanzania tip wheelbarrow-loads of money down the chute when it can scarce afford to do so? To find the answer, let us consider the ingredients of this story.

❏ The seller – BAE Systems, the UK's biggest arms manufacturer.
❏ The purchaser – Tanzania.
❏ The goods – a *military* air-traffic control system.
❏ Purpose – to provide air-traffic control for *civilian* air-traffic control. Admittedly, the military air force might benefit – but for the fact that the Tanzanian Air Force is small and crap.
❏ The EU Code of Conduct on Arms Exports says governments should seriously consider the financial effects of arms sales to developing nations (Criterion Eight; see p.135).
❏ Tanzania's financial standing – poor. 'If it [the deal] goes ahead, it would wipe out two-thirds of the real savings that Tanzania has gained from existing debt relief,' said a *Guardian* editorial.
❏ Who will decide if BAE Systems gets a licence to export the air-traffic control system? Tony Blair.

Who opposes this deal? Well, in the rarefied and arcane language of the international finance markets, the deal is technically described as a 'Crock of Shit'. Even the World Bank and the International Monetary Fund criticised it, describing the BAE

Systems air-traffic control system as 'dated technology'. A report they commissioned noted that the system was an old military one, which didn't cover the whole country, leaving chunks of Tanzania without air-traffic control. It also said the BAE Systems equipment was far too expensive. In fact, Tanzania could have bought a better system for a tenth of the price.

Let me just repeat who made these criticisms – the World Bank and the IMF. When they slag off a deal, you know it is really shit. On a list of the most improbable events ever to occur on the planet, the World Bank and IMF criticising an arms deal would have to appear somewhere in the top ten, probably rated alongside the Catholic Church helping a police investigation into child abuse.

Clare Short described the BAE Systems equipment. 'It was very expensive, very old-fashioned, only covered part of the country. It was rubbish.' Tanzania, Short pointed out, is 'one of the least developed countries … £28 million means some of the improvements that were taking place in education or … children sleeping under bed nets to stop incidents of malaria, all that sort of stuff, it's going to be slower; you haven't got the money to spend on people if you're spending it on obsolete rubbish.'

Half the Cabinet opposed this deal, the World Bank opposed it, the IMF opposed it, the aid agencies opposed it and the British press hated it. Naturally Tony Blair supported BAE Systems and approved the deal.

Why did Blair support BAE Systems? Well, put aside the argument that Blair would support BAE Systems if they were trying to sell syphilis bombs to Kim Jong Il of North Korea. Put that aside, and his only defence was the 'British jobs' line. Blair argued he was not prepared to lose British jobs by refusing the arms dealer a licence, and to give his argument impetus BAE Systems had already started work on the project.

The MoD told BAE Systems to start work on building the equipment before they applied for a licence to do the deal.

Which sounds very iffy. As a general rule, one rarely does the activity one is applying for a licence to do, before getting the licence to do it. Driving, for example, is generally considered a *faux pas* without a licence. Fishing, watching TV, both things you need a licence to do. Or running a pub or selling adult books in Soho, all activities that you can't do *before* you get a licence. Shooting with a shotgun before you have a licence: very bad. Running a home for the elderly without a licence: very bad indeed! However, no licence is required when starting work building a multimillion-pound military system for a Third World country on its knees with debt, a product which doesn't work properly and is opposed by half the Cabinet. Even the President of Tanzania later admitted it wasn't a good deal. Or at least he did to Clare Short. 'I saw him,' says Short, 'on a plane. He said, "You were right. It was a useless project."'

The president's plane

After the air-traffic control system was implemented, the Tanzanian President Benjamin Mkapa bought a new plane for state presidential purposes, worth £15 million. Some believe that this was an extra strain on the country's scant resources. Others believe that it is completely legitimate for the president of a country to be able to travel to all parts of it, and as Tanzania's roads are often dirt tracks, susceptible to seasonal change, getting from A to B can take a long time. Having a plane, they argue, is the most effective way for a president to travel and entirely legitimate. Regardless of which argument is right, it is just a little bit ironic and unfortunate that when the president is travelling around Tanzania in his £15 million jet, he may well fall off the edge of the radar screen on his £28 million air-traffic control system.

ON HOW NEW LABOUR TRIED TO
ARM PRESIDENT MUGABE

It became public knowledge that Tony Blair personally backed a deal to arm one of the forces involved in the bloody conflict in Congo, Mugabe's, only seventy-two hours before UN peace talks were due to take place. This was the deal. Blair agreed to provide spare parts for the Hawk aircraft of the black dictator with the Hitler moustache, Robert Mugabe. Although, in fairness, his moustache is probably more British music hall than Nazi facial hair. The Tory government had sold Mugabe the Hawks in the 1980s and in 1998 he decided to commit some 10,000 troops to the war in Congo, sending some of his ground-attack Hawk aircraft along with them.

Planes, like any other vehicles, need MOTs, new parts and spares. And I suppose those poor little Hawk planes just got worn out with carrying those heavy bombs and cannons. Mugabe's planes needed some £450,000 worth of spares to keep them in the air, which were to be supplied by two UK companies. The names of the companies were never made public. But as BAE make the Hawk planes, I would imagine that they were involved.

For and against
Robin Cook later described (in *Point of Departure*) the effects of the war in Congo as 'three million people brutally killed in a decade and untold thousands raped'. He was against the deal in Cabinet.

AIDING MUGABE

Cook's and Short's opposition to the deal has been well documented. It seems safe to assume that the MoD and DTI therefore supported it (controversial arms licences are a four-way discussion between the MoD, DTI, FCO and DFID). Here are those in New Labour who lined up in favour of aiding Mugabe's armed forces.

1) Tony Blair – presumably concerned that if the deal didn't go through, the UK would lose its reputation for arms customer-care and after-sales service.

2) Alastair Campbell – the Prime Minister's clerk.

3) Ministry of Defence (headed up by Geoff Hoon) – seems to be institutionally incapable of turning down an arms deal. They probably wear camouflage paint in Cabinet meetings.

4) Department of Trade and Industry (headed up by Stephen Byers) – often took a similar position as the MoD, but you wouldn't want Byers on your paint-balling team.

They decided to license Mugabe's arms deal in February 2000. But after escalating violence in Zimbabwe, the licences were revoked and the UK declared an arms embargo on Zimbabwe in May, just over two months after approving the deal. So Mugabe didn't get his arms, but it was not for want of Blair's government trying.

YIDDN', YOCS AND YANKS

Most people who don't do News International or other hard-core hallucinogenic news networks would describe the Occupied Palestinian Territories as a conflict zone and Israel as the occupying force. It is not a hard conclusion to come to; it is Palestinian land and it is Israeli troops who are charging around it. The Cluedo analysis is: Colonel Mustard with a tank invading a completely different board game. Possibly Monopoly, where the Israeli tanks and bulldozers start demolishing houses built in Whitechapel.

This is the story of the Yiddn', the Yocs and the Yanks. The Yocs, in this case, are the British government, and although there are a few Jews in the Cabinet, there are not nearly the numbers envisaged by Abu Hamza or the BNP. No, the British govern-ment is resolutely, though not entirely, gentile – the Yocs. Most of the Cabinet even look gentile: Ruth Kelly, John Reid, Tony Blair, John Prescott – Yocs without doubt. Some might question what it is that makes Prescott look gentile. To which I would answer it is probably that despite his layers of body fat he gives the impression that he has not actually enjoyed one single meal in his entire life. A Yoc. A gentile. He has to be. He just looks like the secretary of a British Legion club.

Israel's broken promises

So the British government decides that the Israelis – the Yiddn' – should not get British arms if they are going to use them in the Occupied Palestinian Territories. Israel agrees to this and says so in a note to the UK in November 2000. But by early 2002 it became obvious that Israel had modified Chieftain tanks, bought from the UK, into armoured personnel carriers and used them in the OPT. British politicians are outraged. 'This is dreadful,' they cry. But, to be honest, what did Britain think the tanks would be used for in the first place? Did they sell Israel the tanks thinking: that'll sort out Tel Aviv's speed bump problem?

Jack Straw is pissed off that Israel has broken its pledges and tells MPs that any future arms exports would have to comply with EU Code Criterion Three, which says: governments shouldn't sell arms or component parts of weapons, 'which would provoke or prolong armed conflicts or aggravate existing tensions and conflicts in the country of final destination'.

Jack Straw is so pissed off with Israel that he reverses the decision in a matter of months. He decides that Israel can have military equipment that will definitely be used against civilians in the West Bank and Gaza Strip, and let that be a lesson to them! However, the equipment bound for Israel is to be sold to America, assembled in America and then sold from America to Israel. That is acceptable to New Labour. So the new British position became: selling weapons to Israel, bad. Selling weapons to America who sell them to Israel, good. Or to put it another way. Yocs sell Yanks arms, Yanks arm Yiddn'.

The equipment

The equipment the UK decided to export to Israel via America was a piece of technology called a Head Up Display unit (HUD). The HUD, other than being a stark and sturdy acronym worthy of an ex-Yorkshire miner, is part of the F16 fighter plane; it is the equipment that enables the pilot to see flight, navigational and attack information in front of the eye, without having to glance round the cockpit at whirling dials on the dashboard.

The HUD is made by BAE Systems. It had to be made by BAE Systems. What other company could it be? Look at the bare facts: they make something that helps kill people, it is used in an illegal occupation and the British government has to break its own rules in order for this to happen. It couldn't be any company but BAE Systems.

The Israeli use of F16 planes to attack the Occupied Palestinian Territories is as regular as the civilian deaths are predictable. Two weeks after Straw announced the deal to supply Israel via America, on 22 July 2002, fifteen Palestinians were killed and seventy wounded when an F16 dropped a one-ton bomb on Gaza City in a heavily populated residential area. The youngest Palestinian killed was two years old.

EU CODE OF CONDUCT ON ARMS EXPORTS

Criterion One: States should respect international law and not export to places with EU and UN sanctions. Furthermore, countries should not do bad shit with WMDs. (OK, I am paraphrasing, but you really don't want to have to read the original document.)

Criterion Two: No arms exports 'if there is a clear risk that the proposed export might be used for internal repression'. God bless the EU; they even give examples of what repression means: 'torture and other cruel, inhuman and degrading treatment or punishment, summary or arbitrary executions, disappearances, arbitrary detentions and other major violations of human rights'.

Criterion Three: No arms exports 'which would provoke or prolong armed conflicts or aggravate existing tensions and conflicts in the country of final destination'. Labour broke this backing exports to the USA, which were then used in F16 planes and sold to Israel. (UK company involved: BAE Systems.)

Criterion Four: No arms exports 'if there is a clear risk that the intended recipient would use the proposed export aggressively against another country or to assert by force a territorial claim'. Labour broke this backing refurbishment of the howitzer cannons (see previous chapter). (UK company involved: Royal Ordnance, a subsidiary of BAE Systems.) Labour also broke this backing Hawk jets to India. (UK company involved: BAE Systems.) F16 parts to Israel can be applied under this one too.

Criterion Five: No arms exports where there is a 'risk of use of the goods concerned against their [own] forces or those of friends, allies or other member states'.

Criterion Six: No arms export if the country receiving them has a record of 'support or encouragement of terrorism' or has a bad record with 'compliance with its international commitments [the law]', or has a bad track record on 'its commitment to non-proliferation and other areas of arms control and disarmament'.

Labour/India: Hawk planes. As the Hawk can train pilots for nuclear bombing runs with Jaguar planes (also supplied by the UK) there is an argument that the deal should not have gone ahead under Criterion Six. India is a nuclear power and alongside Pakistan and Israel has not signed the Nuclear Non-Proliferation Treaty 1970. The NPT was created to stop the spread of nuclear weapons and work to their abolition. (Deal announced 2003.)

Criterion Seven: No arms exports where there is a 'risk that exported goods might be diverted to an undesirable end user'.

Criterion Eight: No arms exports if 'the proposed export would seriously hamper the sustainable development of the recipient country'.

Labour broke this one with a military air-traffic control system to Tanzania. (UK company involved – BAE Systems.)

6

ACRONYMS,
SUBSIDIES AND LIES

CHAPTER SIX

A chapter in which the author examines how much
money we subsidise the arms industry by, answers the
'what about British jobs' argument and is later found
in angry despair. The author loses patience with
BAE Systems and ends up in court.

THE PENIS OF PEACE
AND THE BUS OF DECEPTION

The London gathering of the arms dealers for their trade fair down in the Docklands is called DICEY by protestors, a bastardisation of its acronym. It is self-mockingly referred to as 'our biannual blood fest' by Brinley Salzman of the Defence Manufacturers Association, but the organisers prefer to call it Defence Systems and Equipment International (DSEI). It is held at the ExCeL Centre, a concrete box of an exhibition hall, whose designers mistook size for grandeur. A thousand companies exhibit at DSEI; military delegations from between fifty and eighty countries turn up to visit and some 25,000 folk pass through the turnstiles to gawp and buy. However, among arms dealers who travel the world hawking their wares, DSEI has a rather unique reputation: apparently it attracts more protestors than any other arms fair in the world. And I might proudly add that an industry insider informed me that 'by and a large we have a much better class of protestor too'. Though my source did qualify this statement with this tale: 'At a defence event in Australia the antis [protestors] turned up in a huge papier-mâché penis, with loads of protestors inside it. So there is this huge pink thing, which they called the Penis of Peace, out on the street as part of the demonstration, when suddenly the penis breaks away from the main demonstration and charges at the main doors of the defence fair. Unbeknownst to the police, inside the Penis of Peace is a battering ram. So the Penis of Peace charges at the doors, breaks through the doors and gets into the fair, where the protestors jump out from under the penis and start running around the place causing chaos. More than that, all the protestors were naked and covered in olive oil, so the security had a bugger of a time trying to grab and hold onto them, to chuck them out.' I expressed regret that this type of thing had not occurred in the UK, but my source comforted me, saying, 'But that's Australia, they can do that kind of thing over there because the weather is warmer. You can't expect protestors to do that over here, far too cold.' Penis of Peace apart, the protestors at DSEI do have a reputation among travelling gun merchants, and obviously this is not an affectionate relationship.

On the first day of the arms fair in September 2003, I'm sitting with some friends outside the Thistle Tower hotel by Tower Bridge. The hotel is one of those corporate yuppie sheds and marks the start of the gentrified, soulless expanse of waterfront dwellings that rolls out eastwards along the Thames. Here the City wunderkinds inhabit overpriced loft apartments before they finally burn out and end up pottering around on motorised lawnmowers somewhere in Gloucestershire.

Strangely, the Thistle's welcoming board in the foyer doesn't bear the words, 'The Thistle Tower hotel welcomes arms dealers'. But it should, the place is infested with them. It is this gathering of the gun-floggers that has drawn a small group of friends and colleagues to the Thistle Tower hotel car park. While other protestors will be blocking roads, causing havoc and attempting to shut the fair down, our group has opted for a more personal approach to protest.

Some people like the straightforward approach: make a placard and shout. And believe me, there is nothing wrong with that; it's a tried and tested method of protest. But today this approach is not for us. We want to get within touching distance of them because there are times when a spot of emotional thuggery is called for and that is best at close range. This is what we did.

Two young attractive women colleagues, Sally and Kate, adorn themselves in their best corporate slinky kit. Little black skirt. Lots of lippy. High heels. Bras that are under a year old. They enter the Thistle Tower hotel at about 8.15 a.m., just as the arms dealers are finishing their breakfast and beginning to contemplate getting a cab or the train into the Docklands. Sally and Kate take up position in the foyer holding up printed boards, in the manner that chauffeurs do when they pick up business folk from the airport. The boards are nicely laminated and in bold print bear the words: 'Complimentary bus shuttle service to DSEI exhibition and conference'. This was an entirely genuine offer. We had indeed hired a bus and a driver to take arms dealers to the fair. It was sitting in the car park waiting to be filled.

We had assumed that most of the arms dealers would be male, heterosexual and middle-aged. We assumed they would ogle Sally and Kate. We assumed that they live in a world where minions perform their tasks and where complimentary transport would seem commonplace. This is quite a lot of assumptions to make. Were we right to make them? *Yessireee, Bob!* Within a minute of arrival, Sally and Kate are fielding enquiries. Suited and booted the dealers stand with raincoats draped over their arms, clutching suitcases. 'When does it leave?' enquires a polite chap from somewhere in the Home Counties, up on a company trip.

'About five minutes. Just go to the front door and someone will see you to the bus; the journey won't take too long.'

And out they come, Italian, German, American and British dealers. Briskly they stride in black-laced shoes to our hire bus, which is discreetly parked alongside the hotel. They shuffle in, neatly folding macs and resting cases on their knees as businesslike chatter fills the vehicle. Not one of the dealers knows who has laid on this complimentary bus service for them. They neither know nor care who has done that. These are grown men working in the defence industry getting into strangers' cars. Wow, with a bowl of sweets we could have probably extracted trade secrets, turned them and sent them back into the industry as peace moles.

Just consider for a moment what a wonderful world we live in. These men work for companies that probably turn over millions but the lure of a free ride is still a potent weapon, even among those who fly business class.

And so the bus, now full of arms dealers, begins its ride to the Docklands. The chatter continues while we drive through the morning quagmire that is quaintly called the 'rush hour'. Martin and I are sitting in the front seats next to the driver. Martin is about six foot four, maybe taller. He has a boxer's build and the kind of NHS black-framed glasses that would guarantee bullying on a smaller man. He is half Ronnie Kray and half Eric Morecambe, which is a confusing combination to be threatened with. Martin kneels on his front seat and turns to face our bus full of dealers. He holds a video camera up in his hands and loudly says, 'We're on.'

Clutching the microphone to the hire-bus tannoy system, I turn to face the dealers who are in the seats immediately behind us. 'Welcome aboard our complimentary bus shuttle service to the arms fair.' I try my hardest to sound like I'm flying a 747 and am just saying hello to the passengers. 'We are currently en route to the DSEI at the ExCeL Centre, cruising at an average speed on this road of about 20 to 25 miles an hour. Our altitude is 2 to 3 feet above ground level and we will be approaching the ExCeL shortly. As you are aware, this is a complimentary bus service. However, you are involved in the arms industry, which is the industry that is principally to blame for the creation of Iraq's national debt. The arms industry, indeed some of the companies you may have worked for, sold arms to the dictator Saddam Hussein. He used those guns on his own people, as well as Kuwaitis and Iranians, and then defaulted on the payment. The national governments around the world who underwrote and insured those arms deals paid the companies, ensuring that you fellows didn't go out of pocket, and then transferred that debt on to the national debt of Iraq. So now the Iraqi people are faced with paying those debts. They are literally paying for the bullets of their own oppression. I know that you feel very bad about this and have probably lost some sleep over the matter. So I am going to help relieve you of your guilt. We are collecting money to help cancel Iraq's debt and we are passing round a tin for you to put your contributions in. Please give as generously as you can. Thank you.'

The eyes of a busload of cornered arms dealers stare back at me in silence as a tin is passed to the reticent hands of the nearest one. The business chatter has stopped. They stare at Martin and myself. There is just the sound of the bus engine and small change being dropped into a tin (chink). Passed over shoulders (chink) to people behind them, like a collection plate. They (chink) fidget in trouser pockets to grasp a few coins (chink). There are no complaints, just silence and a bus full of arms dealers, each with a look of mild shock, like a fish being tested for prostate cancer. Martin keeps filming, I keep smiling and (chink) the final coppers drop into the tin, which comes to a dapper-looking Italian sitting at the front. He passes the tin to me without donating, tugs the shirt cuffs that immaculately protrude from his jacket sleeve and says, 'I would give you money. But your tactics! Napolitano! Mafiosi!'

We raised just over twenty quid on two trips. Unfortunately for the populace of Iraq, then faced with paying its international debt, Saddam Hussein borrowed £623 million from the British government alone, for guns and planes and chemical plants. That £623 million was back in 1990, so the red reminder-to-pay letters hit Saddam's doormat some years ago. The interest starts building up, and hey folks, even dictators can go into denial about debt. Even if he wanted to do something about it, what company in their right mind is going to take a call from a man saying, 'I'm Saddam Hussein and I want to consolidate my debt repayments into one monthly manageable sum'?

Falluja 2 – the gas plant in Iraq

Most of Iraq's UK debt was generated via the Export Credits Guarantee Department (ECGD). The acronym sounds innocent enough but it is the financial motor that keeps the British arms industry profitable, aids the creation of debt in the developing world, is funded by the taxpayer, massively assists BAE Systems and remains highly secretive.

The ECGD works under the auspices of the DTI and is charged with underwriting British business deals abroad in what the City terms 'medium- to high-risk markets' – in short, it provides insurance for UK companies working in dodgy countries. So if the country buying the goods decides not to pay the British company supplying them, then the ECGD will step in and pay the money owed to the company. So the company is paid by the British taxpayer. As for the naughty folk who didn't pay their bills, well, the debt owed to the ECGD then becomes part of that country's 'national debt'.

Stephen Kock* was the Midland Bank executive in charge of arms sales. He described the workings of the ECGD thus: 'You see, before we advance monies to a company, we always insist on any funds being covered by the [UK] government's Export Credits Guarantee Department ... We can't lose. After ninety days, if the Iraqis haven't coughed up, the company gets paid instead by the British government. Either way, we recover our loan, plus interest of course. It's beautiful.'**

---

* Though some sources name him as Stephan Koch
** Corner House, *Snouts in the Trough*, 1999

For the banks and the companies it may indeed be beautiful, but this is not necessarily so for those at the end of the stick labelled 'shitty'. Consider Falluja 2, a gas-making plant. Sixteen years after Saddam failed to pay the bills on this, it remains unfinished business. This is what happened. In 1989, a year after the chemical gas attacks on the Kurds in Halabja (which killed over 5,000 people), the ECGD supported a £14 million loan for Iraq to purchase Falluja 2, a chlorine plant. The Secretary to the Board of Trade (as the DTI minister was known then) was Paul Channon, who was told at the time that there was 'the strong possibility that the Iraqis wish to use it for the manufacture of mustard gas'. The British-based company that got the deal for Falluja 2 was Uhde Ltd in Hounslow. Most of the repayments for that particular loan went through, until the start of Gulf War One when Saddam defaulted and the ECGD paid the company £317,684.*

Falluja 2 ended up in Colin Powell's dossier on Iraq's WMD programme, but that is no reason to doubt the fact that this was a genuine chemical weapons facility. By the time the Paris Club got round to cancelling some of Iraq's debt in November 2004, the money owed to the UK for Falluja 2 included some £300,000 worth of interest on the original debt, amounting to approximately £618,000. The Paris Club cancelled 60 per cent of that debt, a further 20 per cent will be cancelled in 2008 (if Iraq complies with its IMF agreements), leaving the Iraqi people to pay off some £120,000 to Britain for a mustard gas facility sold with the minister's knowledge after Saddam Hussein had gassed the Kurds, on a deal underwritten by the ECGD. This one deal is but a fraction of the approximately £240 million the Iraqis will still have to pay the UK even after debt relief.**

---

* All figures relating to Falluja 2 sourced from the ECGD.

** The principal sum of money owed by Iraq to the UK is about £623 million; with interest this will come out at approximately £1,240 million. If the debt cancellation goes ahead as planned and 80 per cent is cancelled, it will leave Iraq to pay 20 per cent of this sum, which is £248 million.

ECGD – the elephant in the room

Much has been made of how wonderful Gordon Brown was to cancel part of the crippling developing world debt. Not as much attention was drawn to the fact that **95 per cent** of the bilateral debt was generated via the ECGD. (Bilateral debt is the debt owed directly to individual governments, such as the UK government, as opposed to multilateral debt, which is owed to organisations such as the IMF and the World Bank.)

It is a violent statistic, which can never truly reflect its own wretchedness nor the scale of suffering involved in its creation. The fact that **95 per cent** of the developing world bilateral debt owed to the UK came from ECGD projects is not a fact that crops up often. No one mentioned it at Live 8. Which was odd, because I would bet that some of the managers from the ECGD went to that show in Hyde Park. I bet they cheered, cried and waved their white wristbands in the air along with the rest of the crowd. And it is right that they should do so. Hell – without the hard work of people like them Live 8 would never have been put on.

But no one mentioned them, not Sir Bob Geldof, not Madonna when she hugged the survivors of famine. Not junkie Pete Doherty after he sang 'Children Of The Revolution' with ex-coke hag Sir Elton John. Billionaire Bill Gates must have forgotten to mention it too. No one pointed to the east of the stage where the home of the ECGD lay, just a few miles away at the Exchange Towers. No one thought the ECGD worth a sentence or two, not even just to point out that one single British government department had helped create the British bit of the debt they were singing to rid the world of. The ECGD was the Elephant in the Park no one mentioned.

SUBSIDISING ARMS EXPORTS

This is a figure you need to remember. If you remember only two figures from this book, make this one of them. Gear yourself up for it. Here it comes. Each export-related job in the defence industry is subsidised by about £13,106.30 per year. Go and write that figure down, remember it and use it in arguments – about £13,106.30 per year per worker in arms exports. If these jobs were in any other sector of the economy, they would have the World Trade Organisation and Peter Mandelson deregulating them before you could say the words, 'The mine workers were never subsidised to that extent.' Every other sector of the economy has to be 'flexible', but not the arms export trade, with a whooping £13,106.30 subsidy per job. So next time you see a BAE Systems or Rolls-Royce executive at an arms fair or lecturing people on the importance of the arms trade for the British economy, you would be fully justified in going totally *Daily Mail* and screaming, 'Get a proper job and stop sponging off the state, you freeloading bastard!' In fact, many of the board of BAE Systems work in other jobs – so they freeload off the state and have other employment. In my book this is the corporate equivalent of working and signing on. BAE Systems essentially works an advanced form of benefit fraud and there should be a hotline to grass up these lazy bastards to the DSS.

Name and shame the arms trade ponces!
Michael Portillo (BAE Systems board member from 2002–6 on £45,000 a year) – ex-Minister of Defence – quit his job at BAE Systems and, as far as I can see, ponced off the state for four years. Works now for TV companies making programmes about Spanish wildlife and coping as a single parent. Once a ponce, always a ponce.

Sir Peter Mason (BAE Systems board member) – chief executive of AMEC, the construction company. Looks like he fondles Corby trouser presses. Oy, Mason, you leech – try working for a living!

CALCULATING HOW MUCH UK
ARMS EXPORTS ARE SUBSIDISED

In 2004 a collaborative report was issued by BASIC, the Oxford Research Group, and Saferworld. It was written by Roy Isbister and Paul Ingram, was called *Escaping the Subsidy Trap*, and it attempted to estimate how much defence exports were subsidised by the UK government. Below is a highly condensed and slightly updated version of their findings.

1) ECGD – £139.95 million subsidy. The ECGD operates in the civil and defence sectors of the economy, dealing with everything from sales of Airbus (which is 20 per cent owned by BAE Systems) and dam-building in Turkey to hotel projects in Ghana and Hawk jets to Indonesia.

The British government finally admitted in June 2004 that the ECGD did provide a 'subsidy' to industry – as it generally charged below market rates for its services – to the tune of £120 million per year (as this is the total budget, the defence budget – 39% – works out at £46.8 million). The following year the government announced the figure of a £150 million subsidy (as a proportion of the defence budget – 38% – this works out at £57 million). However, Isbister and Ingrams take issue with the government's calculation method and argue that if the ECGD were to disappear and the arms companies were to get their insurance on the open market, it would cost them approximately £222 million more than it currently does. For the sake of argument I have settled on a figure in the middle of the two sides – £136.95 million.*

2) Defence Exports Services Organisation – £17 million (figures for 2004/05). DESO is a part of the Ministry of Defence. It was set up in 1966 to help promote British arms exporters. Now let us just consider this for a moment. The British government has an organisation working

---

* The figure is the 2004 and 2005 defence figures added together and divided by 2, to give us an annual figure of £51.9 million. Half the difference between £51.9 million and £222 million = £85.05 million, then add back the £51.9 million to arrive at £136.95 million.

in the MoD to promote British arms exports. Imagine the repercussions if the Department of Health had an organisation working within it to promote drugs sales. There would be uproar, scandal, questions in the House, front-page headlines … it would be a bit much to expect a New Labour minister to actually resign over wrongdoing, but there would still be a fuss.

DESO does provide one useful indicator: it shows the priorities the New Labour government has. DESO employs 161 staff servicing UK arms deals to Saudi Arabia alone. The Export Control Organisation employs a total of 110 staff to license and control the export of weapons. So New Labour employs more people to service Saudi arms deals than it does to control arms exports to the whole world.

3) Defence Attachés – £4.26 million. In 2004 the government announced that approximately 10 per cent of defence attachés' time, in embassies around the world, was spent promoting British arms exports, which gives us the figure above.

4) Defence Assistance Fund – £4.7 million (2004/05). A quango that does trade missions and supports UK defence exports.

5) Armed forces used to promote arms sales – estimated £6 million. From DSEI to Defence Industry Days to teams that demonstrate equipment to potential clients.

6) Research and Development – £483 million. So far the total comes to £204.4 million per year but this does not include two major sources of subsidy, one of which is Research and Development. If British defence exports accounted for 40% of their sales, then it seems reasonable that 40% of the Research and Development money given to the companies by HMG should be included as a subsidy. In which case, according to calculations by academic Paul Ingram, this would have been worth approximately £483 million in 2004. Some argue that the R&D money would go to the arms companies regardless of exports. But folks, I think we should see R&D more as loans. If you can make students repay loans for getting an education, you can make arms companies pay back their R&D grants.

7) Buying British – £200 million (and upwards per annum). The Ministry of Defence has a duty to supply its armed forces with efficient equipment. However, the MoD also buys equipment in order to safeguard British jobs and profitability for the big arms companies. This might seem noble to some but it is still a subsidy if you could get the kit cheaper elsewhere. In July 2003 the MoD signed a deal worth £3.5 billion over twenty-five years with BAE Systems. The deal was not put out to competitive tender, a minimum requirement for open and cost-effective purchasing. It was reported that the other planes on the market, which some said were more suitable for the RAF's needs and which would have come in at about £1 billion cheaper for the taxpayer, were not even considered in the process. The other reason for the deal was to help BAE Systems secure the contract to sell Hawk jets to India (since how could they persuade the Indian government to buy Hawks if the British government didn't buy them). The MoD is committed to buying British for political reasons; if these deals cost more and are less effective than buying from non-British suppliers, then this has to be counted as a subsidy for the arms trade.

TOTAL SUBSIDY PER YEAR = £851.91 MILLION

Mr Richard Lake Olver (chairman of BAE Systems) – this ex-BP man now works for Reuters, the news people, and still finds time to ponce off the taxpayer at BAE.

The *Sun* says bring back national service for these work-shy fops!

Municipal park figure

The Americans use the phrase 'ballpark figure', which I find unsuitable for our needs. Britain does not have baseball parks and their ilk. If we wish to indicate that something is in the right area, though we cannot gauge its precision, I suggest we use the phrase 'municipal park figure', which is far more in keeping with our national pride in commonly owned though slightly grubby facilities. These figures are estimates, they are in no way exact, but they do give an indication of the sums of money we are pumping into the arms export trade.

A municipal park figure of £851.91 million is how much we subsidise arms exports in a year. It is only an estimate. However, even as a municipal park figure, £851.91 million is a lot of money. Do you realise how many doctors, nurses, teachers we could employ with that level of money? ... No, neither do I, but I bet it would be loads and we'd probably have enough money over to subsidise a bevy of buxom opera singers to boot. The MoD estimate that there are between 60,000 to 65,000 people employed in arms exports, which works out at a subsidy of £13,153.23 per job.

Arms companies, like their political allies in the Cabinet, are exceptionally deft at convincing us of the benefit they bring to Britain. The assertion that arms exports are good for the British economy is a myth, no more true than the existence of unicorns, Saddam Hussein's WMD stockpile in 2003 or Graham Norton's modesty. The arms industry is subsidised with *our* money ... well, all right, I have a little fund in the Isle of Man to help with my tax bill, Ken Dodd put me on to it, so technically speaking it has been subsidised with *your* money. But you get the point.

All of this leaves a nagging question: why does the government support the arms trade so much? The arms industry fuels conflict, creates debt in developing world nations, causes people to flee from war zones and become refugees – all problems Britain has to play an international part in solving. The arms industry sponges off the state and is far from being 'good for the economy'. Governments break their own codes of conduct and cause immense embarrassment to themselves by supporting these deals. Why is the arms industry protected and suckled by administration after administration?

A government-to-government arms deal might involve the MoD, DTI, FCO, security services, perhaps even the prime ministers of both countries involved. Few other business transactions (outside oil and energy) can claim to involve that many players in a nation's political elite. Arms deals involve international movers and shakers. In terms of influence, the British government believes the arms industry allows them to punch above their weight on the international stage. America's might and money mean they can claim to be the world's policeman. Britain cannot match that, but as the second biggest global arms dealer we can at least claim to be the world's community support officer.

But the government's infatuation with the arms trade is also run by one other motor, I suspect. It is this. If there was a national poll to choose fifty objects from the last one hundred years that signified 'Britishness', it is pretty much a certainty that amid the red telephone boxes and Minis, there would be Lancaster bombers and Spitfire planes. They epitomise a romantic link with conflict, ingenuity and a national self-image of standing up for the underdog. British governments are as susceptible to this historical romanticism as they are desperate for Britain to be a nation of influence in the world.

FUCK 'EM: STOP THE FAIR

In 2000 the DTI was garnering opinion across Whitehall on the way forward for the ECGD. A leaked copy of the confidential submissions showed that the Foreign Office had said 'the core criteria should be financial … but there is scope at the margins for introducing human rights'. Within three years Cook had moved his ethical dimension from the heart of British foreign policy to the margins of business as usual.

Another three years on and Blair would invade Iraq with the USA, ignoring the calls and pleadings of its citizens. By 2003 New Labour had not only waged an illegal war, it had pimped arms to dictators, bankrupts, thugs and frauds. Leaving a trail of mayhem, deceit, debt, death and handouts. They pumped money into BAE Systems, lobbied for BAE Systems and broke the rules for BAE Systems. New Labour nurtured this malignant cuckoo nesting at the heart of democracy and left room for change at the margins.

No one can kill hope like a politician, nor kindle hatred like them either. I've met a few with a liar's breath and quisling eyes. These men and women are our conduits to power, our means of change. Yet we are their supplicants. We are expected to respect them. Don't make a scene, we are told. Don't do anything that might upset them. Apply to the police to protest and keep the demo orderly. Sign a petition, sign a letter, sign a direct debit, buy the badge, buy the T-shirt. Sponsor a granny. Engage with the process. Join Live 8, join the lobby, join the photo call. Be reasonable in the face of the unreasonable. Walk past the banks that loan the money, past the offices that collect the debt, past the factories that make the weapons, past the departments that break the rules, pay the companies, ignore the bribes, grease the wheels and pimp the guns. Walk past them all, because there is only room for our concerns at the margins.

At times like this, I remember what an old anarchist friend said when asked what changes he wanted to see happen in Britain. He replied, 'Release the ravens from the Tower of London, the rest will follow.'

Down at the Docklands in the ExCeL Centre, the dealers are polishing their wares. At the squatted convergence centre in the East End, activists are plotting and drinking. Two things they are admirably equipped to do. Wednesday would be the big day for the protest, the day the hand-woven gloves come off. Come Wednesday we are going to try to shut the fair down.

At the Docklands Light Railway, the only train transport to DSEI, activists stand next to arms dealers, packed and crowded into the carriages. Aftershave and military haircuts mingle with bad suits and concerned faces. Suddenly a ranter lets rip, just a thin lad in a suit – late twenties, top whack – dressed in a checked shirt and a red corduroy tie. Standing in the middle of dealers and army folk he goes off like a bomb. 'This is not a war, this is barbarism! The invasion of Iraq. This is not a war, it is a blood bath. A war implies that two sides of armies are doing battle. This is not a war, this is slaughter! This is the massacre of civilians. This is not liberation, this is domination. The economics of the arms fair is the economics of death.' In his red face you can see the battle between compulsion and embarrassment. He has to proclaim but is ill-equipped to engage with people, at least with anything other than his sad anger. His eyes avoid contact with the dealers and soldiers. The battalion of thickset shoulders that are packed into suits reduce their talk to a hush; some look away, some look on in contempt. It is embarrassing. His own vulnerability is as painful as the conviction of his words, half strangled and flying out; his eyes are moist. He has travelled down to London for the day to do this. 'This is not a war, this is butchery!'

Teams of lad and lasses are on the network. The Docklands Light Railway is going down. Two women grab the emergency handle and the train stops in the station while they climb onto the roof. Police radios squawk urgently. Another lad is D-locked to the front of a train. The tube, too, is coming down. On the streets below, Critical Mass, the leaderless cycle ride, which has but one rule – spread out in front of the traffic and slow down – is trailed by bike cops in Lycra and fluorescent jackets. The traffic slows. Mobiles ring with news from across the East End.

'Tube's out! Oy,Oy!'

There is something about a mob that makes the hairs on the back of your neck stand on end. One minute you are a polite nice middle-class dad and the next you're part of a surging, leaderless mass. You want to say, 'I am enjoying the sense of individual empowerment that paradoxically comes with a sense of anonymity,' but it just emerges from your mouth as, 'Come on, then! Come on!' The energy is fantastic, charging in mindless directions, a careering crowd with waves of panic that pitches suddenly one way and then another, interspersed with yelps and scrambled running.

On the railway, police climbers are coming in to cut locks and arrest protestors, but the system is backing up. A car parks in the middle of a road on one of the roundabouts into the fair and out jumps a woman who promptly handcuffs herself to the steering wheel, blocking the traffic. Black cabs advise their occupants to risk walking: 'We ain't goin' nowhere.' Looking like an oil spill, the police in black riot gear surge across the train platforms, pushing punters aside and searching out the protestors. Those travellers going to the fair look wary; they hide their ID cards and force conversation in a bid not to stick out.

And in the middle of the pushbikes blocking roads, crusties stopping trains, ranters bearing witness to passengers … in the middle of the sound systems on the back of bikes, the crowds, the whistles and jeers, I get a little carried away. With three friends, I end up chained to a bus full of BAE Systems employees in the Thistle Hotel car park. The very place that only days earlier had been the scene of our free rides for arms dealers.

To attach yourself to a bus that is moving is a reasonably difficult task, so the first job was to stop the vehicle, which we did by throwing hippies at it. This action doesn't harm the hippies in any way. They are quite used to it and afterwards are released into a suitable environment. Once the hippies are sat down in front of the bus, the driver decides to stop. At that moment Bobby, Baggie, Fisheye and myself attach ourselves to the underside of the bus's metalwork. I felt compelled to join them as I was the only one with a reasonably sensible name.

Once under the vehicle, Baggie and I attach ourselves by our necks with a bicycle D-lock to what we thought was the axle. It turned out to be an anti-roll bar and we lay on our backs on the road with our heads propped against it for a while. Fisheye attached himself to a bit of piping with a pair of handcuffs and Bobby felt left out so joined us with a large lump of motorbike chain and a padlock. I am reasonably sure Bobby had bought the chain as back-up, as he later phoned his partner on the mobile to say, 'Sorry, love, yeah, I'm going to be a bit late, yeah, I'm chained to a bus ... yeah, the arms fair, that's right ... All right ... yeah ... sorry, love ... see ya.' The bus is stuck on a small bridge that crosses the harbour. The Thames is littered with little concrete basins packed with yachts and trophy wives, both in need of a polish. From under the bus I can watch the Thames roll by.

The BAE Systems bus, identified by a big sign in the front window that said 'BAE Systems', was now surrounded by hippies all shouting at the driver, telling him not to move or he would kill their friends under the bus. A mini army of hippies and peaceniks, a mass of henna and dreadlocks, screaming hysterically: 'Stay calm! STAY CALM! Baggie and Fisheye are under the bus! UNDER THE BUS!' It is unfortunate that people involved in the peace movement and direct action are named after Muppet characters; Fisheye appearing in the lesser-known work, *Kermit Does Dallas*. In fact, half the people surrounding the bus appear to have a bit of Muppet DNA in them. Looking back on the event, it is a minor miracle the bus driver didn't put his foot down and head off down the Commercial Road, trailing bloody carcasses from his rear end.

The BAE folk stayed on the bus until the police sorted it out and we probably delayed them for about an hour. I am not sure you could call it a victory for the forces of progress. We pissed off people in the arms trade by forcing them to sit on a bus, which they did with a mixed air of vulnerability and superiority. It is not exactly pushing at the frontiers of political change. On the other hand, BAE Systems is subsidised by us, arms human rights abusers, makes pauper nations pay through the nose for its crap, gets the British government, nay the Prime Minister himself, to do its bidding, has the Cabinet acting as its chief sales agent, has had serious allegations made against it of hiding sensitive documents in Switzerland and paying bribes to foreign ministers*, avoids censure or trial and employs Michael Portillo on the board ... considering all of that, four sweaty Herberts chaining themselves to one of their buses is the nearest they get to democratic accountability. So fuck them.

This is the first time I have been arrested. Crawling out from under the bus into the waiting arms of my arresting officer, I am rather embarrassed at how nervous I feel. This should be a moment of rebellious swagger and clenched-fist salutes. But I am slightly shamefaced and visibly shaking in the police van. The officer sitting next to me is a pleasant man, mid-thirties with a face that would have to be called plain. Looks like he was one of the kids who handed out hymn sheets on Sunday morning at church.

'This your first time, Mark?'

'Yeah,' I squeak.

'Don't worry, I'll be gentle on you.'

'What? Oh yeah, right.'

'Seriously, it is just boring paperwork, being nicked is mainly boring. You'll be fine.'

---

* BAE Systems were the subject of an investigation by the *Guardian* in March 2004, which claimed to have evidence to show that BAE was concealing evidence of covert payments to foreign politicians in a vault in Switzerland, a country with strict secrecy rules. BAE Systems denied any allegations of wrongdoing saying: 'BAE Systems rigorously complies with the laws of the UK and the laws of the countries in which it operates.'

The Foreign Secretary of Qatar became a cause célèbre on Jersey in 2000, when local journalist Anthony Lewis unearthed a story revealing that BAE had made large payments into the Foreign Secretary of Qatar's Jersey bank accounts. BAE Systems said 'We have a strong ethical policy and comply with the law ... We will rigorously defend ourselves against any allegations of wrongdoing.' The sheik also denied any wrongdoing.

I think he is a very nice man. I also think I have just made it into the *Guinness Book of Records* for the fastest case of Stockholm syndrome.

Bobby is sitting behind me with his arresting officer by his side.

'Officer?' he loudly enquires in a tone that is half oikish swagger and half innocence.

'Yeees,' replies a gruff voice.

In front of Bobby I wince, thinking: not now, Bobby, I'm getting on all right with my cop.

'Officer?' he says loudly again.

'Yes.'

'I've got a question.'

Oh please don't let it be: 'D'you know your dad?' Please, Bobby. Don't fuck them off. I am new to this and I don't like it.

'Go on, then,' says the policeman in a slightly challenging voice.

'Hypothetically,' says Bobby slowly.

'Yes,' an equally slow voice says.

'I was wondering ...'

'Go on.'

Oh God, Bobby, don't fuck them all off, please.

'If someone phoned up the arms fair and said, "There's a bomb in the building," would it technically be a hoax call?'

There is a very long silence. A really long silence. The officer sitting next to me turns his head slowly to see Bobby sitting behind him, wide-eyed and head angelically cocked to one side in the style of Lady Di. The officer methodically and factually says, 'That would depend if there was a detonator in it.'

Bobby carries on impersonating Bambi's mum; Baggie, Fisheye and I look confused and the police ponder, until one pensively proffers, 'No, I don't think that is the case.'

To this day the question remains unanswered.

Six months later we are all acquitted of criminal damage in the magistrate's court in Stratford, on the technical grounds that we were innocent. It was a lay magistrate's case, so essentially we had three members of the great and the good deciding our fate – trial by Rotary Club. It was a dull affair until one cop came to read out his statement in court. Holding his notebook and referring to it every now and then, he read like a 1950s black-and-white film portrayal of a British bobby. 'I looked under the vehicle and saw the four defendants. "Come out," I said, to which they replied, "No." I then enquired how long they intended to remain under the vehicle. "Indefinitely," was their response. I then enquired as to who was the ring leader or organiser, to which they replied, "I am Spartacus."'

Standing in the dull white mini concourse, dotted with rows of seats, I do what every other person who leaves the dock and enters the waiting area does – I hunch over to check my mobile for messages. As if by parental telepathy, my mum phoned.

'So what have they said?'

'Acquitted.'

'Oh that's fantastic, that's got to be a weight off your mind, love.'

'Well, it is good to prove I am innocent.'

'I wouldn't go that far. I'm your mother, I know what you've done.'

'Yeah, yeah.'

'And how much has this cost?' she says. Now the immediate threat to her son has vanished, my mother's years of reading the *Daily Mail* kick in.

'What, the court case?'

'How much has it cost the bloody taxpayer?'

'Well, I'm guessing but I'd say with legal aid and prosecution time and all that, got to be somewhere around fifteen to twenty grand.'

'Twenty grand! And who's benefited from that?'

'Well … I reckon I've got a good ten minutes of material out of it for the stage show.'

'Twenty grand for ten minutes of material about thuggery! The state has funded you to behave like a thug!'

'Well, BAE started it ...'

As their annual reports show, the ECGD does a large amount of its work with the arms trade:

YEAR	Percentage of defence	Percentage of Airbus (20 per cent is owned by BAE)*	Operating budget
2000/01	48 per cent	21 per cent	£5.662 billion
2001/02	31 per cent	21 per cent	£3.29 billion
2002/03	50 per cent	14.5 per cent	£3.5 billion
2003/04	39 per cent	31 per cent	£2.99 billion
2004/05	38 per cent	38 per cent	£1.99 billion

* Though BAE is looking to sell its stake.

7

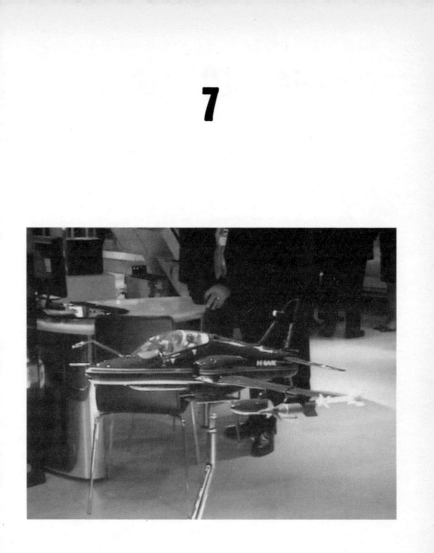

BUNG HO!

CHAPTER SEVEN

A chapter celebrating Britain's ridiculously
poor track record in fighting corruption and bribery.
A British MP sympathises with those poor arms companies
who are forced to pay bribes. The British government is
forced to introduce anti-bribery measures by a skinny
man and a short woman. The author is given
a lesson in common sense.

ALL BRIBED OUT

The tale of the arms industry is one of knighted merchants deal-ing to mad dictators, selling weapons that would make your hair stand on end and then defoliate every last strand, all done with the help of prime ministers and taxpayers' money. But it would-n't be complete without a brief mention of bribery and corrup-tion, which comes neatly packaged with a walk-on cast of Saudi princes, front companies, free holidays and prostitutes. Not to mention the ECGD, which is institutionally pre-programmed to assist bribery by adopting a profound lack of interest in tackling the matter, despite the fact that it lends to companies with a track record of bribing, working in developing countries with a track record of receiving bribes.

Bribery is a habit that most of the major British arms companies indulge in, but few are prepared to talk about in public – a little like middle-aged married men masturbating while their wives are out. Though if you do get caught doing the latter, I recommend you don't use the excuse, 'Well, if I didn't do it someone else would.' Not unless you want to end up on the window ledge of Buckingham Palace dressed in a Batman costume.

The main difference between the two practices is that one of them is wrong ... or if I can rephrase that to avoid confusion among strict Catholics and Taliban supporters: one of the two practices is illegal. One of these was also supported by Patricia Hewitt when she was at the DTI. Can you guess which?

Hewitt, like her boss Tony Blair, talks a good talk. Blair appeared at the G8 summit at Gleneagles banging on about corrupt African leaders, but his vision of corruption only seems to involve one party, the party accepting the bribe. If you had approached him and said: 'What about the multinationals paying the bribes?' I am sure he would have gone into a complete Bertie Wooster tailspin. 'Cripes! Companies actually pay bribes? How cunning! I always thought these bribes just, well ... sort of appeared ... never thought it took two to bribe ... But now you mention it, it is devilishly difficult for a person to bribe themselves ... A chap could get into all sorts of difficulties doing that ... there's probably a verse against that sort of thing in the Bible.'

So a quick quiz for you once again: can you guess when it became illegal for a UK citizen or company to bribe a foreign national? I'll give you a clue. It is somewhere between the invention of the television set and the marketing of the iPod. Any guesses? Would it help if I told you it was post-Spice Girls? For those of you who had a genuine stab at this one, here is the answer, printed upside down: 2002.

It wasn't until 2002 that Britain made bribery of a foreign official a real offence. This is why companies like BAE Systems, when confronted with allegations about bribery, could answer: we have not broken the law, we have done nothing wrong. Even if they had paid money to foreign officials for contracts, they would be technically correct. There was no law to be broken.

The anti-bribery law was rushed through on the back of anti-terrorist measures and was only included because the UK was facing some stern international pressure. The OECD's Working Group on Bribery in Business Transactions had got its members to sign up to a whole load of measures but Britain was dragging its feet. So much so that the chair of the OECD's working group, Professor Mark Pieth, (in 2001), told me that Britain was not doing too well fighting corruption and there was now (he puts this very diplomatically) 'talk about talking about economic sanctions' against the UK. His other comments were less nuanced: 'We have thirty-four members of the group. Twenty-eight have actually ratified and implemented the convention. We have found that, let's say, one third are spic and span, one third are doing relatively fine and one third are kind of sub-standard. There was one country that clearly flunked the exam and I'm sorry to say that was the UK ... It looks as if this government is not really serious about combatting trans-national bribery'. Wow! We could have joined the club of countries with trade sanctions on them. We nearly joined Zimbabwe, Burma, apartheid South Africa and Saddam Hussein's rule of Iraq. Perhaps Britain could have joined a counselling group, where the nations sit around drinking crap coffee and taking turns to stand up and speak. 'My name is Britain and I haven't paid a bribe in eighteen days.'

When I asked Pieth who Britain's peers were when it came to fighting corruption, he instantly listed three countries: 'Turkey, Argentina and Brazil'. When it came to fighting corruption in 2001, that was the gang the UK was in.

So Britain finally got a law to combat bribery. Hurrah! Let us pack up our caravan of moaning nay-sayers – the government have solved the problem. Except that they have not. There are signs that both corporations and government remain institutionally inept in dealing with the issue. The small fact that no company has been convicted of bribery since the law's introduction might be an indication of how seriously Britain takes this new law. Some may argue that no one has been convicted because no British companies have paid bribes, but to believe that requires a level of naivety and faith not normally seen beyond the perimeter of Lourdes. As if to back up this point, the Serious Fraud Office has, at the time of writing, over sixty allegations of bribery on its books, and still no prosecutions.

Then consider the case of the OECD inspection group visiting Britain to assess our efforts to fight corruption and bribery. Meeting with Parliamentarians, the OECD inspectors were greeted by the figure of Bruce George MP, then chairman of the Commons Defence Select Committee. George waded into the discussion with his formidable pale flanks shaking in indignation. According to officials present 'he made an impassioned speech defending the honour of UK civil servants in terms of their susceptibility to corruption'. It was gently pointed out that the subject of the meeting was the bribing of *foreign* officials by UK companies. But this did not halt the by now impressive momentum of Bruce George. The arms industry was one of the most susceptible to bribes, he said. It was worth millions of pounds and thousands of jobs and he would be amazed if many of the big contracts achieved by UK companies were not as a result of bribes. According to Mr George, neither the law, nor the OECD, nor MPs would be able to put a stop to this because the poor old British arms companies have to do it, as everyone else does.

Considering that this man's job was to ensure the MoD was spending taxpayers' money wisely with companies of good standing ... well, considering that, you would have to say that we were fucked. Things couldn't have got much worse if the OECD anti-corruption group had been met by Tony Blair uttering the words, 'Look after your car for a quid, mister.'

Al Yamamah – we're all crazee now
Then consider the Al Yamamah arms deal, between BAE Systems and Saudi Arabia, heralded at the time of its agreement as the

biggest arms deal in the world. The contracts are still active today, with companies continuing to supply and service the agreement.

The deal also featured Margaret Thatcher's son Mark in a walk-on role, who managed to stick his snout in before years later getting caught buying helicopters for coup plotters in Equatorial Guinea. Y'know, folks, let's take the lights down a little here, because I wanna get personal. Whenever I get down and feeling kinda blue, I just think of old Mark Thatcher going to court down in South Africa and I get a warm tingle that makes me feel … well, life ain't so bad. Julie Andrews thought of brown paper packages tied up with string, kittens and noodles. I have Mark Thatcher in court, Jeffrey Archer in prison and George Bush Senior throwing up on the Japanese Prime Minister. Those are the only memories I need to drag me through a lonely winter's night.

Meanwhile, in the equally seedy real world of Al Yamamah, allegations of bribery surrounded the deal, to the tune of some £600 million. The National Audit Office's report looked into the deal and these allegations were suppressed. By which I mean their report was not made public, rather than it was a document that was in denial about its lack of emotional well-being. In fact, the report on those allegations of bribery and corruption wasn't even shown to the MPs who sit on the Public Accounts Committee, the folks whose job it is to oversee financial probity in government.

So I applied to the NAO under the Freedom of Information Act, asking them to release the report. What hope did I have of seeing it? None whatsoever. But it was worth the price of a stamp just to find out if I could hear them laughing in central London when they opened my letter … I swear I could.*

---

* The NAO cited exemptions listed as Sections 34, 27 and 29 (in that order). Section 34: I had requested information that would infringe the privileges of Parliament (as even MPs hadn't seen it and the report had been prepared for Parliament). Section 27: The material couldn't be disclosed as revealing it would have been harmful to relations between the UK and a foreign state (I'm guessing, but let's say Saudi). Section 29: Disclosure of the information would harm the economic interests of the UK.

The question is: if the government are committed to stamping out bribery, why not publish the report on it? Especially as the Serious Fraud Office are investigating BAE Systems over a separate incident, where the company is accused of bribing Saudi Arabia's procurement minister, Prince Turki, in relation to Al Yamamah. The simple answer, I am afraid, is that it appears New Labour are more concerned with protecting BAE Systems than they are with restoring a sense of political accountability and transparency.

NICK AND SUE

On 5 January 2005 very little happened in my world. Stayed in, a bloke came round to fix the computer, a package arrived from Ireland, and my friends Nick and Sue won a court case against the British government.

Nick and Sue both work for the Corner House, the human rights and environmental research group I mentioned in Chapter Three. On first meeting Nick, you would swear he worked at a Steiner school and forced children to play with wooden educational toys in lieu of television. But for all his 'otherworldliness', Nick is probably the most prominent activist of my generation. His colleague Sue is Dr Susan Hawley and she is the leading UK academic on multinationals, bribery and corruption. She also does a nice line in non-corporate garment wearing. Nick and Sue together look like they have just returned from a conference on allergies and wheat-free diets.

Nick and I always meet at Waterloo station. I wait for him under the large clock with Roman numerals that hangs from the station rafters. Nick lollops over with a bizarrely youthful gait. He normally has meetings with lawyers and campaigners that he has travelled up from the country to attend, but we manage to find an hour or so to meet. Hunched over cups, we sit outside the coffee shop opposite platform 12. I can never remember which one of the coffee shop chains it is. In a supreme irony of branding, they all seem to merge into one. This is our spot, under one of the grand arches, half in and half out of the station, and we always sit there. Partly out of routine and partly because neither of us can keep up with the other's attempts to give up smoking.

'Hi, man,' he always says in his posh voice, as he hugs me.

'Shall I get them in?'

'Yeah, that would be great. Anything for me.'

'Which means you want a large cappuccino.'

'Exactly,' he laughs. 'I'll grab a table.'

'Are you smoking?' I ask.

'Yes. Are you?'

'No.'

'Oh fuck.' At this point Nick invariably coughs a racking rasp of his skinny lungs, holds his hands up and says, 'Just get the coffees.'

Nick's work at the Corner House has taken him all over the world. He has compiled reports with Kurds on dam-building in Turkey, he has reported on ecological destruction in Sudan, he has worked on human rights issues and oil pipelines in Azerbaijan. His job is campaigning against the banks and government agencies that finance human rights abuse. Days before I was to go on a human rights fact-finding trip to Diyarbakir in south-east Turkey/Kurdistan, we were, once again, sitting by the coffee shop – half in and half out of the station – and Nick had said: 'You will probably be followed by the Turkish police.'

'Nick, I'm sure I can handle a couple of plainclothes plod. What are they going to do to? They don't want to see "British Comic Jailed in Turkey" in the papers.'

'It's not you I'm worried about,' he said, inhaling the smoke from an absurdly thin roll-up. 'Nothing will happen to you. But it will happen to the people you are with, the people showing you around and translating for you.'

'So don't do anything to embarrass the Turkish cops.'

'Exactly. Always remember the people who will be staying behind when you have gone home.' He sipped the froth, licked his lips and said, 'If anything goes wrong, it will be them that it goes wrong for and you won't read about it in the paper either.'

There is a story about Nick that I never tire of forcing him to retell. He was once speaking at a meeting in Turkey with Kurds. In a dusty plain room, Nick stood under the dull yellow of poor strip-lighting talking to local lawyers and activists. Just as the meeting was due to begin, someone passed Nick a note. It read: 'There is an undercover policeman at the meeting. Please be very careful what you say.' In a land where Kurds have been imprisoned for merely teaching their own language, an undercover cop was a big deal. What was he to do? An incautious remark would have repercussions but a cancelled meeting would be a real step back for local democracy. I always interrupt Nick at this point in the story, impatient for the ending, 'What did you do, tell me again?'

'Well, I started the meeting, got everyone sitting in a circle facing each other and then said, "We have a tradition back home that I think we should follow here tonight."'

The Kurds looked at each other a little confused and worried. One or two glanced at one man in the room. Probably the undercover cop.

'What we do,' Nick continued, 'is one by one we take turns to stand up and introduce ourselves and say a few words about what we want to get out of this meeting. I think that we should do that now, before we start.'

The Kurds tried to suppress their giggling behind their moustaches. Those who spoke English started first and were followed as quickly as the one-to-one translations could take place. In the middle of the circle was one man, the undercover cop, not laughing.

'What did he do?'

'He looked more and more uneasy as it got nearer to his turn to stand up. But he did, he stood up and gave his name and then he said, "Everything that everyone has said here tonight is wrong."'

'And then?'

'And then I thanked him for his honesty, and as his remarks had prompted some disparaging remarks and light rebuke, I said to the room, "Please respect everyone's right to speak freely. This, after all, is a democratic meeting. I want you to respect this man's rights as you would respect your own."'

Once again the Kurds gently heaved their shoulders, suppressing laughter. And as for the undercover cop, he was in conflict, grateful to Nick for having protected his right to free speech, while at the same time anxious to get on with the job of curtailing everyone else's. He left the meeting early.

EasyBribe with ECGD

It was at the Waterloo station coffee shop that Nick introduced me to his colleague Dr Susan Hawley, and it was her methodical and meticulous work that identified a U-turn on anti-corruption measures by the British government.

Trying to stop some UK companies bribing is a Herculean task and nowhere is the shit piled quite so high against the Aegean stable doors as the Export Credits Guarantee Department. Remember that the ECGD provides underwriting for UK businesses supplying goods, such as arms and power stations, in medium- to high-risk markets, such as Nigeria, Indonesia and India. Now, you would have to appear in *Heat* magazine on a pretty regular basis not to connect the words 'arms' and 'Indonesia' with possible backhanders. Yet over the years the ECGD has merrily used public money to back bent deals and managed successfully to investigate precisely none.

So amid the odd raised eyebrow, a small cheer also went up when the ECGD announced new guidelines on fighting corruption and bribery. In March 2003, following the publication of Dr Sue Hawley's detailed report on the ECGD and corruption, the department wrote to their corporate customers to inform them of the 'enhanced provisions in respect of bribery and corruption'. The ECGD extolled the new measures as a 'balanced package ... to the ultimate benefit of all UK companies'.

These measures were simple rules. For example, if a company wanted ECGD backing for a deal they would have to provide details of their commission agents (because commission agents are a notorious route for paying bribes), including any relationships the agent had with the deal. Such a measure would have been invaluable for a company like Alvis (now owned by BAE Systems) when they were selling tanks to Indonesia with ECGD support. Then the ECGD would have known that the commission agent they were paying money to was the President of Indonesia's daughter, Tutut Suharto. Or in the instance of Rolls-Royce working in India on an ECGD-supported deal for the Godavari power station, it would have been useful to know that the commission agent was Towanda Services, registered in the British Virgin Islands, which turned out to be an offshore company owned by the managing direc-tor of the Godavari power plant, responsible for awarding the contract. Indeed a balanced package to the ultimate benefit of all UK companies.

So were the corporations and their trade bodies happy with these new anti-bribery measures? Of course they were. The board members of BAE Systems were ecstatic; they said they would give half the company's profits to street beggars, turn the company HQ into a Buddhist centre and each board member would donate a minimum of one kidney to charity.

For those who have given up sarcasm for Lent, please pay close attention. The ECGD has an advisory committee and its minutes for a meeting in May 2004 said that the anti-bribery measures were 'not ... well received by major customers'. So who had the ECGD upset so much by trying to stop bribery? Well, BAE Systems for one, Airbus (20 per cent owned by BAE Systems) for another, oh and Rolls-Royce. Not to mention the CBI. In fact, the ECGD was forced into a major series of public consultations. By which they meant that they would speak exclusively to industry and no one else, and after these consultations water down the anti-corruption guidelines.

In their 'extensive' consultation leading up to the creation of these new guidelines, which we shall call 'probity lite', the ECGD managed eight meetings with the Society of British Aerospace Companies, the British Exporters Association, the British Bankers Association and the CBI, and precisely none with any major critic of corporate corruption. The ECGD managed to have six meetings with BAE Systems and Rolls-Royce but couldn't quite manage to meet any NGOs who campaigned and worked in this area, like Transparency International or the Corner House. Airbus managed five meetings with ECGD to discuss those rough, tough, nasty, corruption-busting guidelines, but did the ECGD meet with one member of the public on this? No, not one.

The balanced package of anti-corruption measures suffered death by a thousand cuts and all under the approving eye of Patricia Hewitt, then at the DTI. It is astounding even by New Labour's standards that the government should cave in to the demands of bankers and arms dealers who refused to comply with anti-bribery rules.

It was the meticulous work of Dr Susan Hawley who spotted and documented the ECGD capitulation to pressure from the world of business. Hawley and Nick Hildyard decided to take the government to court, despite the fact that the pair of them look barely able to take themselves to the launderette. Sue and Nick argued that the ECGD had not had a proper public consultation, and remarkably the ECGD caved in on the eve of court action, in January 2005.

In March 2006, Sue and Nick, and the Corner House, afforded themselves a small celebration when the ECGD reinstated the tougher measures, much to the chagrin of some of the arms dealers. Here is what they won:

- ❑ Companies have to declare commission agents' details.
- ❑ ECGD previously had to believe corruption had taken place before they could run an audit on a project and had to write to companies outlining their accusations of wrongdoing before they visited. Now ECGD can run random audits to check for corruption.
- ❑ Companies have to give anti-corruption declarations and state they have made the appropriate checks on parent and sister companies and commission agents.

There are still loopholes. For example, if the ECGD want to investigate a company, they have to give them five days' notice, so in effect a company will get a note saying: 'Hide the evidence: you have five days.' I doubt whether this would be an appropriate measure to introduce for other areas of law enforcement. Perhaps the police could send notes to crack dealers, saying: 'The sniffer dog has a cold at the moment, so we'll pop round later looking for drugs.'

It's far from perfect but it's a start
I once told Nick that my son had said to me, 'Dad, you are just like Homer.'

Nick replied: 'In many ways he is right. You tell stories in an episodic manner, using the vernacular—'

'Nick, stop. He meant Homer from *The Simpsons*, not the dead Greek guy.'

'Oh.'

This was part of the team that forced the British government to toughen its anti-corruption work.

At the Waterloo coffee shop, I tell Nick the story of the court case and being chained to the bus full of BAE Systems arms dealers.

'Oh man, that sounds a great adventure,' he says genuinely.

'It was a laugh, but they still get away with it all.'

'Not all of the time. Most of the time, yes. But not all the time … have you got any Rizlas?'

'Yes, but let me roll it for you. Your roll-ups are so thin that convicts wouldn't smoke them.'

'Bastard.' He laughs, then seamlessly adds: 'See, Mark, you won't change everything with reformism, but no one is going to change anything waiting for the glorious revolution either. You can work for change, but you do have to work at it.'

'So the BAE Systems bus was a waste of time?'

'Fuck no! No way, man. That kind of activism is important. Resistance, any resistance is important. It's just that there are a lot of other ways of doing things, too, and one way shouldn't take precedence over another. Remember, use all the tools in the box and work in all of the space you have.'

'Nick, we don't have a huge amount of political space to work in. Blair's as shit as the Tories.'

'Agreed, but there are differences. And we probably have just a bit more political room to work in …'

'It is still fuck all,' I moan almost inaudibly, licking the edge of the Rizla paper.

'You work with what you've got. Make the absolute best use of the little that you have … What the fuck is that?' He laughs as I pass him the roll-up. 'That cigarette is enormous, it is absurdly large.'

Which is true – the cigarette paper barely wraps around the tobacco to hold it together and clumps of brown weed hang out of each end.

'That is ridiculous.' He takes it from me and reaches for a lighter.

'It's a cigar, Nick, it's a cigar.'

A SHORT LIST OF ECGD PROJECTS
WITH ALLEGATIONS OF CORRUPTION

Project: Turkwell Gorge Hydroelectric Project
Country/date: Kenya, 1986
Company: Watermeyer Lesse Piesold and Uhlmann, subsequently renamed Knight Piesold, then Scott Wilson Piesold.
Consultancy services
Corruption allegations: EC delegation alleged that the dam was 'extremely disadvantageous for Kenya' but that government officials – notably President Daniel Arap Moi and Energy Minister Nicholas Biwott – 'nevertheless accepted it because of high personal advantage'. Allegations include: illegal contracts, failure to account for expenditure, overpayment of contractors.
ECGD involvement: £17.5 million guarantee. Paid out claims of £2 million, recovering £1.2 million from government of Kenya. Gave the guarantee despite credible allegations of corruption. Failed to insist on proper audit of the project by Kenyan government. Denied backing the project until 2001.

Project: Ewaso Ngiro Hydropower Scheme
Country/date: Kenya, 1990
Company: Knight Piesold (now Scott Wilson Piesold).
Conducted feasibility study and environmental impact assessment.
Corruption allegations: World Bank criticised the Knight Piesold contract for being 'five times what such services would normally cost'. Concerns also raised over 'procurement practices and financial mismanagement'. Knight Piesold denied allegations of wrongdoing and were subsequently cleared by World Bank auditors. Kenyan minister investigating allegations of corruption was murdered.
ECGD involvement: £37 million export credit. Paid out claims of £8.12 million, recovering £5.74 from the government of Kenya. Gave guarantee despite international concerns over corruption. Failed to investigate allegations of financial mismanagement.

Project: KAFCO Fertiliser Plant

Country/date: Bangladesh, 1991

Corruption allegations: Allegations of extensive bribery of ministers in government of military dictator General Hussain Mohammad Ershad, who has since been deposed. Described by ministers in new government as 'most corrupt deal in Bangladesh's history'. Contracts highly unfavourable to Bangladesh. No competitive tender despite requirements of Bangladeshi law. Allegations have never been officially investigated.

ECGD involvement: £20 million investment insurance to Citibank. Almost total failure of any due diligence procedures.

Project: Lesotho Highlands Water Project

Country/date: Lesotho, 1993–7

Company: Kier International, Sterling International, Balfour Beatty and Kvaerner Boving Ltd.

Corruption allegations: Chief executive of the Lesotho Highlands Development Authority, the state body responsible for the project, convicted of receiving bribes.

ECGD involvement: Total support amounting to £215 million. Continued to give guarantees after first corruption suspicions arose. Failed to implement adequate due diligence. Failed to institute proper investigations, stating only that it had asked the companies themselves for information. Failed to pass on allegations to Serious Fraud Office.

Project: Coco Palm Apartments and La Palma Beach Hotel

Country/date: Ghana, 1994

Company: International Generics Ltd.

Corruption allegations: Described in Ghanaian press as 'a pyramid of fraud', with chief beneficiaries alleged to have been President of Ghana's family. Hotels were to have been built in two years but were not completed for seven. Both projects were crippled by debt and alleged financial mismanagement.

ECGD involvement: Underwrote two loans by Bank of Scotland worth £22.3 million. Paid out £18.4 million on the projects, recovering £10 million from government of Ghana. Inadequate due diligence. ECGD acknowledged in 2001 that there were serious corruption issues with the projects and passed allegations to Serious Fraud Office. No prosecutions resulted due to difficulty in establishing that a criminal offence had occurred in UK. Claims paid out despite corruption allegations.

Project: Godavari Power Plant
Country/date: India, 1995
Company: Spectrum Power Generation Ltd.
Corruption allegations: Allegations that commissions paid to SPGL's managing director to secure contracts.
ECGD involvement: £50 million guarantee for ANZ Grindlays Bank for Spectrum Power Generation Ltd to support involvement of Parsons Power Generation Systems Ltd (subsequently Heaton Power Ltd) and Rolls-Royce Industrial Power (India) Ltd – both subsidiaries of Rolls-Royce plc. Inadequate due diligence on both commission payments and financial mismanagement.

Project: Defence Equipment Package
Country/date: Qatar, 1996
Company: BAE Systems. Vosper Thornycroft.
Corruption allegations: Allegations of corrupt payments worth at least £100 million, channelled through Jersey banks. Foreign Minister of Qatar admits accepting substantial commissions from companies but denies these were bribes.
ECGD involvement: Two guarantees worth £5.5 million and £222.9 million. Inadequate due diligence. Failure to acknowledge or investigate bribery allegations.

Project: Dabhol Power Plant
Country/date: India, 2000
Company: Kier International.
Corruption allegations: Allegations that bribes were paid in the awarding of the contracts.Indian court has stated that it found 'indications' which 'suggest corruption by those responsible for the deal'.
ECGD involvement: £30.5 million in reinsurance for Kier International. Additional insurance for three UK banks through Overseas Investment Insurance scheme (amounts unknown). Backed project despite well-known corruption allegations.

Project: Defence Equipment
Country/date: South Africa, 2000
Company: BAE Systems.
Corruption allegations: Allegations of corruption, nepotism and misuse of power. Former defence minister and ministry officials alleged to have channelled contracts through firms that benefited relatives.
ECGD involvement: £1.6 billion guarantee to BAE Systems. Gave support despite allegations of corruption. Has made no apparent effort to investigate the allegations or pass them on to the Serious Fraud Office.

Project: Yumi Yet Bridge Development Programme
Country/date: Papua New Guinea (PNG), 2001
Company: Mabey and Johnson.
Corruption allegations: Deal described by official of PNG's Planning and Monitoring division as 'sinister and highly suspicious'. Project challenged on grounds of value for money. As yet unsubstantiated and uninvestigated corruption allegations have started to emerge.
ECGD involvement: £35.7 million guarantee. Inadequate due diligence. Several months prior to the signature of the contract, PNG Auditor General's office reported allegations of financial

mismanagement, fraud and misuse of resources at the Department of Works and Transport, which is responsible for the bridges project.

Project: Philippine Bridges
Country/date: Philippines, 2005
Company: Mabey and Johnson.
Corruption allegations: Accusations of corruption and overcharging are now being made in the Philippines. Mabey denies any impropriety, saying the allegations are made by rivals or are politically motivated. Many bridges led to nowhere.
ECGD involvement: £90 million guarantee. Went ahead with further phase of the project despite well-documented allegations of over-pricing and evidence that many bridges were 'white elephants'. Corruption allegations have since emerged.

Sources: 1) Dr Sue Hawley, *Turning a Blind Eye: Corruption and the Export Credits Guarantee Department*, Corner House 2003
2) House of Commons Environmental Audit Committee, *ECGD and Sustainable Development*, July 2003, 'Corner House Evidence'
3) Leigh, D and Evans, R, 'British Family Firm Accused of Getting Rich by Building Bridges to Nowhere', *The Guardian*, 20 December 2005

PART TWO
AT THE MARGINS

8

STEPPING AWAY
FROM RESPONSIBILITY

CHAPTER EIGHT

A chapter in which the author asks if it is possible to like an arms dealer, and can arms dealers admit to their responsibilities in the supply chain of weapons?

GETTING A LIFT TO THE TRAIN STATION WITH THE MAN WHO SUPPLIED THE KALASHNIKOV USED IN THE HUNGERFORD MASSACRE

The driver of the white Mercedes is Mick Ranger, the man who supplied the Kalashnikov rifle used by Michael Ryan in the 1987 mass murder in Hungerford. As we head out along the M11 to Stansted, clocking Eddie Stobarts and cruising the lines of orange cones, Mick discusses *Fawlty Towers* – his favourite TV comedy programme – detailing the acute embarrassment he felt on Basil Fawlty's behalf. One hand leaves the wheel as he casually slips on a pair of shades. They are Cool Hand Luke shades, big and gold-rimmed, the kind of shades men thought might get them laid back in 1971. Mick stops squinting into the winter glare of the Essex sun and shifts back in his chair. The flow of traffic is not too bad but there is the threat of ice on the roads. And for a moment, Mick Ranger, international arms dealer, managing director and CEO, gets stuck behind a gritting lorry.

As a rule, folk don't tend to imagine international arms dealers boxed in by yellow council vehicles throwing spitefully small brown/pink stones at the windscreen. And I, for one, feel cheated. Mick's an international arms dealer – we should be hanging out with Mark Thatcher, ordering helicopters, drinking brandies, sweating like mercenaries and behaving like ponces. We should dine with presidents on rare game meat and talk loudly with our mouths open. Our briefcases should be full of banknotes and our birthday cakes full of women. We should be a reason people voted Labour in 1997.

Mick Ranger would probably describe himself as a working-class lad made good. I would describe him as North London made Essex. Same difference really; it's the bit of the Venn diagram where social sciences meet geography. His North London accent harbours a regular disbelief at the way of the world. It's the voice of a 1950s *Daily Express* reader. It seems to have been purpose-built to utter phrases like, 'You will not believe what they have gone and done now.' It is this tone of voice that is being employed as Ranger describes his stranded shotguns left high and dry on the continent as the result of a shipping error. The guns are for mercenaries in Iraq who have got the job of guarding the embassies and today they should be at Heathrow ready to be picked up. They are not. The airline moving his shotguns is Virgin; normally they 'have no qualms about moving the type of goods I trade in. They're, in fact, one of the good guys, decent guys that appreciate that the arms trade is there for everybody to make money out of that can legitimately do so'. Mick Ranger ponders and identifies the reason his shotguns have not been shipped to Heathrow; it is the fault of one Virgin employee. His shotguns have 18-inch barrels and 'civilians here can't have a shotgun that's less than 24 inches, but the majority of military shotguns are normally 18 or 20 inches'. So the Virgin bloke has got twitchy and is going to refuse the shipment.

'Well, he might have been a bit shocked when he saw the guns—' I begin.

'No, no, no, no, it doesn't matter, I have the correct paperwork, that's all he should be bothered with.' Mick Ranger sighs, as much with incredulity as with anger. 'Totally unnecessary, total waste of my time, delaying my shipment.'

I had met Mick Ranger for the first time a few hours earlier that same day. He is a polite man with a quick if uneasy smile and the kind of striding gait that is compulsory to all men of six feet four. He is a trim sixty-year-old, with combed-back hair receding slightly and greying gently at the sides. Everything he wears today is black: black leather slip-on boots, black jeans, black T-shirt and a black shirt half buttoned up. Standing tall and rigid, he looks like a Munster impersonating Johnny Cash.

He had agreed to take part in some filming for a Channel 4 show I was doing. It was good of him to come along, to 'put the good face of the arms industry', to use his words. It was especially good of him as the filming was going to take place at Lord Williams Upper School in Thame, where students from the school's Amnesty International group were going to put questions to him. In all fairness to Mick Ranger, this is not something that many arms dealers would be prepared to do.

The school is a mix of old brick structures with stone arched doorways and newer prefabs that smack of Grange Hill. All of which sit on the rolling green tracts of Oxfordshire farmland. And in a small room, sitting in front of a group of pupils, is Mick Ranger, who wastes little time getting on to the subject of his wrath. 'More and more airlines won't take guns,' Ranger explains. 'They want to show a clean face to the world, they don't want to get involved in arms movement anywhere. It's political correctness.'

The assembled semi-circle of teenagers didn't appear that concerned about this particular issue. Perhaps because as members of the school's Amnesty International group, an arms dealer's transport worries were not top of their agenda.

So what would Ranger like to see changed in the world of arms dealing and export controls?

'Less prejudice against the arms trade.'

Beating prejudice against arms dealers? It sounds like an 'awareness training course' waiting to happen. I can see it now: a small room in the Greater London Assembly building, me, Mark Thatcher, maybe a couple of other gunrunners, all with name badges, taking turns to feel each other's pain.

The students offer up a range of questions, from the meticulously arcane: 'What effect would an introduction of extraterritorial controls being placed on small arms have on your business?' to the more expected: 'How many guns have you sold?' and the deceptively innocent: 'Does your mum approve of what you do?'

To which the shortened answers to the above are: 1) Quite a bit. 2) About a hundred thousand. 3) She sadly passed away and therefore can't comment.

'Everything I do is legal,' says Mick Ranger, who claims his turnover is around £2 million a year. 'There's enough good business [so] you never have to need to bother to go the wrong way. Once you're established in the trade, if enough trade comes to you, you don't even have to think about the dodgy ones.'

Mick Ranger almost sits back to let the £2 million sink in with the students.

'What experience do you need to be a successful arms dealer?' another pupil asks.

'Well, obviously the experience is within the trade itself and you gain that experience as you go through it. But success in any business, in any job, has got nothing to do, I've found, with degrees. [It] is just common sense and the will to work. I've got no GCEs [sic], I've got no degrees.'

A shocked fascination descends as Mick Ranger gets into his stride. For a moment I am not quite sure what he is up to, but Mick is oblivious to any curious grimaces from my direction.

'I've done pretty well,' he continues, 'and I think it's down to just getting on with the job and the will to work. And I hope you guys never forget that, 'cause that's the main thing you need to succeed in life.'

I look round the room to see if anyone else is doing a double-take. It dawns on me that Mick Ranger thinks he is giving a class careers talk. While the kids ask him about moral responsibility, Mick Ranger thinks he is some kind of keynote inspirational speaker for students in the school Amnesty group.

The pupils warm to him, though. They actually quite like him. Oddly enough, I warm to him too. Ranger appears candid, chatty and friendly, none of the things the students expected him to be. But this doesn't stop them being critical of him, and the slightly knotty topic of the mass murder of sixteen people at Hungerford has been raised. Ranger supplied the Kalashnikov semi-automatic rifle to Michael Ryan 'via a third party, via a gun shop in the West Country, but I didn't give him the licence to buy that. That was the police'.

Looking around the room I ask, 'Anyone else has a question?'

'I've got one,' says a lad with his hand half up. 'Do you detach yourself from where you send your weapons, do you think of the effects?'

'The thing is you've got to stand back and let someone else make the decision. It's not our job. Our job is just to sell the goods, if we're allowed to by the authorities ... This was said to me in 1987, after the Hungerford massacre, when it worked out that one of the guns I'd imported actually got to the guy that did the evil deed. People are saying to me "What do you think?" and I've got to take a step back and say I didn't give him the licence to buy the gun.'

Another hand raises, half formal-classroom style, half auction-house bid.

'Even though you didn't do anything wrong by selling the weapon, don't you regret selling it to start with, because of what it did?' says a student.

'Of course, yes, but actually the figures that came out at the time actually said that he killed more people with the pistol [a Beretta 9mm] that he got from somewhere else than he did with the Kalashnikov that he got from me ... the media honed in on the Kalashnikov being the evil weapon rather than the pistol, which he did more damage with.'

I have to confess that I have never seen anyone before suggesting, as Mick appears to be, that the Kalashnikov used in Hungerford has been scapegoated and unfairly blamed for its role in the murders. It's tempting to suggest that political correctness is to blame.

Ranger is statistically right. Ryan killed eight people with the Kalashnikov and eight with the Beretta. However, if you include Ryan's suicide, the Beretta goes to pole position and was responsible for nine deaths on 19 August 1987.

By the end of the questions Mick Ranger must feel he has made a good impression because as the pupils thank him for coming, he rises from his seat and with total sincerity says: 'So, are any of you destined to be arms dealers, then?'

My eyes are open wider than a roadie's arse crack, but the kids don't miss a beat.

'Dunno. Is it worth it money-wise?' says one, leaning back in his seat.

'Oh sure,' says a motivational Mick.

'Is it worth it morally too?' chips in another.

'Oh yeah, sure. As I said, we have to step back and say somebody else has taken the decision that this deal has gone through. It hasn't been our decision.'

'So you say the money outweighs the morals?'

'Again, you keep saying morals,' says a genuinely perplexed Ranger, 'but I'm not making the decisions who has the guns. And if I wasn't doing the deals I was doing, somebody else would be doing the same ones. Simple as that.'

Except that it is not as simple as that. From Prince Charles to Ranger, people have excused the arms trade by arguing that if they didn't do it, someone else would. While true, it is not an excuse you can use in other areas of antisocial activity. Try defending dealing in heroin by standing in court and saying, 'Well, if I didn't do it someone else would.' Oh, and if you ever do try that line of defence, let me know where to write to you.

Child pornography is another area where a dealer could technically argue: 'If I didn't do it, someone else would.' Again this would invariably be true. But a dealer would have to have some fairly intense masochistic tendencies to try that defence. There are a host of things that will always be done by 'someone else', from using prostitutes, to selling fake cigarettes, even trying to punch Phil Collins, but they still remain crimes. Legally and socially there is such a thing as individual moral responsibility. But does Mick Ranger know that?

The raisin appraiser's son

The mundane, day-to-day banality of arms dealing fascinates me, probably as much as the trade's role in conflict and barbarity. Mick Ranger's phone is constantly ringing as he fields questions about paperwork and returning calls. All of this is peppered with his fury at a petty official, the airport employee who will not let his shotguns on the plane. It is all too easy to identify with the feeling of hopelessness and rage in the face of incompetent bureaucracy. Just as it is all too easy to be alienated by the fact it is shotguns we are talking about being delayed. Shotguns destined for Iraq for some mercenaries. These paradoxes make trying to like someone like Mick Ranger a confusing affair. In the grand scheme of arms dealing, he isn't BAE Systems, he isn't a huge multinational, impersonally arming all and sundry. But he is an arms dealer and isn't it inevitable that if he has sold 100,000 guns, then one or two of them will end up in 'the wrong hands'?

He is a slightly weird but pleasant enough bloke, who just happens to have provided the gun used at Hungerford. Other arms dealers might have packed up at this point, but Mick Ranger has managed not only to stay in business but to prosper.

But at some point he must have wobbled and wondered if he had any responsibility. At some point he must have wondered: 'Do I have a responsibility for what happens – does the blame for Hungerford reach me? And I wonder how he keeps going.

After talking to the students, Ranger offers to give me a lift to Stansted airport, from where I can catch a train back into London. Sitting next to him and staring down at the circular metal Merc logo at the end of the bonnet, I ask him why he likes guns.

'I've been interested in guns all my life, even when I was a child I was interested in guns, you see,' he explains.

'Did you go hunting? Did you—'

'Oh no. No. Never. Not on your life. Never killed animals,' he interrupts emphatically. 'I absolutely detest those people who go shooting, you know – African wildlife, what have you.'

'Like trophy hunters and all that?' I say.

'Oh yeah.' Then he warms to his philosophy. 'If a tiger comes into my room, into my house, I've got the right to shoot him,' says Mick, as we speed down the motorway. 'But,' he continues, 'that is my bit of the world. We've got no right to go into their world ... certainly not to shoot them.'

Ranger grew up in the North London suburbs in the 1950s. His father worked for the Australian Dried Fruit Board.

'He was on *What's My Line* many years ago,' said a proud Mick Ranger. And he is right to be so. For you youngsters who live on a diet of *Big Brother*, crystal meth and teen pregnancy, *What's My Line* was an old black-and-white-TV show. A panel game where show-business folk would try to deduce the employment of each mystery guest by asking series of questions, to which the mystery guest could only answer yes or no.

'Was he?' I exclaim in mild admiration.

'Yeah, as a raisin appraiser.'

Mick Ranger started in the motor trade, and after a chance meeting with a police firearms officer, joined a gun club. It was a short step from shooting to owning guns, then to trading them and eventually to running a £2 million-a-year company called Imperial Defence Services Ltd.

'You don't actually set up an office: "International Arms Dealer: come and get your weapons from me" – nobody's going to come because nobody knows you. You know, it just led from one thing to another, it went from a part-time business to a full-time business.'

Imperial Defence Services Ltd is run out of Hertfordshire and employs four people. I had previously met one of Mick's employees at an arms fair. He was a pleasant enough man, balding, mid-fifties, 1980s grey suit and pre-NHS teeth. He, like Mick, had the air of a hobbyist. Which is not to say he was unprofessional, merely that these are men who earn their living out of their hobby. They reminded me of the types of men you find in railway modelling shops.

There is a difference though. Men in modelling shops might know too much about double-0-gauge railway tracks, but they rarely have problems getting their stock of shotguns onto a Virgin plane. The Hornby choo-choo boys don't ship Bushmaster machine guns to Aegis, the mercenaries working in Iraq. Nor do the modellers get the *Observer* newspaper writing articles about them under the headline 'Exposed: Global dealer in death'. Mick has, though. An undercover journalist accused Mick of quoting to supply AK47s for Syria in the knowledge that the weapons would go on to Iraq. Mick turns up in Oxfam reports and gets mentioned at Parliamentary select committee hearings. There must be days when Mick wishes he had gone into raisin appraising.

'No country or its needs are of difficulty to us'
Since 1987, Mick Ranger has sold approximately 100,000 small arms, the odd surface-to-air missile, anti-tank weapons and a large quantity of rifle grenades and heavy machine guns. His website boasts: 'Our business is truly global, with no geographi-

cal limitations, therefore no country or its needs are of difficulty to us, with the sole exception of countries currently under UN embargo. We are able to fulfil defence requirements no matter where the buyer is situated.' In the world of arms dealers this is quite a mission statement. EU arms sanctions or UK government obstacles mean nothing to Mick Ranger; he only fears UN embargoes. That and Kryptonite, which for a fee I am sure he would be happy to supply.

If an advertising executive translated Ranger's website into a 15-second TV ad, Ranger would sit in front of a warehouse full of guns and missiles. The script would run: 'I'm Mick, and I deal whatever guns you want, to whatever place you want them. Pistols to tanks. Whatever to wherever.' Mick would then strike a smiling pose in front of the weapons, while a high-speed voiceover says, 'UN destinations need not apply.'

Ranger's claim that no destination is a problem is backed up with offices and agents in Bulgaria, Cyprus, Nigeria, Australia, South Africa and Vietnam. Indeed, up until recently his website was even more open about making use of other countries' laxer arms controls. The Ranger H-P pistol (9mm automatic) is Imperial Defence Services Ltd own make of gun, named after Mick, and according to the website 'can only be obtained from this company, *who will either export it to clients from the UK or Bulgaria when easier for export licensing procedures to certain destinations*'. (my italics)

Every country in the world has a different set of rules and regulations for arms trading. Some are a lot laxer than others and a dealer like Mick Ranger knows which countries are the best to work from. 'Bulgaria used to be good,' he says. Vietnam is another place he does a lot of work from. 'Albania used to be great, you could get a licence in a week.' He has a warmth in his voice remembering the official in charge of the Albanian state arms company. 'What you'd call a likeable rogue,' says Mick Ranger.

I am sure it is entirely possible to see an arms dealer in Albania as a likeable rogue, but I suspect most of us would regard him as an utter twat. The point is that Mick Ranger knows the laws he needs to obey and those he can simply walk round. He can and does legally sell weapons all over the world. In the absence of comprehensive laws to control the arms trade, where Ranger sells to is as much down to him as it is down to governments.

Mick's morals

Back in the white Mercedes running along the tarmac veins of Essex, Mick Ranger is recounting his school days back in the 1950s. 'Each lesson would start with the teacher saying, "Right, let's have your guns," because it was natural that kids had guns … their fathers brought back from the war, and they played around with them, and nobody took a blind bit of notice. I remember one day as though it was yesterday, fifty-two years ago it would have been. A young kid, he had a strip of white hair. He brought a hand grenade to school, this is junior school, and the teacher said, "What are you playing at, boy, bring it out here," and the teacher just unscrewed the detonator from the top, looked inside, saw it wasn't live and put it in his desk and said, "You can get this from me at the end of the day." Imagine what would happen nowadays?' he says, with incredulity creeping back into his voice. 'They'd call out the bomb squad: headline news on the papers!' He trails off in mild exasperation at the thought of the creeping intrusion of the nanny state.

The urge to grab the handbrake and slew the car into a jack-knife leaves me as suddenly as it came, but for a second I want to drag Mick onto the hard shoulder, cup his head in my hands, stare into his eyes and ask, 'Exactly why is it wrong to be concerned if an eight-year-old child brings a hand grenade into school?' But perhaps I am being churlish.

Schools might have been awash with weapons in the 1950s but back then 'there were four armed robberies in London' in a year, according to Ranger. Though he can't quite remember where he heard that fact. Today, though, there must be 'four a day in London', he exclaims, though I don't think I should push him on his data; he is making a point rather than quoting a statistic. So thinking that Mick might have some interesting observations to make about the illegal gun trade, I ask why he thinks there has been such a dramatic increase in gun crime.

'Lack of moral, um … uh … uh …' Mick searches for the right phrase. 'That's the wrong word, isn't it, the demise of people's moral attitudes,' he says thinking out loud, before triumphantly concluding, 'Nobody gives a fuck any more, do they? Nobody cares.'

'So you think it is moral degeneracy?'

'Sure, that's pretty right, sure …' he says, his shades fixed on the road, before he starts to casually pontificate on the murders of Jamie Bulger and Damilola Taylor. 'What possesses children to do things like that? Something like that they blame it on TV, but you know I used to watch violent films as a kid, you know, and I didn't go around shooting people.'

Let me tell you, folks, if you ever get a lift in a car with an arms dealer, it is always a relief to learn that they can watch a Dirty Harry movie without thinking, That looks enjoyable, I'll give that a go.

'And,' he continues, 'I didn't know anyone who did go around killing people or maiming, it never, it-it-it never came into our thoughts.'

Which once again is nice to know. None of Mick's friends killed anyone. It's at times like these that I wish I had more bunting at home. On reflection, though, it would be even nicer if Mick's clients could boast the same Buddha-like urges of peace and tranquillity.

He continues: 'Things that happen nowadays, [it] is the decline in moral attitudes. It's phenomenal compared to what it used to be.'

'What do you think caused that?'

'No idea. No idea, no idea … it's just the way society has degraded.'

As we slip between the three lanes avoiding slow vans and heavy lorries, we chat about how the 'the English gun industry has gone the way of the English motorcycle industry'. He tells me of his trip to Nairobi: 'One of the biggest disappointments of my life.' And he recounts his visit to the Killing Fields in Cambodia, 'The Khmer Rouge's Auschwitz … Oh it was terrible, absolutely diabolical really, dreadful, you know, but unfortunately these things happen.'

Indeed they do and Mick spots the pitfalls of the logic looming ahead of him. Killing Fields bad. People killed with guns. Mick Ranger sells guns. Mick Ranger bad.

'But in reality I s'pose what happened in Cambodia is not really much worse than what happened in … where is it … I can never remember.'

'Rwanda?'

'Where the Tutsis and the Hutus hacked each other to bits. Not much difference really.'

Talking about man's inhumanity to man is safer ground for Mick. So it seems logical that in his version of the Rwandan genocide the problem was two groups hacking at each other. Rather than the prepared and planned genocide that it was, where one group, the Hutus, butchered another group, the Tutsis. In his version of this particular history, human beings are always going to be doing this sort of thing and you'll never stop them. But there is another version in which those who prepared, orchestrated and carried out the barbarity are individuals. These individuals can be caught and punished for their actions. In this version, humans have a responsibility to each other. A responsibility I suspect Mick finds it easier to ignore.

We glide on past the slip-roads leading to the wilds of Essex, past the leafless trees whose copses dot the winter farmland, and past sales reps in company cars weaving lanes, jacket off, hunched over the steering wheel, one hand clutching a cardboard tube full of coffee while they shout into a Bluetooth earpiece. Sealed in a glass and metal bubble, they hurtle down the highways screaming at someone miles away, back at head office or at home. A bloke in a florist's van, probably full of bouquets proclaiming undying love and tenderness, thrusts his arm out of the window, extending the middle digit of his hand in the direction of the car in front of him, which has cut him up and hit the brakes. All the traffic is slowing. There is an accident on the other side of the road, which, like it or not, we are slowing to gawp at.

Once past the wrecks, Mick returns to the not insignificant matter of Britain's moral decay: there is too much petty crime, too much CCTV, shop assistants are not polite.

'How old are you?' he asks.

'Forty-two.'

'Forty-two, OK, right, so you grew up in a different era to what I did, you grew up in the promiscuous time of the 1960s, when sex was freer.'

'I was born in sixty-three. So I kind of missed it,' I point out to no avail, as Mick is continuing regardless.

Referring to his youth he says: 'You know you thought you were doing well if you got your hand down a girl's blouse on the fourth date. Nowadays if they're not shaking themselves at you within about half an hour of meeting, there's something wrong.'

I have an uneasy feeling that Mick Ranger is suggesting that sexual promiscuity might be a contributory factor in the rise of gun crime.

Hungerford

Michael Ryan was twenty-seven when he killed sixteen and injured fifteen people over a 58-minute massacre in Hungerford, a small town off the M4. He was a member of a Home Office-certified gun club and his gun ownership was entirely legal; his shotgun licence application had been countersigned by his doctor. He was given permission to purchase and own the Kalashnikov 7.62mm semi-automatic on 30 July 1987; a week later he bought the gun at Westbury Guns in Wiltshire. Mick Ranger had supplied the Kalashnikov to Westbury Guns; it was one of many he bought from Chinese manufacturers Norinco. The one he sold to Westbury was just one of 'five or six hundred I sold in the year leading up to Hungerford'.

The first person to be killed by Ryan was a 33-year-old woman, Susan Godfrey; she was picnicking with her two children, four and two years old, in Savernake Forest when she was abducted, taken some 75 yards away and shot thirteen times in the back. The gun that killed her was the Beretta pistol. Ryan's next victims were his next-door neighbours, Mr Roland Mason and his wife Mrs Sheila Mason. Mr Mason was killed with the Kalashnikov and Mrs Mason with the Beretta pistol.

In the car and away from the school students, Mick Ranger is slightly blunter on the topic.

'I didn't pull the trigger.'

'Right,' I nod.

'It's a business and you've got to appreciate that as a business. And we have to walk away if we've done things correctly and then things go wrong.'

'Yeah.'

'If through no fault of our own things go wrong and we'll have done everything in our power to make sure that the deal has gone through correctly and legitimately and the paperwork's been checked up on, and then the deal gets into the wrong hands, how can we be responsible for that?'

This is the fifth time today I have heard him talk about 'stepping away' or 'standing back' from events that have 'gone wrong'. The words, his words, are about physically removing oneself from an incident, about not becoming involved. It is a partial admission that if he stopped to look and stare it would have an effect upon him. He might be moved to take action by what he saw, maybe to cast doubt upon his role in it. So he has to walk away.

The white silhouette of a plane starts to appear on large blue road signs, so Stansted is nearby. From there I'll grab a train into London and Mick will head back to his Hertfordshire home and hub of his arms business. Tomorrow he'll try and pick up the 18-inch shotguns.

'We've all got a line that we won't step across, sure, course we have,' he tells me.

'What's your line?'

'I won't supply illegal guns to anybody. I wouldn't do anything that's illegal in the arms trade.'

But given the loopholes in the arms industry, that still leaves him with plenty of room to operate in. And Mick Ranger's global business, which is able to 'fulfil defence requirements no matter where the buyer is situated', has helped put 100,000 guns into the world.

Arms dealers will sell as many guns as they can to as many people as they are allowed to. This is the way business works, from a fruit and veg stall to a City stock-market trader. No one runs a company with the objective of selling less each year, though Rover comes close. If a dealer was flogging fruit there would be no problem, they could sell to whomever they pleased, whatever they pleased and however much they pleased – except to the odd diabetic and sufferer from Crohn's disease. But weapons are different, because weapons take human life. Admittedly a host of other things take human life too, anything from kitchen knives to microlight planes to Rottweilers, but they are not designed or intended specifically to take human life. Kitchen knives are not marketed as 'The ultimate in divorce!' Microlights don't come with the strap line 'Fly 'n' die!' Nor does Crufts have a best-in-show award for running pensioners to ground. Weapons are different. They are designed to take human life, they are forever updated and upgraded in the quest to kill, immobilise and incapacitate greater numbers of people for smaller amounts of effort. And it is this fact that defines an arms dealer. More than perhaps any other occupation, an arms dealer is defined by his or her job.

9

NEW LABOUR
AT THE MARGINS

CHAPTER NINE

A chapter in which the government's accomplishments are considered. Some change has come at the margins of the arms trade. The author gives the government the praise it is due, and then promptly finds another loophole.

SHOCK TO MY SYSTEMS

It is not exactly taboo-busting to suggest politicians may not be surfing in the choppy waters of progressive thought. If you ever want to disprove the pseudo-science and religious desperation of 'intelligent design' – the theory that there must be a God because life is so complex and beautiful – you could do a lot worse than citing politicians and AIDS as primary examples of undivine ugliness. If, as the Bible says, man is born in the image of God, then we only have to look at Peter Mandelson and Tessa Jowell to realise that either the Bible is wrong or that an eternity of hell with Satan does have an upside.

These are deeply held beliefs and so it pains me to do this. There is no polite way of saying what I need to impart to you, nor of gently leading you to the brutal conclusion and shocking statement that lies in wait for you in the next sentence. So I shall just have to say it bluntly: when British politicians say 'on arms control and torture equipment Britain has got some of the strictest regulations in the world', they are being relatively honest. Please let me reassure you that I too find the image of a truthful MP alarming and disconcerting to the point of nausea. I am desperately sorry and it grieves me greatly, but in this instance they are basically right.

For those of us who find this grim image too threatening to our value system, let us briefly consider the vision of John Prescott reclining on his departmental office sofa, his quadruple chins thundering with pleasure. Feel better? Probably not, but let us continue ...

Let's assume that MPs enter Parliament with noble intentions. Pretty quickly the daily grind of political point-scoring and personal grudge-settling becomes a full-time job, while running the country is a more cash-in-hand affair, akin to delivering leaflets for curry houses and minicabs. What puts progressive laws on the statute book is more often than not campaigning and public outrage, rather than an innate desire within governments to create a veritable Garden of Eden for all humankind. That said, there was some change, at least at the margins there was.

Robin Cook's declaration in 1997 that there would be an 'ethical dimension' at the heart of British foreign policy was a stillborn pup. Abbreviated into the 'ethical foreign policy', it joined our ever-growing lexicon of oxymorons, comfortably complementing some of our old favourites like 'Channel 5 News' and 'UN Peacekeepers'. Overall, the new ethical foreign policy looked remarkably like the old unethical one, which frankly couldn't have got more unethical if it had been constructed by child slaves from fresh ivory.

Despite this, Cook and New Labour did manage to introduce some changes, including: signing up to the landmine ban, outlawing torture equipment and updating the law. The law controlling the sale of arms dates back to 1939, which makes it four years older than Mick Jagger for God's sake, so obviously in need of some repair.

This is how the law came into being. Armstrong Whitworth epitomised Britain's bigger companies. They were quite happy to arm whoever they could, including both sides in the American Civil War, a British tradition that has carried on to this day (see Saddam Hussein). Come 1914 and World War One kicked off, which meant productivity went through the roof. It also went through the walls, the windows and a few million human bodies. British and German arms manufacturers decided that though there was nothing in law to prevent them from trading with each other, it would be best if they did not for the duration of World War One. However, with the military build-up and arms race that preceded World War Two, the British government decided to intervene rather than leave it to self-regulation and the first export control act came into being in 1939: the Import, Export and Customs Powers (Defence) Act 1939. No act of Parliament had altered the law since then. So New Labour's new export controls may not have been the most headline-grabbing legislation but they did nonetheless need doing and thus the Export Control Act 2002 goes in the credit column.

LAYING DOWN THE LAW

Export Control Act 2002 – The parent act for the offspring that follow …

Export of Goods, Transfer of Technology and Provision of Technical Assistance (Control) Order 2003 – controls dual use goods and makes the technology for military goods and systems licensable.

Trade in Goods (Control) Order 2003 – arms brokering controlled and extraterritoriality applied to 'restricted goods'. (No Brits can deal in WMD, long-range missiles and torture equipment from anywhere in the world.)

Trade in Controlled Goods (Embargoed Destinations) Order 2004 – arming countries with EU, UN or OSCE arms embargoes becomes illegal and extraterritoriality applied. No Brits anywhere in the world can arm embargoed countries.

Landmines

Clare Short signed the Ottawa Convention outlawing anti-personnel landmines in December 1997, along with 121 other nations. It was a momentous occasion. Landmines have killed hundreds of thousands of people in the past few decades, predominantly civilians, and here was most of the international community declaring an end to it. Yes, there are countries that have still not signed up to it, including the USA, Russia and China. Yes, there are loopholes; the treaty bans anti-personnel (AP) mines but not anti-tank (AT) mines, which can still be activated by civilians. But it is a vitally important landmark and without it thousands more would have died since 1997.

That said, signing up to ban landmines wasn't exactly contentious. Even Haiti, Zimbabwe and Sudan signed up for it. Anyone on the left of Princess Diana was against landmines. Even serial killers were against them. Murdering bastards they might be, but I bet they loved Princess Di. The issue was so clear-cut that even Nazis in comas opposed landmines … I don't know Prince Charles's position on this one. But he wasn't on the left of Di.

The torture list

Then there is Robin Cook's torture list. On 28 July 1997, Cook announced to the House of Commons that: 'We are committed to preventing British companies from manufacturing, selling or procuring equipment designed primarily for torture and to press for a global ban.' With these words Cook started the UK's attempts to end the trade in torture equipment.

While this may be a relatively small area of concern compared to the overall picture of arms sales, military interventions and British support for some fairly unpleasant regimes (by which I mean murderous thugs), it is notable that most ministers go down in history as having helped sell military hardware rather than restrict it. Cook should, in fairness, be remembered for doing both.

An even bigger shock to the system: the EU joins Britain

It has to be seen as a plus point that Britain developed a policy against the production and sale of torture equipment before most of Europe. True, the rest of Europe does include the Czech Republic and Lithuania – countries not exactly noted for their historic opposition to the arms trade. Anyway, the Council of the European Union drew up common guidelines to ban the export of 'goods which could be used for capital punishment, torture or other cruel, inhuman or degrading treatment or punishment'; thus attempting to stop the export of torture equipment from the EU.

Admittedly, the European Union is a subject that draws hatred and indifference in equal measures from the British. And even the measure of indifference is calculated in yards. For some people in Britain, hating the EU is an instinctive act of patriotism and ignorance akin to not knowing the second verse of the national anthem, and those people are called, Kent. Ah, Kent. The patio of England.

However, what is reasonably accurate is that nine times out of ten, any new rulings coming out of the EU that are covered in the British press are met with automatic vehemence, regardless of the content or truth of the matter. The examples are well known: they want to regulate our sausages! We won't stand for it. We will fight for our traditional way of life. We have always had pig eyes and minced dog bollocks in our bangers and we always will.

The EU could announce a directive to stop under-fives sucking on discarded nuclear waste and the *Sun* would publish: 'Come off it, Brussels!' Continuing: 'Those barmy Eurocrat killjoys are trying to sap the fun out of our kids and their glow-in-the-dark toys. To the joyless pen-pushers the *Sun* says, "Get a life!" or at least a half-life!'

Lacking bangers or bananas meant that the EU common guidelines issued on June 2005 received scant mention in the UK press. The guidelines force all twenty-five member states to put into law the new regulations. This surely is a positive contribution to stopping the sale and use of torture equipment. Though I wouldn't be surprised if somewhere in Kent a bloke is grumbling, ''Course the French don't want to torture, they ain't got the stomach for it. They're all too busy bumming each other and going to the ballet. That's what happened in '39. Hitler had only to wait for a new production of *Swan Lake* to open in Paris and wallop, he was in.'

The EU directive became UK law in July 2006 and bans the production and sale of electric chairs and gallows, which I don't think we made too many of, but better safe than sorry. As far as torture equipment goes, 'thumbscrews' and 'shackle boards' will be added to the UK list. I'm not sure how thumbscrews managed to avoid the British torture list before. Possibly Britain's torture trade was more modern and thug-centric than the European Spanish Inquisition-based model of human rights abuser. I don't know – I'm making it up.

The EU regulations do come with a commitment to update the list of 'prohibited'/'controlled' goods to 'take into account new data and technological developments'. 'Does Britain have a commitment like that?' I hear you ask. My reply is: don't be stupid. It only took a hundred and sixty-four years after the abolition of slavery to get round to abolishing leg irons.

HANDS ARE THICKER THAN ANKLES

At this point it is worth remembering one of the enduring attributes of class difference in Britain. In judging impropriety, the middle class are easiest to shock. While the suburban middle classes are quick to drop their jaws and clutch their cheeks in horror at the thought of a government minister taking a loan from the Paymaster General, or of cruising Welsh MPs or Lib Dems having sex with anyone, let alone rent boys, the urban working class have a far more stoical attitude. You could walk into a pub in Bermondsey declaring that Tony Blair and George Bush had just been photographed wearing goats' heads and sacrificing schoolchildren and the response would be: "Course they 'ave ... they're all fahking at it ... Oy, Cliffie, put an 'alf in that, wil yer?' The Prime Minister could announce that the government will cut taxes for the poor, charge the rich for breathing and personally clean the floors of every voter in their constituency and the reaction they would get: 'Wos their fahking game, aye? Wot they up t'? Dirty fahkers, up t' summit, inaye?'

Likewise, if the government gave the impression they had outlawed torture equipment, the response would be: 'Wossa catch? Wossa get-aht? Those slippy barsteds always leave a way aht fer 'emselves.' Which is true, and in the case of arms control the government is particularly adept at creating loopholes. Here is one of them.

The government have two categories of military goods listed on the unsurprisingly named UK Military List: 'restricted' and 'controlled'. Most military goods are 'controlled': an exporter applies to the DTI and as long as it is not too dodgy in the eyes of HMG, a bit of bureaucracy occurs and bingo, you get your licence. The 'restricted' category applies to three types of military goods: 1) Weapons of Mass Destruction; 2) long-range missiles and 3) torture equipment. The 'restricted' list, as its name would imply, is not of banned goods; you can still get a licence to export this stuff, but potential dealers should assume that they won't. But the government can still issue a licence for it. So torture equipment is not torture equipment if it has a licence – enabling New Labour to boast of having one of the 'tightest sets of regulations in the world', but leaving enough room for business to be accommodated.

Now, there is one type of handcuff that does need a licence: shackles over a certain size – 165mm to be precise. This is because hands are thinner than ankles. Big handcuffs could be used as leg cuffs (which is why they are restricted), but they can also be sold and marketed primarily as handcuffs for the larger criminal. Cuffs for fat felons. Restrain your wrists, not your diet. Tether the tubbies! Hiatts, a Birmingham-based company, produce a make of 'oversized' handcuffs that go by the brand name Big Brutus.

The UK government has issued a number of licences for 'oversized' handcuffs, twenty-four of them, in fact, between 2000 and 2004. As the only other British company to do this size is Chubb, it makes sense that either Chubb or Hiatts are the folk being granted these licences to export supersized cuffs. Now the cuffs could be used for really big burglars, they could be used for film props, they could be used for a whole set of legitimate reasons. But take a look at some of the places they are going to …

LICENCES GRANTED BY UK GOVERNMENT FOR PL5001 (OVERSIZED HANDCUFFS/LEG IRONS) FROM 2000 TO 2004

❑ Australia: 1 licence issued in 2000 and 2001, 2 licences 2004 (4 licences in total). Not too hot on aboriginal rights but do have a lot of big fellas … 4 licences' worth?

❑ Barbados: 1 licence issued 2003. Who knows on this one?

❑ Canada: 1 licence issued 2001. Could be used for film props.

❑ Cayman Islands: 1 licence issued 2002. See Barbados.

❑ Cyprus: 1 licence issued 2002. Don't like conscientious objectors of compulsory military service or Roma. *Hmmm.*

❑ Egypt: 1 licence issued 2004. *You're pulling my chain!* After reading Amnesty reports on this place, I wouldn't trust the Egyptian police with a fucking yoyo, let alone a handcuff/ leg iron. The authorities use normal handcuffs to bind people's hands behind their backs and then hang the victim off the ground by the cuff.

❏ Hong Kong Special Administrative Region: 5 licences issued 2001, 2002, 2003, 2 licences 2004. *Whoa there, Scooby!* Five licences in four years in an area not noted for large people. Hong Kong doesn't produce tub guts in the quantity that, say, the USA does. Next-door neighbour China. This lot of licences is more dodgy than a backpacking imam from Finsbury Park.

❏ Malaysia: 1 licence issued 2003. *Hmmmm.* This is the kind of place the Rev Ian Paisley would really be able to relax in on a short-break holiday. The police forced the deputy prime minister into confessing to sodomy, which carries a prison sentence. That might give you an idea of the human rights situation.

❏ New Zealand: 2 licences issued 2001, 2002. Not as squeaky clean as they like to think.

❏ Philippines: 1 licence issued 2004. On the face of it, this has to be a no, but let's be optimistic and assume the 'supersized' wrist cuffs/average-sized leg irons were for a film set …

❏ Sweden: 1 licence issued 2001. Sweden did blot its human rights copybook by illegally handing over two Egyptian asylum seekers to the CIA, who dropped them off at Egypt for a spot of torture and detention. But I don't think they do it themselves on a regular basis.

❏ Trinidad and Tobago: 1 licence issued 2002. Reports of torture and cruel treatment in prison. Still keep the death penalty. This has to be a big factor when considering whether or not to send the 'mega cuffs'.

❏ United Arab Emirates: 1 licence issued 2001. Still like to flog foreign domestics but, hey, who hasn't lost their temper with the cleaner. Wouldn't trust this lot with a barge pole as you can guess where it would end up.

❏ USA: 3 licences issued 2000, 2001, 2002. Oh for fuck's sake – haven't they seen *Green Mile*? Home of the trophy photograph. For some reason US soldiers just can't wait to get home and show their parents pictures of themselves forcing Iraqis to masturbate. So we have Abu Ghraib, Guantanamo Bay, plus a home-grown prison system that uses leg irons, shackles, electro-shock and the death penalty. These deals stink higher than an out-of-date anchovy in a cream eclair.

I applied to the FCO under the Freedom of Information Act, asking what companies had sold the oversized cuffs and which institutions had bought them. Jack Straw had previously said that he saw no reason Freedom of Information requests about arms deals could not be answered, so I should have known I was wasting my time and a stamp. The FCO refused to answer the requests, firstly saying I had asked for too much information, and after a brief scuffle citing customer confidentiality.

But I bet the government has broken their own policy on torture by licensing oversized handcuffs to those destinations. 'Wait a minute,' you may cry. 'Mark, you may have proved that the cuffs went to countries with questionable human rights regimes, but you don't know what institutions the cuffs went to nor their purpose.' And you are right. But if there is not one dodgy deal in that lot mentioned above, I promise I will sit outside the Department of Trade and Industry for a whole day with a big banner reading: 'I didn't trust the government and look at me now!' More than that, with the aid of a loudhailer I will shout, 'I am so sorry, I was wrong to doubt you!' in the direction of the minister's office until I am arrested. I will give the Labour Party every penny I make from writing this book, if there is not one licence that gives cause for concern in that list. Now there's a challenge for the government … all they have to do is say where the oversized handcuffs went to.

The government has introduced laws to outlaw torture equipment but we don't actually know if the government has abided by these laws itself. Given New Labour's track record of not abiding by measures they themselves have introduced, like EU Codes of Conduct, it is hard to think the best of them.

10

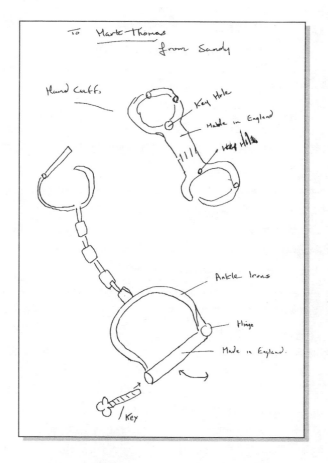

TORTURE IN THE
TIME OF TERROR

CHAPTER TEN

A chapter in which 'Made in England' is found on numerous British prisoners' wrists and the author visits the maker's factory to find out why.

FAX AND FACT IN THE LAND OF AL QAEDA

You may not know it, but the world's entire philosophical thought and discourse can be distilled into a couple of questions.

The first one is: why are we here? When people ask me that I reply, 'Gravity.' (Though I normally can't answer their follow-up, which is, 'What am I asking you for?')

The second big philosophical question that has perplexed our finest thinkers for centuries was answered live on *Trisha*. I'm paraphrasing but it is basically this: respect each other and best not to shag your mum's boyfriend. For me the really big question, though, has to be: is violence ever justifiable, and if so when? The short answer is: whenever Richard Madeley is within striking distance but only with an open hand.

Since the al Qaeda attacks on the World Trade Center in America in 2001 and the bombings on the London bus and tube in July 2005, there has been a debate bubbling near the surface of public consciousness. 'If,' the question goes, 'you get hold of exactly the right person involved in a terrorist plot and by torturing them you get information that prevents a terrorist attack and saves lives, isn't this act of inhumanity justified?'

No.

'Aha!' the questioner ripostes. 'So you are prepared to let innocent people die but will protect the rights of terrorists?'

No, again, because the more pertinent question regarding torture and terror is: if by torturing someone you don't prevent a terrorist attack but actually give cause for others to take up arms against you, would torture then be acceptable?

Now which scenario is more likely to occur?

See, folks, what separates humans from animals isn't the violence, it's our ability to scrutinise mass-media-promoted state value systems – that and the Nectar card points.

I am contemplating this while waiting for a fax to come through. In a world of wireless laptops and the paperless office, the fax essentially farts ink in binary down a telephone wire. It is a throwback to an era when steam was king, spinning jennies were machines and not a brand of Ecstasy and ten fingers guaranteed you were posh. With such a ponderous lineage it is not surprising that this particular fax is coming through at an agonisingly slow pace. If it had got any slower we would have gone back in time.

What is coming through on the machine is a hand-drawn picture of sets of handcuffs. The bold and crude pictures show two sets of shackles, one set of handcuffs and one set of leg irons, drawn by Sandy Mitchell. These are the leg irons and handcuffs Sandy was forced to wear when he was imprisoned in Saudi Arabia. The most telling part of the drawings is an ink line to a specific point on each of the cuffs; at the other end of the ink line are the words 'Made in England'. These are what he was forced into every time he was hauled from his cell to be tortured.

A series of bombs had gone off in Saudi Arabia in 2000 (one in Riyadh in November killed UK citizen Christopher Rodway) and in a spectacular act of self-denial and a desperate effort to convince the world that it did not have a problem with Islamic militancy, the kingdom's security forces arrested Western workers for these offences. To this end the three men, Mitchell, Sampson and Schyvens, were taken to the Mabatha Interrogation Centre and tortured into admitting their involvement in the bombings. The Saudis publicly insisted these crimes were the consequences of a vicious turf war in the illegal alcohol business. Meanwhile, the real culprits, al Qaeda, were left alone by the authorities to grow, reorganise, recruit and bomb again. By ruthlessly pursuing and torturing the innocent, Saudi Arabia effectively pardoned al Qaeda.

Sandy's cuffs

When Sandy was arrested he was forty-four and worked as the chief anaesthetic technician at the Saudi Security Forces Hospital in Riyadh. He spent thirty-two months in prison for a crime he did not commit. 'The first nine days,' he said, 'were spent in the interrogation centre. I was chained to the door ... always hung by the left hand to the top of my cell door so that I couldn't sleep. There was one cuff around my wrist and the other attached to the door bars. So all during the night we were beaten and tortured and all during the day we were kept awake. So it was just total sleep deprivation.'* The torturer's name was Ibrahim Al Dali, a member of the Saudi Secret Police and a state prosecutor. Sandy is trying to take Ibrahim Al Dali to court for torture. The human-rights-loving British government are supporting the Saudis' legal appeal to avoid a trial.

In *Saudi Babylon*,** written by Mark Hollingsworth with Sandy Mitchell, they describe how Sandy was shackled, suspended from a metal pole by his knees and had his buttocks and the soles of his feet beaten. Reflecting on the handcuffs and leg irons, Sandy Mitchell said to me, 'and that was the most disgusting thing in fact, was that those instruments were provided by our country'.

---

* Interview with MT on 6 January 2005.

** Mainstream Publishing, 2005.

There was a time when 'Made in England' was stamped onto more things than it was not. The more nostalgic of you might want to pause for a moment in silent contemplation of Hornby model trains, Morris Minors, Raleigh bikes, toasted fruit bread and tea from a thermos with a cork in it. Now 'Made in England' is found on leg irons and footballers' tattooed backs.

Sandy Mitchell is far from the only British citizen to find the infamous refrain on the shackles that bound him. Patrick Foster was detained on trumped-up charges in Saudi Arabia in 1995, and yet again the shackles that held him were 'Made in England'. In 2002 the UK government's dossier on Iraq's human rights abuses listed the jailing of Mr Hussain al-Shahristani, who spent eleven years in prison for refusing to work on Saddam Hussein's nuclear programme, a brave and noble stand. On the day Foreign Secretary Jack Straw published the dossier, Shahristani said, 'When I was in jail I was held with British-made handcuffs.'*

Honour bound

At least five British men held in Guantanamo Bay, the US detention camp in Cuba, saw 'Made in England' on their cuffs. Shafiq Rasul, Asif Iqbal and Rhuhel Ahmed all come from the West Midlands and became known as the Tipton Three. As a rule of thumb, if you ever find yourself referred to as part of a collective noun that involves a town name and a number, you're in the shit. Especially if the town name and number is printed on a T-shirt under the words 'Free The'. The Tipton Three are no exception to that rule.

A regular part of their existence in Guantanamo Bay was interrogation. Shafiq says he was 'shackled in a three-piece shackle, which basically meant my hands were tied, in front of me, and then attached to a belt which went round my waist. The chain of the leg irons I had around my ankles was about a foot in

---

* Asia Africa Intelligence Wire, 4 December 2002.

length which meant I could not walk properly but rather had to shuffle'.* Once in the interrogation room the men were 'long' and 'short' shackled. 'Long shackling' is the procedure where a prisoner's chains are attached to a metal ring embedded in the interrogation room floor, which gave them enough room to sit on a chair. In 'short shackling' prisoners have to squat on their haunches, put their arms between their legs and their chains are attached to the metal ring. Prisoners were kept in this position for hours on end.

It was Asif Iqbal who said: 'One thing that always stuck with me was that the handcuffs had 'Made in England' written on them.'** The Tipton Three are augmented by a fourth British citizen and former inmate of Guantanamo, Jamal Hareeth, who said he remembers 'Made in England' on his wrists.*** To the names of Jamal and the Tipton Three is now added Moazzam Begg, to bring the number of UK citizens up to five.

British equipment used on British citizens in a manner that would be illegal in Britain.

LET'S TACKLE THE SHACKLES

One of the most recognisable human rights lawyers and defendant of a number of captives in Guantanamo Bay is Clive Stafford Smith. At six foot four, maybe even five, he tends to stick out anyway, but today he really sticks out. It's mid-morning on a weekday and Clive Stafford Smith is dressed in an orange prison jumpsuit, dancing in the middle of the road alongside some simi-

---

* Detention in Afghanistan and Guantanamo Bay – statement of Shafiq Rasul, Asif Iqbal and Rhuhel Ahmed. July 2004. Available at: http://www.ccr-ny.org/ v2/reports/docs/Gitmo-compositestatementFINAL23july04.pdf.

** As above.

*** Author's interview with lawyer Robert Lizar, 6 January 2005.

larly attired legal interns. Which is not what you normally stumble across if you live by the small industrial unit in Perry Bar, Birmingham.

I have chosen the far more dignified option of standing on a flatbed truck, dressed in orange with a black hood on my head, holding a banner next to an inflatable palm tree. The banner reads 'Tackle the Shackles', and Clive is dancing to the music of Seize the Day, a folk band with whom I share the flatbed.

Seize the Day don't conform to the traditional image of folksingers: they are witty, beardless and prone to get naked if the protest calls for it. Though it's worth celebrating this difference, we should also give thanks that neither the Chieftains nor Shane McGowan employ this same tactic. Theo, the lead singer, had earlier explained that a lot of the movements in Latin American and West Indian dance come from slavery. 'This is what I was told. It's all about moving the bits of your body that you are able to wearing shackles. See,' he says, demonstrating the restricted arm and leg movements. 'It's all in the hips,' he adds with a wiggle. 'So it is completely appropriate that our song about Guantanamo Bay uses a South American style.' He pauses, then smiles and says, 'With a bit of a Rocky Horror – let's do the Timewarp crossover.'

Which goes to explain why an eminent human rights lawyer is shaking his booty in an orange boiler suit. All of this is for the benefit of Hiatt, the British company whose handcuffs keep cropping up in Guantanamo: attached to belly chains, combined with leg irons and manacles and shackled through the rings on the floor. Stafford Smith noticed the company name when he visited his clients in the camp. Hiatts 'Made in England'.

The Hiatt office is on Baltimore Road. On one side of the street is a series of small industrial units; the other is a respectable working-class area. Cars are off-the-road parked; someone has left a kid's pink bicycle out in the front garden. Two houses up is being decorated so most of the paint has been taken off the house exterior, and even though an old mattress is discarded in the front garden it had been leant against the wall in an effort to be tidy. Hiatt has a small brick wall by the pavement, about six or seven courses high, which marks out its thin stretch of front garden. The garden is a few shrubs with alopecia and an anaemic rosebush that sits in an oval of dirt in a narrow strip of grass. The Hiatt building itself is a brick one-storey affair, with light-blue metal window frames and a 'Shopkeepers against Crime – Business Watch' sticker in the middle of a pane. Centrepiece is a rising concrete porch reception, a kind of half-arsed attempt to be art nouveau. It is all very ordinary and all very far away from Guantanamo Bay.

The flatbed truck sits half on the pavement and half in the road directly in front of Hiatt. 'At Guantanamo Bay, it's the US of A., shackle-shuffle every day at the Club X-Ray,' sing Theo and Shannon to a crowd of local press, a few cops and some curious local residents who have come out to sit on their walls to watch the show. 'Wear a chain on your wrist, do the Islamicist, Bosa Nova with a twist and it goes like this.'

Stafford Smith is joined in the road by local MP Lynne Jones and Dr Dave Nicholl, alongside the legal interns who've come along for the day.

'Put your hands on your head,' sings Theo.

The assembled group place both hands on their heads like they have all been arrested.

'And shackle-shuffle to the left.'

They awkwardly move to the instructions.

'You do the monkey squat and then –' to which everyone drops down to their haunches, some still with their hands on their heads – 'you shackle-shuffle back again.'

With the local press pointing cameras and everyone in orange, following instructions and adopting awkward poses, it looks like the filming of a Hare Krishna workout video.

It's fun and folk enjoy the atmosphere, but there is a ghost at the banquet: Omar Deghayes, imprisoned in Guantanamo Bay.

As a British resident, lacking a UK passport and merely living with his family here, he has no representation from the likes of Margaret Beckett and the British state. He is left without charge or trial, and he has just entered his fifth week of hunger strike. His brother Abubaker is here to speak, as is Dr Dave Nicholl. Dr Nicholl steps up to the mic on the lorry and begins. He talks of faith, of friendship with the Deghayes family, of suffering, and he talks of Hiatts and their complicity.

'I wrote to Hiatts. I wrote several times and I have received no reply. And I want to say –' he looks around him at the truck, the blow-up palm trees, the loudspeakers, the band, the people dressed in orange, the press, the police, the residents, the shut Hiatt office with its workers sent home and the windows barred with metal shutters – 'I just want to say ... that this is what happens when you don't answer your mail.'

Hiatts

This is not the first time Hiatts has been linked to controversy. The commercial company director for Hiatts, a certain Mr TR Fellows, wrote a brief history of the company. Rather delightfully, he records, 'In the year 1780, when Birmingham was little more than a village, any passer-by walking down the well-known thoroughfare called Masshouse Lane, might well have stopped out of curiosity to look at a new sigh (sic) which had recently gone up at Number 26. This intimated that a certain Mr Hiat was a maker of Prisoner's Handcuffs, Felon's Leg Irons, Gang Chains and Nigger Collars "to the Trade".'

This account appeared on the website of Hiatts' sister company in the US, Hiatt-Thompson, and remained there until 1999, when, in its dying moments, the twentieth century caught up with them. With their roots in the slave trade, it is not surprising that Hiatts continued to be a noted producer of leg irons. Slaves might even have been wearing Hiatts leg irons when they had to dance on deck of the ships that abducted them.

According to the company, they stopped manufacturing leg irons in the UK in 1996, a year before Robin Cook classified them as torture equipment. However, Hiatt-Thompson, the sister company set up in the US in 1987, has sole trading rights for the Hiatt brand and continues selling leg irons globally, under the Hiatt name.

The musical manacles of Geoff Cross

It is a shame that Geoff Cross, the boss of Hiatt, has chosen to stay away. Not unexpected, I hasten to add. Having a mini protest carnival in front of anyone's reception area can hardly be described as a normal day at work. But I would have genuinely liked to meet him. To him I suppose we are just idiots with nothing better to do with our time than upset law-abiding hard-working businessmen ... which in my case is true.

As manufacturers and dealers of 'police and security equipment', Cross must regard his work as useful, possibly vital. After all, it could be his handcuffs that are used by the police to restrain muggers, or violent drunks, or the suspects accused of attempting to blow up the London Underground. This would be something to be proud of. Trouble is, the same type of equipment has a tendency to turn up in Amnesty reports. Which can't be that much of a badge of honour. No one rushes home with Amnesty reports shouting, 'Gather round everyone. Look at what Daddy's helped do!'

Though arms dealers and their ilk are not fantastically sensitive folk, I have spoken to one who casually mentioned during a conversation about electro-shock batons that he had 'sold thousands of the bloody things to the Saudi Arabians – they use them as vibrators over there'. Another example of the industry mentality is an advert for leg irons sold by the Kejo company. Under a picture of the shackles run the words: 'These heavy-duty leg irons are made in South Africa and are the same type used on the famous Mr Mandela'.* To boast that you can supply the equipment that held the world's most famous political prisoner under one of the most shameful and vile regimes of the twentieth century shows a certain lack of awareness. It is akin to RG Industries running an advert for the Rohm RG14 revolver under the slogan: 'The gun that nearly killed US President Ronald Reagan'.

As an industry, arms dealers seem incapable of accepting that the rest of the population views their activities with mild distaste at best. I phoned a South African company to discuss purchasing electro-shock stun batons. The operator said, 'Wait one moment please, sir,' in clipped South African tones. 'You need to talk to another department. I will just put you on hold while I get them for you.' With that, music was piped down the phone at me. The music they chose to play to potential buyers of electro-shock was Elvis Presley's 'Love Me Tender'. Most arms dealers would not find this incongruous.

I would genuinely love to see Geoff Cross and Clive Stafford Smith going head to head and trying to see each other's viewpoint. But I suspect you've got more chance of seeing the Pope line-dancing at a gay bar than there is of that happening. Though less inclined to speak to the press these days, Geoff Cross has been vocally enthusiastic about the use of leg irons. He even claimed to have played the piano wearing a pair, just to prove how comfy leg irons can be, oblivious to the fact that Saudi jails don't contain Steinways as a rule. Piano wire? Maybe. But so far there are no reports of Saudi guards screaming, 'Confess to everything or we will make you sing British music-hall songs to your own accompaniment.'

In truth Cross's character is perhaps not the most important obstacle to change. The simple fact is that Sandy and Moazzam and a host of others have been hung up, stretched out and shackled down with 'Made in England' on handcuffs because no one

* http://bodyarmour.safeshopper.com/25/20.htm?531

had ever bothered to include handcuffs as police and security equipment. Handcuffs don't need a government licence. And until that simple measure is included Britain will continue to abet the ill-treatment of its own citizens.

11

BROKERAGE: THE ZEN ART OF GUNRUNNING

CHAPTER ELEVEN

A chapter in which the author meets up with a prosecutor who tried to put a gunrunner on trial only to find the law unable to help him do so. The idea of international arms control appears on the horizon.

THE BASIC INGREDIENTS TO EVERY WESLEY SNIPES MOVIE EVER MADE ... EXCEPT *THE VAMPIRES*

In August 2000 a man was arrested in the Hotel Europa in Italy, not far from Monza. In his room the police found quantities of cocaine, half a million dollars' worth of diamonds and a bag full of documents, some of them false, detailing arms shipments. His name was Leonid Minim, and he was a Ukrainian-born Israeli. The police had received a tip-off about the drugs from the prostitutes he used. And frankly it's a huge relief to finally hear of an arms dealer who actually behaves like one. Arms dealers should be red in tooth and claw. Who would want it any other way? That would be like opening a tabloid newspaper to find the headline: 'Vicar in stable marriage!' or 'Cherie Blair pays for own holiday!' No, that would not do, not at all. Vicars should have affairs with parishioners (preferably organists), Cherie Blair should freeload from that nice Signor Berlusconi and arms dealers are best served sleazy. Minim seems ideal. Though what one has to do to piss off prostitutes to the extent that they inform the cops, I daren't guess.

Minim's case was reported to the public prosecutor in

Monza, who, on hearing of a man found in a hotel room with coke, diamonds, hookers and false arms certificates, must have surely thought: Ah fuck it, I'll take the afternoon off, most of the case work seems to have been done here … it's not as if this one is going to end up with a hung jury.

In reality, Mr Mapelli, the public prosecutor, did no such thing. He got to work investigating the documents found in the Hotel Europa, while Minim stayed in a slightly different type of B&B than he was accustomed to. For the drug offences he was given a prison sentence of two years and four months.

The documents showed Minim was involved in buying and shipping guns and ammunition to the Liberian President Charles Taylor, who as well as being an autocrat and kleptomaniac, was also accused of war crimes and crimes against humanity by the UN. And as if things couldn't get much worse than that, Minim was also involved in the transportation of some of those weapons to the Revolutionary United Front (RUF) in Sierra Leone. Both countries were under UN embargoes at the time. The Cluedo analysis for Liberia: Professor Plum, in the library, with the candlesti— hang on, who's nicked the candlestick? As for Minim, he had been caught breaking a UN embargo, he was illegally trafficking arms and it is not every day that a bagful of evidence drops into a public prosecutor's lap.

A few weeks before his arrest, Minim had completed a deal to ship 113 tonnes of arms and munitions to Taylor, using End User Certificates from the Côte D'Ivoire and Burkina Faso. Alarm bells should have sounded at the prospect of former Soviet bloc armaments going to Burkina Faso. According to the arms trade bible, *Jane's Defence Weekly*, Burkina Faso's military is equipped with NATO weapons. Why would a government want to start equipping its troops with new equipment (from the former Eastern bloc) incompatible with its older equipment (from NATO)? Why would they suddenly ditch all their current allies and suppliers?

Minim used a Gibraltar-based brokering company, Chartered

Engineering and Technical Company Ltd, to purchase the weapons from the Ukrainian company Ukrspetsexport. The weapons were flown to Ouagadougou in Burkina Faso, they arrived 13 March 1999 and, according to Major General Felix Mujakperuo, commander of the ECOMOG* peacekeeping forces in Sierra Leone, the plane waited by the VIP terminal while the weapons were transferred to another plane to Liberia, from where some of the weapons were diverted to the RUF in Sierra Leone. This particular shipment consisted of 3,000 AKM (Kalashnikov) assault rifles, fifty machine guns, twenty-five rocket-propelled grenade launchers (RPGs), five Strela-3 (also known as SA-7) missiles and five Metis anti-tank guided-missile systems, as well as ammunition for these weapons.

Mapelli

The public prosecutor's office in Monza has all the hallmarks of a relatively new Italian building: an off-the-road car park, a smattering of steps leading to a public walkway, a concrete block full of earth and some recently deceased municipal vegetation. The ground floor of the building is made up of big black frames and large sheets of glass with pull-up blinds made of flimsy metal strips, the type that go 'whoosh' when you pull them sharply. The upper floors of the building are a bright-orange cement finish. Slightly Bond villain meets arty council flats.

Over the front door is posted *Procura della Repubblica Presso Il Tribunale di Monza*. Mr Mapelli is waiting by the front desk. He is a tall muscular man with a charcoal-grey jacket that looks like it was chosen for him. His hair is cropped close, the way men of a certain age like when their hair starts to recede – no point in trying to hide the baldness. His clothes might suggest a cop who has been put on desk duty but he is a generous and

---

* ECOMOG is an armed force made up of troops from various member states of the Economic Community of West African States.

charming host, breaking into easy smiles and speaking with a slight lisp that gives him a dash of boyish vulnerability.

The office is big enough to swing a cat but I wouldn't want to try anything further up the food chain. Not without a mop and plenty of disinfectant. Hanging from the wall is one of those free company calendars with a six-inch crucifix above it. The crucifix is a subdued one by Catholic standards, lacking trails of blood and an agonised face. The air-conditioning unit is stuck on the wall at waist-height in the corner and I bet it rumbles like a trucker's belly when it is switched on.

'Minim was a very special case.' Mapelli speaks slowly, finding the right English words, as he leans back in a beige-covered metal-frame chair. 'Because,' he continues, 'the documents showed the evidence of the journey by air of the weapons and munitions, and Minim declared to me that he had sold the arms and munitions to Charles Taylor.'

It can't be often that a prosecutor finds the evidence and the confession ready and waiting for them. 'It was the first and only case in my job [like this],' smiles Mapelli spreading his hands, appealing to an invisible judge. As well he might, because for all Mapelli's work and good fortune, the case could not be tried in Italy. Minim was free to go. He had bought arms from Bulgaria and the Ukraine, used Ukrainian planes to transfer the arms to the Côte D'Ivoire and Burkina Faso, from where they were flown on to Liberia and Sierra Leone, and the deals were paid for by a Swiss company and involved the hiring of a Gibraltarian broker. He had broken international sanctions. Yet none of this occurred in Italy. According to the Italian Supreme Court no offence was committed on Italian soil and therefore he should not face trial. Neither Bulgaria nor the Ukraine had the legal wherewithal, let alone the political will, to put him in the dock. So, once he had served his sentence for drug offences, Minim was free, and the UN international embargo broken with no consequence.

'Naturally I was very disappointed and sad but I am happy to have tried,' says Mapelli. 'Maybe I made it more difficult for the arms traders to arm child soldiers in Africa – it is a warning.' But despite this there is a sense of frustration that neither Bulgaria nor the Ukraine could or would put Minim on trial. 'It wasn't the lack of evidence in this case. Minim told me: "Yes, I bought munitions; yes, I took it from Ukraine to Liberia and Sierra Leone, and Charles Taylor then paid me in cash." The problem in this case is who is the judge?' Without common international law on the arms trade it will remain like this, a point Mapelli concedes: 'If there is not a common [international] rule it is very easy for arms traders and brokers to slip through the loopholes.'

CRIME AND PUNISHMENT

Let's take this opportunity to issue a challenge to the Right Reverend Ian Paisley. Dear Ian, if you are reading – and I bet he has this book slipped in behind a copy of *What Sash Monthly* – dear Ian, I dare you to shout 'Fuck the Pope!' in Vatican Square. And none of your doing it at midnight either … I dare you, when *il Papa* is on the balcony doing a prayer to the masses. OK, there are a few questions that might arise from this dare, aside from the need to request Gerry Adams of Sinn Fein to shout '*Tiocfaidh ár lá*' at the Cenotaph in London during the wreath-laying, to redress the sectarian imbalance. The point of this challenge is that if Paisley were to utter such a comment he would face some severe penalties, including being lashed by nuns wielding rosary beads as if they were motorbike chains. Paisley would be charged with breach of the peace or some other offence, the police would cart him off to jail and he could face a fine, maybe even imprisonment. Which is more of a penalty than Minim the gunrunner ever faced.

It is heart-breaking that an Italian shoplifter faces a greater punishment for nicking a roll of dental floss than Minim does for breaking a UN embargo. A nudist by the Tivoli fountains would face a greater penalty. A persistent jaywalker or a man who drops his bus ticket in the street would at least be threatened with a fine. But for breaking a UN arms embargo and supplying weapons to murderous scum – nothing!

A kleptocracy ruled in Liberia where children faced summary execution if they did not join the armed forces to fight. So it is worth saying it one more time: the man who armed this violence did so without justice, for his crimes received a punishment of – nothing. Minim got nothing for gunrunning to the RUF and to Taylor. Once again we find ourselves rolling down the tracks of logic that wind up at a junction called: 'What is the point of the UN?' If a UN arms embargo is this easily broken, why bother having one? But while it is entirely reasonable to heap scorn on the UN for many things, it is not entirely the UN's fault if national governments do not enforce UN embargoes. It is up to individual governments to introduce domestic law to make the arms embargoes effective. To that end the European Union has started to move in the right direction.

The European Union Council passed a Common Position on the control of arms brokering in June 2003, making it compulsory for all EU member states to bring in new laws if they didn't have them, or update old ones if they did. Arms brokering is simple in concept and practice. Rather than an arms dealer exporting guns from the UK directly to the buyer, the arms dealer acts as a middleman. The UK dealer could arrange the sale and shipment of guns from, say, the Philippines, directly to, say, Malawi without any weapons physically touching British soil.

A quick example

Back in 1996 the Tory government was in power. For the benefit of younger readers I should explain. A Conservative government ... well, it is similar to a New Labour government but its supporters tend to be older and more overt in their hatred of foreigners. Back then, mobile phones were the size of house bricks and though people were not mugged for their phones, you could mug with them.

The journalist Martin Gregory made several programmes about torture equipment being sold by UK dealers, including David Knights, who ran a company called SDMS in West London. Knights offered to get electro-shock weapons to Zaire, having sourced them from South Africa, saying, 'We would prefer to ship them direct to your client, if that is possible, particularly if it is coming from South Africa and the client is Zaire, that will save time obviously. And, erm, we can get it done through England, but we don't want to do it, technically the goods are illegal here …'*

Knights exported to some states with questionable human rights records, including Egypt, Sierra Leone, Burma, Kenya, Tanzania, Bahrain, UAE, Libya, Bulgaria and Angola, amongst others. Knights said that the purchasers were the police or military authorities.

In 1998 Knights was investigated by the Metropolitan Police for supplying 200 electro-shock weapons to Cyprus. After eighteen months the Crown Prosecution Service declared that they could not proceed with a prosecution as he had not broken any law, because he had brokered the weapons. The *Evening Standard* reported the police as saying, 'This decision now means that any company or individual can now trade in these weapons with impunity, provided they don't come through Britain.'

Is this position common enough for you?

All of that changed on 1 May 2004, when the Trade in Goods (Control) Order 2003 came into force. The law says: 'No person shall directly or indirectly:

---

* *Back on the Torture Trail*, Channel 4, broadcast 13 March 1996.

❑ supply or deliver;

❑ agree to supply or deliver; or

❑ do any act calculated to promote the supply and delivery of restricted goods.

The UK had introduced brokerage laws and the rest of Europe was obliged to do so too, if it had not already done so. There are problems with the EU Common Position 2003. It gives no time limit for countries to get the work done by and it isn't too precise about what countries should do either. Should brokers be registered? Answer: up to you. Should there be extraterritorial controls? Duh? You decide. Should it cover embargoed countries? Your choice.

In typical EU style it is hammered in the white-hot forge of fudge and compromise. What is generally accepted by campaigning groups trying to control the arms trade, and by certain parts of the arms industry too, is that to have effective brokering laws this is what you need:

❑ Brokers should be registered, both nationals and visiting foreign dealers.

❑ The law should apply to all arms, military equipment and components.

❑ Extraterritoriality needs to be applied on all arms brokerage deals. This means that any UK citizen conducting an arms deal from anywhere in the world is still subject to UK law.

❑ All UN and EU embargoes should be legally enforced.

If we could get that to apply across Europe it would be a start in reducing the amount of arms out there in the world. After all, the EU is the biggest exporter of small arms, according to Small Arms Survey, bigger even than the US.* And although the EU

---

* http://news.bbc.co.uk/1/hi/world/africa/3135146.stm

BBC News, 24 September 2003, 'One gun for every 20 Africans', based on 2003 Small Arms Survey which says that, 'The European Union as a whole is the largest small arms exporter, followed by the US and the Russian Federation.'

Common Position is far from perfect it does at least give campaigners something to work with. This may sound too legalistic for some on the Left, who argue that nothing can really change until after the revolution. And far be it from me to criticise that view for being simplistic and lazy. Or to accuse the adherents of creating a recipe for sitting on one's arse – no, I would not do that. I wouldn't dare accuse the British Left of being self-indulgent, irrelevant and vain at the expense of millions in the developing world. I respect the British Left too much, and I even have my name down on the list to help out with the catering once the revolution starts. I'm doing the sandwiches. So as soon as the barricades go up in Whitehall, someone will text me and I'll have the wholemeal baps round to the frontline.

Meanwhile, New Labour got round to introducing brokering laws in 2004. Two years later, in 2006, seemed a reasonable time to assess if the laws had worked. And what better way to robustly road-test the law than with a group of schoolchildren setting up their own arms company …

12

BROKERAGE ... THE STORY OF THE AFTER-SCHOOL ARMS CLUB

CHAPTER TWELVE

'... and after I finish my homework I'm going to buy some weapons.' A chapter in which a group of school students prove the loopholes exist in arms export control by becoming arms dealers and by brokering equipment.

ROUND ONE: LORD WILLIAMS UPPER SCHOOL, THAME, OXFORDSHIRE, UK

Mick Ranger, the Kalashnikov-supplying arms dealer who visited Lord Williams Upper School in Thame to talk to the Amnesty group there, finished his chat with a question for the school pupils. After all the students had questioned him on export law, illegal arms deals and moral responsibility, it only seemed fair for Ranger to put one back to them. He turned to the students and asked, 'So, are any of you destined to be arms dealers, then?' Ranger's question was a genuine one, though considering he was talking to an Amnesty group perhaps it was a tad optimistic. Ranger might have been trying to mentor a room of 15- to 18-year-olds into arms dealing, but the pupils looking back at him had beaten him to it. They had already set up their own arms company as part of an extracurricular project for a Channel 4 *Dispatches* programme I was making (which was broadcast on 3 April 2006).

Their company, Williams Defence, was named after their school. Once the company was up and running, they chose who was on the board and whose name was to be used in communications, and once a week at lunchtime they would meet up. They would send out business enquiries, check up on responses and buy equipment. It is exactly the kind of radical preparation for the globalised world of business that the government would approve. Indeed, the students' entrepreneurial acumen proved to be so effective that they now own several New Labour City Academies, one of which they have relocated to China where pupil costs are lower due to a flexible student force.

For the benefit of the quizzically concerned, Andrew Adonis and the smattering of *Daily Mail* readers who have been given a copy of this book by their angry university-attending offspring: this was a project to assess the government's arms controls. The students studied the human rights implications of the equipment, interviewed everyone from MPs to arms dealers and magistrates, visited the select committee hearings for the Quadripartite Committee (which oversees the government's arms licensing policy and practice) and presented them with their findings. To those readers with a more Dickensian approach to education, I would merely say: it was the government that wanted to introduce active citizenship classes. Well, I can think of no finer act of citizenship than holding a government to account over its arms licensing system.

Williams Defence was supervised by 31-year-old teacher George Lear, who organises the school Amnesty group, founded five years ago at the pupils' request. The group had already become involved in the world of direct action as part of the Make Poverty History campaign, in the summer of 2005. 'It was the students' idea actually. What it was, we turned up at the town hall in Thame on the day of the summit with a huge white band made of linen, which we got from the market. The white band had "Make Poverty History" on it in big letters and we wrapped it round the entire town hall. So the front door said: MAKE POVERTY HISTORY,' says a smiling and enthusiastic Lear. 'Someone from the town hall staff came and said it was a health and safety problem, but then they cleared off and left us.'

You could be forgiven for thinking that the students who took part in the Amnesty group were the more serious-minded of their peers, but this would belie their sense of fun, enquiry and individuality. Ed tended to plaster on an innocent expression before asking questions like, 'Does your mum approve of you being an arms dealer?' Tim and Chris had a penchant for digital radio and Led Zeppelin. And Mykala and Ellie kindly explained to me the difference between an 'emo' and a 'goth', with the patience of people used to dealing with confused and desperately unhip dads. In short, they were a normal bunch of state-school pupils.

Mission unimpossible: objective

Their mission was quite simple: to test the government's heralded laws on torture equipment and brokerage. Robin Cook had said, 'We are committed to preventing British companies from manufacturing, selling or procuring equipment designed primarily for torture and to press for a global ban.' How far had New Labour got? Until 2004, brokerage was a major loophole for arms dealers. The law now says that anything on the UK Military List should be licensed, even brokered deals where the equipment doesn't touch UK soil. So was the loophole closed? The students were about to find out.

There were limitations on what the students could do. They could not buy anything that required an End User Certificate (i.e. firearms), so guns were off the menu. But this still left the students some scope in the 'police and security' field, as Sandy Mitchell's and the Guantanamo prisoners' experience proves. Just because equipment isn't listed as military or security doesn't mean it can't be used in inhumane ways.

So armed with a video camera to record their experiences (plus myself and a *Dispatches* researcher at the end of a phone if they needed us), the students got on with the job of finding out if they could find, buy and transport equipment designed for degrading or ill-treating their fellow humans.

It's like eBay for bastards: method

America – Land of the Free, Home of the Brave and Shopping Mall of the Enormous – is the biggest arms exporter in the world, but its supremacy is being challenged by the manufacturing powerhouse of the Far East. So the students of Williams Defence initially looked to that region to source various 'police and security' items. Some of the goods they have on offer are ... well, let's just say that the equipment is not for the squeamish. And like most of the world's products, services and indeed peccadillos, they are all available online somewhere. Ironically, the Chinese torture products might be available online for all and sundry, but the Chinese themselves can't access the websites that condemn their use. (Thanks, Google! Your data censors and firewalls developed in the free-market *über*-capitalist world have saved the day for the dictatorship of the proletariat!)

So the task Williams Defence had was to track down the companies that dealt in this field. Find out what products they were selling, see if the equipment is included on the UK's Military List, and if not, email an enquiry, place an order and phone DHL. The students' emails obviously looked like they were coming from a bona-fide arms company. They didn't do the classic pupil letter: 'I am a doing a school project on the arms trade and was wondering if you sell things you can hurt people with.' Though if they had, it's a cert that someone would have replied with a goody bag of company stickers, brochures, a free testicle-crushing vice and a best-regards slip. No, the students had formed an arms company and it was the company that was going to contact the manufacturers. The reaction to their product enquiries was mixed. Some didn't reply, some took a while to get back, and some were keener than a dog in a prosthetics factory.

Results

The final tally of purchased goods was: thumb cuffs (imported into the UK), wall cuffs (imported into the UK) and a sting stick (brokered to the USA and then imported into the UK). Here is a quick assessment of whether these items do more harm than good.

The thumb cuffs do what it says on the tin ... and more. The two cuffs form part of one solid metal bar. The cuffs inner rings are serrated, so if you try to move your thumbs they get cut to pieces. Generally these are applied by forcing the victim's hands behind their back with their thumbs sticking away from their body.

The wall cuffs are made by a Polish company who exhibit at police and security fairs throughout Europe. The cuffs can be mounted in any position or height, on a wall or door frame, and can be used for keeping a prisoner upright for sleep deprivation, or just to put them into a good torturing position.

PURCHASED GOODS SUMMARY

Item/price: Thumb cuffs: $3.65 per pair if the order was for over 2,500 pairs

Company/country of origin: Shyh Sing Enterprise Co Ltd, Taiwan

Sent to: UK

Evidence of use: In China, Tibet

Legal status: Legal to export and broker from from UK until end of July 2006. After the programme was aired on Channel 4, sources close to the government said the thumb cuffs would be 'restricted', i.e. given the same legal status as leg irons and torture equiment.

Item/price: Wall cuffs: £9.00 a set

Company/country of origin: Eltraf, Poland

Sent to: UK

Evidence of use: Many reports of prisoners being cuffed to walls come from the USA, China, France, Burma, Egypt and Argentina, among others.

Legal status: See above.

Item/price: Sting stick or wolf stick: $7.50

Company/country of origin: Rubber Impex, China

Sent to: USA, then on to the UK

Evidence of use: Chinese anti-riot police (oxymoron of the year!) used these in Lhasa in 1999. Used in Nepal 2003, Philippines 2003 and reports of Cambodian and Burmese authorities having these weapons.

Legal status: Legal to export and broker. Not included on the Military List. Because of EU trade regulations, the UK government claims it cannot prohibit or add the sting stick to the Military List without going through the EU.

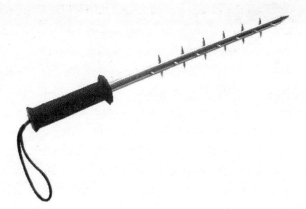

The sting stick is a heavy bar with spikes and a rubber handle for grip. It is basically a mass-produced version of a club with nails in it. Williams Defence had a sting stick sent to the USA to prove that a UK company could broker the deal without any need for licences. The sting stick was then imported into the UK.

Williams Defence: conclusion

Some American readers may find the idea of school students purchasing and shipping weapons normal, believing as some do that children should be armed in order to protect themselves at school. However, those of us familiar with the notion of each action having a consequence would rather not have students dealing weapons, and the fact that they can raises some serious questions.

For some American readers those questions will be: are their prices competitive? Do they ship to Waco? Can we fix red, white and blue tassels to the sting-stick handle? But, for those of us who regard a duck hooter as a comic device rather than an essential piece of hunting equipment, the first question is: shouldn't we have a register of arms dealers and brokers? If there was a register, then the students would not have been legally able to run their company. A register of arms brokers and dealers would compel them to inform the government of their intended business and have the government give their approval. Or not give their approval, as the case may be. After all, the idea of a released Abu Hamza, Ronnie Knight or even Jeffrey Archer going into the arms business would give some cause for concern.

The second question all of this raises is: why is it possible to broker this equipment? It is clearly designed to cause humiliation at best and more than likely torture. There really is little reason to possess a sting stick other than to threaten or cause harm to another human. It could be argued that the stick's purpose was to control farm or zoo animals, but I wouldn't want to do that near the Animal Liberation Front. So why isn't it on the list of controlled or restricted goods? Shouldn't there be a method of including these things on the list, rather than waiting for an Amnesty school project to link up with Channel 4 and a fat dad to attempt to embarrass the government into action?

In drawing up a list of 'restricted' torture equipment, the government provided a number of loopholes for dealers to crawl through. The first and most obvious flaw is that no matter how often a government updates the list of torture equipment, it can never be definitive. New equipment is created all the time and people can be tortured with just about anything, from a ballpoint pen to Metallica CDs.* This leaves a whole host of equipment that is designed specifically to torture that is simply not on the list and not covered by the law. Indeed, even the Export Group for Aerospace and Defence (the arms industry's export-control lobbying group) describe the attempts to list torture equipment item by item as 'deeply misguided and doomed'.

---

* 'One regular procedure that was described by people who worked at Camp Delta, the main prison facility at the naval base in Cuba, was making uncooperative prisoners strip to their underpants, having them sit in a chair while shackled hand and foot to a bolt in the floor, and forcing them to endure strobe lights and screamingly loud rock and rap music played through two close loudspeakers ... "It fried them," the official said, explaining that anger over the treatment the prisoners endured was the reason for speaking with a reporter.' *New York Times*, 17 October 2004. But I am actually guessing that Metallica was used.

The obvious answer is to have a catch-all clause. This would say something along the lines of 'anyone exporting equipment, regardless if it doesn't appear on the Military List, that they suspect could be used for torture should contact the authorities, who will assess it'. This type of clause already exists for dual use WMD items – any supplier who thinks the goods they are selling could be used for WMD has to report it to the government. (For further examples, see the box: The Foot Heaters.)

Presenting our findings to the minister

Waiting in the long corridor that stretches past the committee-room doors, each numbered in red gothic paint, a host of campaigners, NGO staff and civil servants sit on the leather benches or gently pace, check their watches and chat, or distract-edly draw shapes with the tip of their shoes on the carpet. The Quadripartite Committee is about to question the minister in charge of arms licensing and the Export Control Organisation, Malcolm Wicks. In honour of his visit, four police officers are hanging about by the entrance, in case anyone wants to kidnap him. Though I have a feeling they would be hard pressed to recognise Mr Wicks in the event that he was taken.

I am standing next to one of the Men In Black. MIB is a term of endearment for friends and campaigners who wish to remain anonymous and track down information on arms dealers. I wish I could tell you they spoke with gravelly voices and only ever used the phone when they were sitting in a darkened room under a triangle of light from an angle-poise in the corner. But they don't.

I casually mention to an MIB: 'I have no idea of what Wicks looks like, have you?'

'Nope,' says the MIB, master of the northern minimalist approach to discourse.

At which point all the smartly dressed men and women along the corridor stand up and focus their attention on one man in a dark suit.

'That has got to be him – all the civil servants are fawning.'

'Bloke in the middle?'

'Yes, he has to be the minister – no one is taking the piss out of his pink tie.'

I wander five paces down the corridor, take a punt and hold out my hand to the man I hope is the minister. 'Mr Wicks?'

He takes my hand and quizzically raises an eyebrow. 'Yes.' He is about five foot ten, trimmed grey hair, fifty-odd and well groomed. I'll wager he has more aftershave than Q-tips in his bathroom cupboard and a nostril-trimmer to boot. His accent puts him somewhere south of the Thames. His suit and tie put him in the stalls at *Queen the Musical* by Ben Elton. Middle-aged, middle-brow, middle-management.

I explained that the students wanted to meet Mr Wicks, he is the minister responsible and they want to present him with their findings.

'So you're looking for a bad guy?' he mumbles.

'No, we have got our bad guy.'

'You're looking for a fall guy.'

'No, we are looking for the person we should be handing this stuff to; we are looking for the person with responsibility for this stuff.'

'I'll have a think about it during the committee.'

And off he goes through the gaily numbered doors, followed by a sheaf of civil servants.

Outside Parliament is College Green, a strip of grass opposite the arse end of the House of Lords. A Henry Moore sculpture sits to one side, its location ensuring that it remains one of the few bronze works of art on public display not to have been stolen for scrap metal recently. The green has provided a location for many TV networks to interview politicians from. It is near Parliament, so the poor dears don't have to stray too far, and it has a nice view of Big Ben in the background. Some MPs from the Quadripartite Committee have said they would come over to meet the students, so at least someone will talk to them. It is here that representatives from Williams Defence wait to display their entrepreneurial prowess. They huddle together, red-faced and misty-breathed, their buttons done up to the collar against the cold, waiting, when from across the green a figure starts towards us. Nearly unrecognisable without minions, it is the minister.

The sting stick is a problem. Neither the Sergeant-at-Arms nor Black Rod are happy, and it is not just the anachronistic nature of their employment that is causing this distress, though that will undoubtedly contribute. The sting stick is a problem. The police pointed out that it could be viewed as an offensive weapon, and should the stick be displayed in public they might arrest us. The logic being that the sight of the stick might provoke members of the public to violence. I argued that Simon Cowell was allowed out in public and he was far more likely to provoke violence, but made little headway. This left us in a bind. How could we present the stick to the minister without breaking the law? To be fair, the police were aware of the irony at work here: namely that school students could legally broker this stick across the world but couldn't present their findings to an MP. But to be fairer, irony was never the police's strong suit, favouring sarcasm as they do.

'Right then!' the brisk minister announces his presence, and automatically stands in the middle of the group.

'We're Lord Williams Upper School,' volunteers George Lear.

'Right,' says the minister, indicating he has listened, understood and the speakers may proceed with the next point they wish to make.

'And we set up our own arms company and brokered these,' say the students, handing over the thumb cuffs to the minister.

'What are these? Where did you get them?'

'These are thumb cuffs.'

'And you ordered these over the internet?'

'Yes.'

At this point I felt the need to tell the minister about the sting stick, so cutting it from its packaging I open the box containing the weapon and look around to see if there are any police about the place. 'This is a sting stick. The police have said we could be arrested if we get it out, but you should feel how heavy it is.'

I offer the box containing the weapon to the minister and to my surprise he picks up the sting stick. Holding it in one hand, as if gauging what damage he could do, Malcolm Wicks, minister at the DTI, stands on College Green opposite the House of Lords. I look at the students and I get the feeling I am not alone in wanting to scream, 'POLICE!'

In fact, the urge to do it is almost irresistible. Just to see his face as we all run from him, leaving him standing there with the sting stick. All of us screaming, 'Nutter! He's a fucking nutter! He's got a weapon!' We should manically run across the green shouting and waving, 'Save the school children!'

'He's attacking the kids!'

'For fuck's sake, save the kiddies!'

Should we scream or should we lobby?

Time slows as a leafless tree moves fractionally in the noiseless breeze. I can see the single beat of a pigeon's wing as it alights on the Henry Moore. I have cosmic inner peace in this torrent of traffic and politics that surrounds central London. Two routes open before us and one of them involves a government minister being wrestled to the ground and handcuffed. The other involves more campaigning, letters, petitions and work. The comedy option frankly has the upper hand. Reform or revolt? If only we could multi-task and do the two. If only we could get him arrested – but he would see the funny side and agree to change the law anyway.

'You're trying to get me arrested,' says the minister.

And the moment goes, the pigeon crashes on the sculpture with a squawk and we have chosen from our options. 'If we can

get these, anyone can. So we want to see a register for arms dealers and brokers,' says Simon, a student with cropped black hair.

'Would you send me a report or a letter, detailing what you
have done?' says the minister.

'We'd be happy to,' says their teacher, George Lear.

'OK. Great. Thank you,' says the minister, using the universal words for: 'It's all over, I'm going now and leaving you here.'

And the award for Best Government Vacillator goes to …

In April 2006 Dr Kim Howells from the Foreign and
Commonwealth Office was answering questions in place of his
boss Jack Straw at the Quadripartite Select Committee hearing.
Howells was asked by the committee chairman about the items
brokered by the students. 'Given the items that the government
has already banned because they are instruments of torture,' said
Roger Berry, 'is there any reason why thumb cuffs, wall cuffs and
sting sticks cannot be immediately added to the list?'

The thumb cuffs and wall cuffs would be added to the
Military List; as for the sting stick, Dr Howells said it was a
'matter for negotiation at EU level'. His civil servant Graham
Glover added: 'It is a Commission and EU competence matter.'

The committee's sense of incredulity was summed up by Paul
Keetch MP, when he said: 'What you are saying is that the British
government cannot stop the export of these items if they believe
they are potentially being used for torture, that is only something
that the EU can do?'

'It would be something that the Commission would have to
regulate on is my understanding,' said Mr Glover.

According to the Foreign Office, the government can't add a
sting stick to the Military List unless the EU agrees on it first …
oh, the *Daily Mail* will love this.

ROUND TWO: LORD WILLIAMS UPPER SCHOOL, THAME, UK – GUILTY ANYWHERE

Extraterritoriality is a concept that is a lot easier to grasp than it is to pronounce. If a UK law has extraterritoriality, it means it applies to all UK citizens no matter what country they are in. Britain already has examples of this concept in action. British law applies to British paedophiles even when they are not in Britain. So the law follows the law-breaker over the border.

Extraterritoriality already applies to all 'restricted goods' (i.e. WMD, long-range missiles and torture equipment). This means no British dealer can have anything to do with long-range missiles without a licence, and it doesn't matter if they do the whole deal in Peru or Mali. No licence = criminal offence, anywhere in the world. Which is the beginning of some positive attitudes towards controlling the arms trade. Dealers will find holes to crawl through antimatter, so extraterritoriality is quite an effective way of covering the problem of legal responsibility. The law also applies to countries under UN and EU arms embargoes. So no British dealers can have anything to do with a deal to provide arms to Congo, for example, even if they are based in Congo. If they are British, then they are subject to British law.

The problem is, having applied this law to missiles, why not to small arms? Small arms kill half a million a year; long-range missiles do not. So a British citizen can nip on board the Eurostar and deal arms with impunity on the Continent. 'Oh, what is the likelihood of that?' you may cry, to which I reply: 'British people travel to France in flocks of white Transits to save duty on beer: it is a year-long migration. This is a force of nature so elemental it rivals the wildebeest migration of Kenya. If people go to these lengths for a few quid saved on twenty trays of lager, do you think the dealers wouldn't go to the Continent to make a few quid doing guns?' Get a grip. Think what an arms dealer would do for the kind of money to be found in the defence industry. Especially as all you need to be an arms broker is a bank account (offshore), a mobile phone, a Blackberry and an internet address. You don't even physically need an office – you can use a postal address.

The small arms of Williams Defence

Chris and Tim are fifteen and as well as possessing the endearing gaucheness of adolescence are part of Williams Defence, the Oxford school's arms company. They are standing with me in Newry, technically Northern Ireland. On the other side of the border, in Ireland, Chris and Tim can legally deal in about 99 per cent of the equipment on the UK Military List and there is nothing the UK authorities can do to stop them. Ireland has no brokerage laws, and therefore they can operate with impunity, and Britain has no extraterritorial controls over small arms. The border between Ireland and the North lies at the Newry Bridge. Bureaucratic intransigence on the part of both sides has provided a visible line for this boundary, as neither side will take responsibility for any part of the road belonging to the other. Which means two types of tarmac and road markings converge to physically create a line to illustrate the border.

On the northern side of the border stand Chris, Tim and I. Williams Defence has an Irish office and with a single bound we step into it, across the different shades of tarmac. Having traversed a good two feet into the Republic of Ireland, we get out the mobile and start calling up arms companies.

It is slightly worrying calling international arms dealers from a country roadside, not least because you don't want to be forced mid-conversation to shout, 'Will you keep off the fucking kerb!' as a juggernaut thunders past. And it is slightly disconcerting that Chris and Tim's voices sound so youthful and might not be too convincing as arms dealers. There are quite a few 'what-ifs' to contend with. What if Tim or Chris accidentally blow the façade by mentioning homework or their teacher. What if the conversation gets awkward, what if faced with a prolonged and anxious silence the pupils blurt out, 'So ... er ... what music do you like, then?'

To give us a slight safety net I am pretending to be a personal assistant working for Williams Defence. I will get the conversation going with the arms companies and then hand over to Tim or Chris, who will be the company managing director and use the name George Lear. It was decided a while ago that it would not be advisable to use the children's real names, so all communications were to be done in the name of their teacher. So if an international arms dealer was really going to get upset and come after someone, it would be their teacher. Which seems fair.

The first company we call is Daudsons in Pakistan, on the trail of hand-held grenade launchers. 'Hello, Mr Daud, it is Mark Thomas here, the secretary for George Lear,' I stutter as we stand alongside an old tractor rusting on the edge of a field. ' ... Yes, we are just in the middle of a client reception and have some quick questions to ask about the grenade launchers ... Will you hold for one moment? I have our MD Mr Lear here. I'll just get him.'

I pass the phone to Chris, who is all of fifteen and playing the part of MD for all he is worth.

'Hi, it's George Lear here, Williams Defence,' he says with schoolboy charm. 'We want the hand-held grenade launchers to go to Syria, for the army to do some tests.' He leaves the sentence hanging in the air.

'Oh well, I don't know. Syria,' Mr Daud ponders.

I am wearing headphones so I can hear the conversation and my heart sinks at Mr Daud's reticence. This trait of expressing disappointment when things go right is one that comedians and journalists share. George Bush is elected and most of the world is hugely depressed; me, I am overjoyed at the wealth of material and stories coming my way. As a human being I should be pleased that Mr Daud, the arms dealer, is not prepared to supply a repressive regime with grenade launchers. I should take pleasure that at least one person won't flog this stuff to any braid-wearing yahoo, but we have come a long way to find out about the innate goodness of the human soul.

'Is there a problem with getting the grenade launchers to Syria?' Chris continues with a nonchalant air, which suggests he could be discussing an ill-toasted muffin or a billion-dollar jet plane.

'Well, there could be, there could be,' replies Mr Daud.

I hang onto the headphones. I am childishly gutted that Mr Daud appears to be showing some form of common sense. In my rush to condemn the arms industry, perhaps I have tarred them all with the same brush. Forgetting that an industry is made of individuals, each with the potential for their own personal morals to affect their work. Here was Mr Daud from Pakistan expressing what seemed to be genuine concerns about exporting to Syria.

'You see,' he continued, 'they have a very bad reputation for copying things. We would have to have an assurance that the Syrians were not going to copy the design.'

Relief floods into my veins like a breached dam as Mr Daud confirms that his biggest worry is not the fact that Syria is a sponsor of state terrorism and a human rights-abusing regime to boot. No, the biggest worry Mr Daud has is that they might steal his designs. He later offers us a deal of $420 per grenade launcher. Hurrah! Outside I am calm. Inside I am bunting and street parties. Arms dealers are bastards and once again profit triumphs over human compassion! Yes! YES! YES!

All is right with the world. Let the trumpets of joy shower the heavens with song. And as if to celebrate the intrinsic fallibility of humankind, some birds start singing in the hedgerows. I smile at Chris and make a mental note to get professional help when I get home.

MKEK, the Turkish arms manufacturer we met in Chapter Three, offer sub-machine guns and pistols and are happy to get them to Mali. Like Syria, Mali is a place that has no EU or UN arms embargo on it but Britain would not normally license arms to either place. Syria is a bad egg, so Britain won't flog guns there, and Mali is a member of ECOWAS (the Economic Community of West African States), and they have a moratorium on arms sales in the region, which Britain observes. So here are Chris and Tim, our fifteen-year-old arms dealers from Oxford, legally able to broker guns to places that the UK would not permit, from a roadside in Ireland.

Next up is Truvelo, a South African shotgun manufacturer, who were charging $1,165 per Neostead pump-action shotgun, though the price comes down to $1,137 each if you are buying a hundred. Tim and I spoke to Ingrid Beisiegel at Truvelo.

'We have an order for shotguns to go to the West Bank, an Israeli settlement. Will it be a problem to get the guns to Israel?'

Ingrid replies in clipped Afrikaans tones: 'No, we can't do that.'

'Sorry?'

'No, we can't do that. The South African government will not license arms sales to Israel.'

'Oh dear.'

My smile, left over from Mr Daud, starts to slip. Would Truvelo comply with their own government's policies and intentions rather than attempting to circumvent them? Was Truvelo going to display some moral muscle?

'But what we can do,' says Ingrid, 'we have a dealer in Switzerland who might do the deal for you. They will buy the guns from us and they will sell them into Israel.'

My heart leaps. Once again an arms dealer has behaved like ... well, an arms dealer.

THE GUN THAT KILLED PC BROADHURST

Of all the deals set up in Ireland by Williams Defence Eire, perhaps the most significant was for some handguns from a Croatian company, and this is why. PC Broadhurst was thirty-three years old and married when he was killed. He was executed in a Leeds lane on Boxing Day 2003. He had been shot but was still alive as he lay in Dib Lane unable to escape. He pleaded for his life with the gunman, who seconds later shot him in the head at point-blank range. Along with his colleague PC Neil Roper, Broadhurst had stopped a stolen car, a BMW, which happened to contain the US criminal David Bieber, who was working as a bouncer/dealer. Bieber was wanted in America in connection with the contract killing of a fellow bodybuilder and the attempted murder of his former girlfriend. He had slipped into the UK on a tourist visa and adopted the name Nathan Wayne Coleman. Seven years later he killed PC Broadhurst. Some police suggest that Bieber was a hitman and was on his way to carry out a killing when the officers stopped him.

In the 2004 trial of Bieber, recordings picked up by the police radio mics were played to the jury. They were the tapes of PC Broadhurst pleading with Bieber not to kill him. Bieber was sentenced to life. The gun Bieber used to kill PC Broadhurst was an HS95 semi-automatic pistol manufactured by a Croatian company called IM Metal. The question is: how did it end up with Bieber?

Interpol investigations tracing the weapon were led by Alan Shiers of the National Criminal Intelligence Service. He is retired now, but striding into the pub where I met him he looks every inch a copper: ruddy-faced, with a smart black overcoat, white shirt and nondescript tie he exudes essence of Old Bill as if it were an aftershave. I'd put money on he has never attended a seminar on effective delivery of performance indicators to community stakeholders. Shiers looked like a no-nonsense copper, get the bad guys and bang 'em up. He had worked in the Merseyside drugs squad before moving to Interpol and NCIS, where he specialised in tracking firearms. He was ideally suited for the job when the Yorkshire police approached him for help tracing the HS95.

We are sitting in a pub that drinkers would call a proper pub. There is no menu featuring mussels or Thai food, just sausage and mash. There are no corporate CDs playing world music. There are no couples sharing a chilled bottle of wine. There are a handful of builders, a darts board and a layer of nicotine on the ceiling that in a few years time will transform into a stratum of coal. We order a coffee, the one concession to modernity in the pub.

'I forget the name of the DI [detective inspector] who asked me to help trace the weapon,' says Shiers, 'but she called and explained the case and asked if I would help. So I started making enquiries via Interpol. Circulated a request for information and got a reply from Holland.'

'Did you find the person who sold the gun?'

'Well, we pinned it down to a person who had already been arrested for firearms offences. He had the HS95 with the next serial number to the murder weapon. It is a fair assumption that the murder weapon came through Holland and this particular guy.'

Interpol say the tale of the gun starts on 17 September 1998 when, according to documents I've seen, the first batch of weapons was bought from the Croatian company IM Metal by a front company. The bogus arms company was registered in the US at 15 North East St, Dover, Delaware and was called Metropolitan Capital Investment Co. They purchased 500 HS95 semi-automatics. In February 1999 Metropolitan Capital Investment Co purchased another batch of HS95s, this time 1,200 guns. A second front company, called Liberty Enterprises Ltd and registered in the British Virgin Islands, bought a third batch of 1,000 semi-automatic pistols on 10 March 1999. 'Initial enquiries by Interpol indicate that neither company exist,' said the official document. Using dodgy paperwork to get the guns out of the factory gates was the first step on the journey. The document continues: 'The pistols have been recovered from both criminal and terrorist groups.' In 2001 ETA, the Basque terrorist group, used a gun from the same batch of weapons to assassinate the president of the Aragon section of Partido Popular, the ruling party in Spain at the time. The network of gunrunners not only included ETA, but covered Belgian and Albanian criminals, the Kosovo Liberation Army, and ganglands in Germany and the Netherlands. They were also found in the Republic of Ireland. The report concludes: 'The fact that the weapons were recovered from Albanian criminals and the KLA, suggest Albanian involvement in procurement and subsequent diversion. The Dutch black market appears to be the main source of former Yugoslav weapons in circulation in Europe ... brought into Holland by drug smugglers, probably using HGVs.'

So the HS95 that killed PC Broadhurst started in Croatia with IM Metal, who made the gun, was bought by a front company, transferred by Albanian criminals to a gunrunner in the Netherlands and from there to David Bieber, who fired the gun at PC Broadhurst's head, killing him.

IM Metal ... HS Produkt

IM Metal no longer exists. It has changed its name to HS Produkt and still makes pistols. The upgraded version of the HS95 is the HS 2000 9mm semi-automatic pistol. Subject to the same bits of paper that should have been produced by the gangsters buying the HS95s, HS Produkt were happy to quote a price to Williams Defence to supply the guns to a private military company in West Africa. The guns cost only 240 euros each and could be delivered to Zagreb airport. The Oxford school pupils, working out of Ireland, can buy the kind of gun that killed PC Broadhurst. They can buy it from the renamed company that sold it to the gangsters. And as long as the Croatian authorities tick the paperwork, the students could have armed mercenaries in Africa, and the UK government couldn't do a damn thing to stop it.

ROUND THREE: SCOIL CHRIOST RI PRESENTATION SCHOOL, PORTLAOISE, IRELAND

Portlaoise is a rural Irish town about an hour south-west of Dublin by train. Its most obvious claim to fame is that it boasts not one but two prisons. High-security terrorist prisoners used to find themselves at home in Portlaoise, but the Good Friday Agreement seems to have knocked the stuffing out of that particular section of the penal marketplace. It's a friendly town, where the new houses quickly give way to the countryside. The statue of the Virgin Mary in the middle of a roundabout is a particularly good one. Standing a good eight feet high, she has a halo above her head. Haloes being ethereal and somewhat transparent they are difficult things to sculpt, so this halo is a flat grey disc. It looks like the Virgin Mary is standing under a satellite disc picking up a signal. Our Lady of the Sports Channels – though she might be getting more adult-orientated programming.

There is an old cemetery in Portlaoise. Pitched on the side of a high mound that springs dramatically upwards from the road, it is straight out of a Tim Burton set. Its green slopes, dotted with slanted and tilting gravestones, are ringed with a wrought-iron fence as twisted as a toilet-scrubber's face. Next to the cemetery is the local store, Browns. They sell everything from newspapers and birthday cards to a whole chicken and chips, cooked, wrapped and salted. Opposite the cemetery and Browns are the gates to the Presentation Secondary School, a Catholic girls school. The building is grey and modern, in slight 1960s decline.

I am here to see a nun about a gun. Past the big sheet of sliding glass at the reception and the school cabinet with trophies and shields, up the echo of the staircase lined with pictures of children holding candles, and along the dark corridor is Sister Barbara's room.

'Come on in,' she says, as brisk as she is friendly. 'You'll be wanting a cup of tea after your journey. Do you want a cup of tea?'

'Yes, that would be lovely. Thank you.'

'It's no bother. Here, there's some biscuits. Sit ye down and have a biscuit.'

Sister Barbara is wrapped in a long grey cardigan and the only hint of nunnishness in her outward appearance is her black trousers. She has clear eyes behind her metal-framed glasses, and short silver hair. Her physical frame is slightly wiry like her glasses, and slightly shortish like her hair. Sister Barbara is a direct woman, who expresses her moral outrage with sharp and deep intakes of breath while muttering, 'Och, go on.' I don't know how old she is but I find out later that she is thinking of retiring next year.

While the wind blows and batters the land outside her room, inside we are snug; the kettle steams and burbles to the boil. For several years she has run a human rights group, with the students meeting at lunchtime to exchange information and plan campaigns. Her classroom is covered in posters mainly made by the students. 'Free West Papua' declares one over a home independence flag. A large sheet of paper is covered in photos of the girls' Fairtrade campaign in the town and handwritten student accounts. Next to this is a banner-cum-chart showing how much money is spent on the arms trade. Sister Barbara appears to be the ideal candidate to run the Irish equivalent of Williams Defence.

The Irish human rights group AFRI (Action From Ireland) had worked with Sister Barbara before on various school projects. It was AFRI who recommended I get in touch with Sister Barbara with a view to setting up a school arms project in Ireland. It was AFRI who kindly agreed to mentor the project, should it happen.

'You'll like Sister Barbara,' said Joe Murray from the group. 'She's grand. I'll be shocked if you don't like her.'

There was little chance that I wouldn't. Sister Barbara is talking, over a steaming cup, about the time she was working in Somalia. 'We had to go over the border every day from Kenya. It was a small medical team, but the bandits thought we had brought food, so they attacked and started shooting, it was terrible, we were all lying on the floor.' There is a sharp intake before she continues. 'And d'you know, the people we were helping, the people in the clinic, crawled on top of us to protect us with their own bodies. Their own bodies, mind. Amputees. Some of these people had arms missing. Some had their legs missing and still they protected us with their own bodies. It was very moving. Very moving.' She pauses, takes a deep breath and then offers me a Mars Bar and a word of encouragement to eat it. 'Go on,' she says. And I, your humble atheist narrator, have to hold myself in check from falling in love with a nun.

Promises in limbo land

Ireland is one of those countries that hasn't quite got round to introducing brokerage laws yet. There are five countries in the EU that have no arms brokering controls: Cyprus, Portugal, Greece, Luxembourg and Ireland.* The EU might compel them to do so (under the EU Common Position) but they have not got round to it yet. So Ireland languishes forever pledging and constantly on the cusp of introducing the laws. Not surprisingly, arms brokers have and can work from Ireland with no restrictions. In fact, Leonid Minim, the Ukrainian/Israeli gunrunner who broke UN sanctions by transporting massive arms shipments

---

* Italy and France are in an odd legal situation; they have some laws that cover some brokering activities but have updated them to cover all brokering activities.

into Liberia and Sierra Leone, was until recently a board member of an Irish company.

So six convent schoolgirls and one nun (after some lengthy chats with myself, the team working on the show and Joe from AFRI) decided that they should try to inject some urgency into the Irish government's thinking. They do so by setting up an arms company called Seachtar Associates, meaning 'seven' in Irish. Like their Oxford counterparts, they are normal intelligent teenagers. They chat frantically in huddles about boys, basketball and local gossip. Claire talks about Eminem. 'He was great live. Fantastic. My friend and I went. We're on the video. For a second, like.' She flicks her hair in self-mocking importance. She wants to train as a hairdresser. Mary is in her final year and is shrieking in disbelief as one of the girls confides: 'I am the only person in my family to break the pledge.'

'No!'

'Yes, all the others took the pledge and stuck to it.'

'What pledge?' I stumble into the conversation.

'Not to drink alcohol before I'm eighteen,' she says smiling, before embarking on a tale about the local park and some boys. Just normal school students, who happen to email arms companies across the world in their lunch breaks, and sometimes come in early to school so they can phone across the different time zones to chat to the dealers.

Just normal schoolgirls, who made contact with a Korean company to broker electro-shock stun batons, which though illegal to possess in Ireland can still be brokered. Seachtar Associates sent a baton to a human rights activist in California, to prove they could. To prove that Ireland needs to introduce brokerage laws. Six convent schoolgirls and a nun were even asked if they would consider being agents for the Korean stun batons in Ireland. On top of that, they imported leg irons into Dublin. It was then that they decided it might be appropriate to call a press conference to announce what they had done. But before they could do that, there was one more surprise in store.

ROUND FOUR: SCOIL CHRIOST
RI PRESENTATION SCHOOL,
PORTLAOISE, IRELAND

Sister Barbara has a fine and robust sense of humour. Which is just as well, as the story I'm about to tell ended up being written about in the Irish press. The day after the *Sunday Times Ireland* wrote this story up, I spoke to Sister Barbara on the phone, over a cup of tea.

'Have you seen it?' she says. 'The *Sunday Times*?'

'No.'

'Ohh.' She inhales. 'The story is fine enough but the head-line! Oh dear Lord!'

'What was it? What was the headline?'

'"Undercover Nun In Arms Deal Sting"!'

I stayed on the phone while I laughed. By the time I had finished, the phone company were ready to announce new dividends to shareholders. In fact, I wondered if now might not be a good time to retire. Headlines like that don't come along every day of the week, and it would be nice to bow out on a high. Hell, I'd forgo my name on my gravestone if I could have that carved on instead.

This is how it came about. An Israeli arms dealer was the object of the 'arms deal sting'. He sold us one of the most bizarre weapons in the world – a mini cannon stone thrower. Obviously he had no knowledge at the time that he was doing business with a comedian, a Catholic nun and six schoolgirls. Had he known that, then he might not have volunteered to come over to Ireland to give us a demonstration of how his invention worked. But he didn't, and he did, and that is how Sister Barbara and I ended up in the tale of the 'Undercover Nun In Arms Deal Sting'.

It had started, as it often does, with the Men In Black phoning, and a slightly incredulous northern voice saying, 'You wouldn't be interested in a stone thrower, would you?'

'You what?' is my ineloquent reply.

'Stone thrower.'

'Why do you want a machine to throw stones? Are the Saudi Arabian adultery courts working to quotas now?'

'It is for "crowd control" apparently. The picture I've got is of this machine mounted onto the top of a Land-Rover. You should find out more.'

It was not long before the girls at Seachtar Associates were doing just that.

The MCS mini cannon stone thrower

The MCS was developed and made by the Israeli company RD Peled. It hurls approximately 600 egg-shaped stones a minute, can cover a distance of 100 metres and has been deployed by the Israeli security forces. It can be mounted on a vehicle or a tripod; a sample one costs $7,500.

So we buy one* and RD Peled ships it over to Dublin, having sent us a note saying: 'We would like to let you know that in order to pass customs and security checks without delay we will write that the product is for agricultural use.' This is a tad naughty, as Israeli arms exports need two licences: one to begin negotiations for a deal, and a second to actually export. Like Olli Salo back in Chapter Three, who changed the labels on the crates to get guns to Zimbabwe, Mr Peled too is playing with labels in warehouses to avoid licensing and control of his military equipment.

A stone's throw away

First thing in the morning on a farm in Portlaoise, Ireland, and the crows are scrambling round the sky. Spring was on its way but got delayed, so the trees were still leafless as the crows infested their branches. In the middle of the field is the stone thrower,

---

* The company Williams Defence Eire was used to buy it, but the deal on this one was arranged by the Channel 4 team.

erected and on a tripod. It has a hopper for pouring the stones in, which feeds them into the motorised drum, which rotates very, very fast and throws the stones out of the front of the contraption.

Sister Barbara and I are standing next to Rafi Peled and his wife Dinah, the company of RD Peled. At a guess I would say they are in their fifties. Rafi's cropped black hair and still strong physique would turn a few heads at an Israeli Darby and Joan. He has the thick gnarled hands of an engineer. Dinah, who has the better English, is still trim, with cropped hair like her husband. His winter coat is unbuttoned, and he has the manner of a man used to working in the open. Dinah remains wrapped against the elements.

The stone thrower is powered by two car batteries and makes a noise like a loud hover lawnmower when it is switched on. Rafi holds the handle, points the machine into the air, releases a mechanism to let the stones into the cylinder – and BOOM! The stones clink and clank loudly with a fast erratic rhythm. They fly out from the metal cover like a vicious mist, a hurtling black cloud of stone, hundreds and hundreds of stones spraying an area, arcing high into the air. It takes only seconds, then the machine is switched off and silence descends. Even the crows are shocked. Rafi stands back with a big grin, holding out his arms and grunting, 'Uh-huh uh-huh,' in a what-do-you-think-of-that kind of way.

'I have to know,' I say, 'is this lethal?'

'No, it is not for killing!' Rafi says emphatically.

'But if I got in the way of it ...' I say, gingerly stepping towards the front of the inactive machine.

'No, not for killing.'

'But if I stood here,' I say in front of the machine.

'Then I will kill you.'

'Right.'

'It is lethal at twelve metres.'

From 300 yards away, five of the girls watch through a top-floor window of a lone house the events that are taking place in the field. They are wired into the cameras dotted around the place and can hear the conversation.

'If I wanted to get this equipment into somewhere sensitive in West Africa, could you label it agricultural equipment?' I ask Dinah.

'Sure,' she says. 'No problem.'

'You can move it without having to get the licences.'

'Sure.'

'Would Sudan be a problem?' I ask, punting a country with a record of genocide and a UN arms embargo to boot.

'No, no problem.'

Later Dinah says: 'We can even change the colour.' She is referring to the giveaway military green.

'Oh right, to silver or something ...'

'Sure.'

And so the conversation goes: the stone thrower has been sold to the Mexican authorities; Rafi thinks it would be ideal to use in Darfur to control returning refugees should they get unruly; they can label it as agricultural equipment to get it past customs.

Until finally the girls from Seachtar Associates walk down the wooden steps, out of the house, along the gravel driveway and across the field. Dressed in their school jumpers and tracksuits, a group of 17- and 18-year-old convent schoolgirls walk up to Mr and Mrs Peled to ask them how they can sell something that can take a human life in so bizarre a fashion.

As the girls walk towards us, Rafi jokingly turns to me and says, 'You want me to get rid of them?'

'What, with that?' I say, looking at the stone thrower and having a serious sense-of-humour failure.

'Yes, you want me to stop them?' he says with a grin.

'No.'

I inform Rafi he is being filmed by Channel 4 and the girls, being the new owners of a mini cannon stone thrower, have a few questions for him. The grin goes.

'How can you sell this when it could kill someone?' says Maeve, who is possibly the feistiest of them.

'No, it does not kill.'

'Yes, it does. You said at twelve metres it would kill someone.'

'No.'

'Those rocks will kill someone.'

'It could not fire rocks,' says Rafi, gripping the stone thrower. 'It could fire plasticine balls.' He motions his hand in a flicking gesture to indicate the balls leaving the machine. 'Or sweets. It could fire sweets.'

'Sweets!' says Maeve. 'Sweets!' I have never seen such awesome incredulity.

'Sweets,' attempts Rafi, slightly desperately.

'Has the Israeli Defence Force deployed many sweets against youths in the intifada?' I casually enquire. But Rafi will no longer talk to us. So we all go back to the farmhouse, leaving RD Peled in the field.

'He didn't make sense,' say the girls, excitedly chattering over each other.

'First he said it would kill you, then he said it wouldn't.'

'Then he said it would fire sweets.'

'And then he refused to answer.'

'I think he is just very angry. And I would be too if I was in his position,' I say. It is no fun being caught out smuggling military equipment, offering to get it into sensitive places as agricultural equipment, talking of how it could be used in Sudan and has a lethal range despite being 'riot-control equipment'.

Mr and Mrs Peled walk off into Portloaise's country lanes. I turn to one of the TV production crew and say, 'Would you make sure they get in the car?'

The Peleds have been driven from their hotel some forty

minutes away in a car that we, the TV crew, had hired. If they stomped off down the narrow roads on foot they would end up lost in five minutes, and it would be a hellish walk even if they knew the way.

'They are not going to get into the car. They say you paid for the car and you are a no-good bastard,' says one of the crew, a young journalist called Sally Freeman. 'I told the driver to follow them. Sooner or later they will have to realise that they are lost and that the driver knows his way back to their hotel.'

THE PRESS CONFERENCE

We drive in a van from Portlaoise in rural Ireland to the capital, heading for a hotel conference room that is filling up with Dublin's press, all ready to hear of the girls' exploits. A couple of TV news cameras are setting up, radio mics are swarming about the place. Some radio folk pick up chats with some of the girls one by one as we arrive, while print journos slouch against the walls and scribble with disinterest like old pros.

Fittingly for Ireland, the hotel decor has an air of apparent neutrality. It is a small room, with brown Formica bar-room tables set at one end of it for the girls to sit behind. The chairs have thin, square, red cushions and gold-painted metal frames. The wallpaper is some kind of off-white, pale pink, yellowy nondescript, and was old and staid when it was put up. The hotel staff walk past in their red waistcoats with a workaday look that says, 'When you've been in this job as long as I have, you've seen it all before.'

The girls might be in their smart uniforms but as they are not in the school they have all opted to wear make-up, a punishable offence within their educational boundaries. Maeve, Lara, Mary, Margaret and Claire, with Sister Barbara at the end of the row, are all slightly nervous. They have each prepared their statements but I worry that the press might react cynically to them.

'Haven't you been exploited by a telly company?' I imagine a cold voice asking in a bored fashion.

As if to accompany that thought, a bored-looking print journalist leaning distractedly against the wall catches my eye with a smileless gaze. I grin automatically back at him; he picks up his open notebook covered in the hieroglyphics of shorthand. I raise my eyebrows, giving my best 'Are there any questions I can help you with?' look. He stares back with the blank sneer of a high-court judge, then turns away. I continue to smile like a beaming idiot.

The TV news cameras are set up on tripods; their bulky presence almost dominates the room, it is so small. Radio mics with station logos printed on the fuzzy windsocks are set up around the front table. Sister Barbara gently coughs, pours some water from the glass jug at the table and manages to sit casually bolt upright, a position that comes with ease after years of attending mass. She looks small, even in this room.

'Good afternoon, my name is Barbara Raftery and I am a Presentation teacher in Portlaoise,' she begins formally. 'Over the past years I have worked with students in the school on human rights issues, fair trade, arms trade, child soldiers and debt, and I have worked with some of the organisations you see here.' She reads on as the odd camera clicks and crouched figures move their microphones nearer to her. She explains how AFRI approached her about the project. She explains the law to the journalists, and her viewpoint: 'Now as much as we may dislike the sale and use of weapons, there is a great distinction between regulated arms brokering and unregulated arms brokering.' The room is respectfully quiet, save the clicking of cameras and the bustle of the odd journo trying to place their microphone nearer Sister Barbara.

The students then take turns telling each part of the story of how they brokered electro-shock equipment from China to America. Each girl introduces herself by name and age.

'Hi, my name is Claire, I'm seventeen years old,' she says, reading from her card but looking up at the gathered press, not frightened to give them a good stare. 'We are an international business with a very broad range of clients and we cater for dictators, torturers and corrupt police states.' She stops and looks up at the room, makes sure they have caught what she is saying, then continues, before handing over to another girl.

'My name is Maeve and I am eighteen years old. Like any start-up we had to decide where we were going to position ourselves in the market. Did we want to specialise in submarines or did we perhaps want to deal in riot and security equipment?' says the next member of Seachtar Associates, who then goes on to explain that AFRI put up the money for them to buy samples of electro-shock equipment and broker them from China to America.

And so, up and down the table, the girls take over from each other, telling the story. Each of them looking at their notes, double-checking before they read them out, looking like they are doing last-minute revision. Margaret explains: 'Just before Christmas we bought one [an electro-shock baton] from a South Korean dealer. Shock batons are illegal in Ireland so we couldn't bring it into the country, but that is not really the point. If we really were arms brokers operating out of the country then we wouldn't be buying for the Irish market anyway. We had the baton sent to a friend and a human rights activist in California because the US has no controls on importing stun batons.' When Margaret finishes, she blushes, then does what each girl has done in turn. Once they have finished reading, they turn to quietly watch and support whoever is reading next.

Another student, Mary, unwraps leg irons that were bought from South Africa and imported into Ireland by the girls. She holds them up for the cameras, the clicking intensifying as the leg irons are brought out of the box and displayed to the room.

Finally Laura reads her message: 'We call today on Bertie Ahern and the Irish government to urgently introduce effective brokerage laws. We urge the government to introduce brokerage laws to ensure the brokerage of all military goods is covered. From leg irons to tanks, but, in particular, torture equipment and small arms should be covered.' She finishes and puts down her piece of paper with her handwritten notes.

Without prompting, the room of journalists automatically gives the girls a spontaneous round of applause. I hold back proud tears, revelling in the girls' audacity and conviction. They believed from the start their actions and words would prick the conscience of the Irish government, who in turn would bring in new laws to control arms brokering. I had forgotten the power of the word. For all my family history, for all of our shouting from pulpits, I had forgotten. I sit awkwardly on a chair with a flimsy red cushion, my emotions threatening to force a sob. Rocking slightly I let out an embarrassed laugh. Laughing in wonder that a nun and a group of convent schoolgirls could wrench an atheist into remembering the power of the word. I have remembered the power of testimony.

We might be at the margins of the arms industry but today we are dominating the arena we can work in. A few weeks later the Irish government announce they will introduce brokerage laws by the end of the year.

THE DEMANDS MADE BY THE AFTER-SCHOOL ARMS CLUBS

Williams Defence (UK)

❑ That the government introduce a catch-all clause for torture equipment, forcing any supplier to refer to the authorities any equipment that could be used for torture – regardless of whether it is included in the UK Military List or not. (This is also the view of the Export Group for Aerospace and Defence, the arms industry's export lobby group.)

❑ That all armaments, especially small arms (pistols to rocket-propelled grenade launchers), be subject to extraterritorial controls. So no British dealer can avoid UK export law by setting up the deal outside of the UK. (This is also the view of the Defence Manufacturers' Association – the arms industry lobby group.)

❑ That all arms dealers and brokers be forced to register with the UK authorities, who will decide if they can or cannot deal in arms. (This too is supported by the DMA.)

Seachtar Associates (Ireland)

❑ That Ireland introduce brokerage laws controlling the arms trade from Ireland.

❑ That this law covers points 1 to 3 of Williams Defence demands.

THE FOOT HEATERS

There is a trade website called PostOffer, where you can buy, sell and set up deals for all sorts of stuff. From quality baby toys and accessories to reproduction old masterpieces, from German hair-removal kits to reflective clothing. It is basically the *Exchange and Mart* for small businesses but more low-rent; *Loot* for arms dealers.

When I last looked an Israeli arms dealer was trying to flog off Eastern European rocket launchers and ZU-23-2 air defence systems, which is 'an efficient and reliable anti-aircraft weapon'. Which even for the casual browser could come in handy. Consider a child's birthday party. The kiddies' entertainer is booked, sandwiches made and paper plates acquired. But there is still one thing preying on the parents' mind. What to do if the helium party balloons escape and fly over the wall into the neighbour's garden? The ZU-23-2 air defence system could be the answer to your prayers! And what children's clown wouldn't give the performance of a lifetime staring down the barrel of an RPG rocket launcher.

Scrolling down the offers and products on the site I wondered: do al Qaeda internet-shop?' Perhaps a young member of the Taliban sits in a cave downloading specification sheets for rocket launchers, while Osama bin Laden looks over his shoulder tutting.

'What's wrong with going to an arms dealer and giving them money for
it?'
'Oh, Osama, come into the twenty-first century, why don't you.'
'Duh! I'm still pissed off at centuries fifteen through twenty.'
A silence descends upon the cave, till the youngster reproachfully asks,
'Shall I smash the computer and add Bill Gates' name to the list?'
'No no,' a distracted Osama says. 'See what kind of warranty they come
with, then put in a bid.'
Osama wanders off shaking his head with an incredulous smile. 'We've
left Bill Gates off the list?'

In amongst the company information sheets, the adverts and product columns on PostOffer sits an entry from Bangladesh, HN Associates are advertising for offers for a Bangladeshi government tender. 'We are looking for Intelligence/Security Equipment for Police' reads the page, which goes on to list the items they require. The list starts like a run-of-the-mill police and security catalogue:

Cordon tape with stand – 10 units
Vehicle-mounted search/flashlight – 10 units
CCTV with 8 cameras – 10 units

It all looks like reasonably bog-standard equipment for a defence service, until you get to Item 17: Interrogation face light – 08 units

Hey, wait a minute … interrogation face light … they must mean those angle-poise lamps that TV police use. A darkened room, a sweaty suspect on a chair and a fat cop in shirt sleeves who suddenly points the lamp into the suspect's face and shouts, 'Just give me the names!'

Item 18: Interrogation foot heater (digital control) – 08 units
Item 19: Interrogation chair with accessories – 08 units
Item 20: Interrogation hanger (remote control) – 08 units

In the middle of an international business-supply website, in the full glare of the worldwide web, HN Associates are offering companies the chance to tender for torture equipment. Tucked away between sump pumps and fridge freezers is a chance to supply an 'interrogation foot heater'. OK, so most of us don't actually know what an 'interrogation foot heater' is, but it sounds like something Joseph Mengele would design should he ever be employed by Argos. Logic dictates that if someone wants to create an interrogation room, they are not going to want a device that will soothe and massage away the aches and pains of the day with a relaxing foot heater. If they did, then surely it features in Amnesty reports, with nameless victims giving testimony, 'I was dragged from my bed at gunpoint, taken to a spa and forcibly invigorated with aromatic oils before being dumped blindfolded in an alleyway.'

The chairman of HN Associates is listed as Mr Chowdhury. I phoned him posing as a potential supplier. His English is good and he turned out to be polite but slightly nervous, which confused me. I would have thought that someone advertising a request for torture equipment on the web would be fairly blasé about the whole thing. I expected a bored secretary to answer the phone, with a professionally cheerful voice full of sibilant s's and elongated o's: 'Hello, HN Associates, torture tools without the torturous delay, how can I help you?'

Mr Chowdhury informed me that the foot heaters are for Bangladeshi Defence Forces Intelligence (DFI) and are to have a digital control and a temperature range from 20 degrees C to 200 degrees C. If you can think of a logical reason as to why the Bangladeshi DFI would want a foot heater with that temperature range, in an interrogation room that does not involve torture, please feel free to email me*. Though, please remember Bangladesh isn't noted for its cold weather and lack of footware.

Out of a sense of fairness I feel compelled to mention that the Bangladeshi DFI are not total bastards, as the specification for the foot heater states, 'While heating, NO INJURY or NO BURN should occur', so employee health and safety are clearly uppermost in their minds. It is that kind of care for their torturers that must make DFI such an enjoyable and rewarding place to work. They probably have a sign up in the interrogation chamber, probably above the interrogation chair, that reads: 'Days lost to work-related accidents – nil'.

Mr Chowdhury also felt the urge to state that as the tenders are 'pure government purchase', it was important to note that the tendering

---

* Mark can be contacted at mthomas@likeineedyourfuckingapprobation.co.uk

process would 'be followed by World Bank-prescribed purchase procedure through international tender.' Which seems to mean that the contract will be put out to open competitive tender, as a closed tender process could invite corruption or nepotism. This means that Bangladesh is ethically sourcing its torture equipment.

The important point here is that any British citizen could manufacture, sell or broker these 'foot heaters' perfectly legally. Foot heaters are not on the Military List. So they don't need a licence. A catch-all clause for torture equipment would make anyone thinking of supplying the order to report it to the state, who could decide if it was for torture or not. And act accordingly.

13

FAIR COP

CHAPTER THIRTEEN

A chapter in which the author is escorted around the DSEI arms fair by a military minder while being wanted by the police. Discovers illegal electro-shock equipment on offer at the fair and is protested at.

WE'RE GOING TO THE FAIR

As I get older time seems to go by quicker – except for when I am watching anything on the TV with Ross Kemp in it. So paradoxically the biannual arms fair comes around faster than it takes a single episode of *Ultimate Force* to finish.

From cooking with Quorn to anal sex, the motivation for human enquiry is frequently a potent mixture of curiosity and devilment. Indeed, the aforementioned acts are often preceded by the thought: I wonder what would happen if I did this? It was curiosity and devilment that made me apply for a press pass to the 2005 London arms fair. Instead of ambushing buses full of arms dealers, I could enter the fair legitimately. Visiting company stalls, picking up brochures and chewing the fat with arms dealers might not seem as adventurous as abseiling into the fair with a bunch of hairy anarchos dressed as a dove of peace or indeed charging at doors as a penis, but it avoids court and you never know what might happen. From the organisers' point of view, you don't need to be a rocket scientist to work out that my presence at a British arms fair is only marginally more desirable than that of Tony Martin, the burglar-murdering farmer. Personally, I can think of few better images for DSEI than Tony Martin wandering around the guns stalls while trade journalists shout, 'Seen anything you like, Mr Martin?' and 'Oy! That bloke just nicked your wallet!' But you can see why the DSEI organisers, Reed Exhibitions Ltd, might get a tad upset at that prospect. So I am perplexed when the reply arrives from the organisers saying my press pass has been cleared and that they look forward to seeing me. In fact my exact thoughts were: are they fucking me about?

The publishers Ebury Press double-check the press pass, I double-check the press pass, we triple confirm it and basically do everything to ensure I will get in short of taking hostages. Everything is fine. Though there will be no women with garlands to greet me, they will not deploy fat-dad mines at the entrance either.

The driverless train of the Docklands Light Railway clatters as its path cuts a concrete line through the air over the heads of East London. Dull pillars made duller with graffiti prop the structure that winds like the Thames it follows. Over shawls, scarves and a sea of baseball hats, the carriages with the pre-recorded announcements carry the men of the arms trade, thousands of them, to the London arms fair. The company reps, the multinational men, the traders, experts, clients, national delegations, government men, sales departments, design teams, brokers and trade press all thundering to the fair on a driverless train, blissfully unaware that they are travelling on such an obvious and blunt metaphor.

The ExCeL Centre with its three capital letters, like pop stars with only one name, should always provoke a weary response. It smacks of 1980s advertising agencies and the kind of pretension that doesn't easily exist outside of cocaine habits and prog rock. The eXcEl* Centre even has its own stop on the Docklands Light Railway: 'Custom House for ExCEl' says the sign. Visitors simply get off the train, skip up the stairs, over the bridge and straight onto the concourse for the centre.

---

* Well, they started it.

Police in luminous jerkins are all over the area like a glow in the dark rash. The visitor assistants look gauche by comparison, they look poorly paid and are forced to wear bluish-black chauffeur outfits with peaked hats. They look like gay Thunderbirds puppets. They look bored.

ANGUS

After a three-hour delay at security I am escorted into the arms fair to meet my minder. The deal is this: I am allowed into the arms fair but I am to have an 'escort' with me at all times. My escort is Angus Taverner, ex-army officer, now working in 'crisis media management' with his own company, Perdix Communications Ltd. He is also a recently promoted colonel in the Territorial Army. Angus is a Sandhurst-meets-the-Soviets type of minder. He is a stocky chap, with a pudding face and a balding blond hairline. His accent is typically army officer: Home Counties but prone to the odd bout of Ealing comedy cockney phrases, 'Not 'arf' or 'Ruddy lingo'. It is a curious mix of posh meets 1970s Radio 1 DJ. As for his dress sense, and I speak as a man who has none himself, Angus could wear a tutu and a pink jockstrap and he would still manage to look like an army chap in civvies. He is ultimately an entirely pleasant man whose job it is to follow me everywhere. 'I need the loo; you'll have to excuse me,' I say at one point.

'Good idea. I'll come too.'

And off we trot, the minder and the minded.

The press day takes place twenty-four hours before DSEI opens its doors to the punters, so the companies are still finishing putting up their stalls. Workmen wheel trolleys loaded with pot plants to various destinations, saws buzz and hammers nail, signs are raised, displays are polished and wooden crates dot the exhibition floor. An atmosphere of genial panic prevails. Angus gives me a guided tour nonetheless. The EXCeL Centre is a massive hangar divided into two sections by a central corridor that is lined with coffee shops, snack bars and the odd restaurant; the designer must have spent a lot of time in airport food halls, for it lacks none of their charms. Angus and I wander in and out of the two halls, meander along the docks and the parked-up warships, and bump into an old friend of his, a woman army-type.

'Hi, Angus. Congratulations on the promotion.'

'Thanks. Yes, it is rather good.'

'What are you doing here? I thought you were doing crisis media.'

'Yes, I am. Meet the crisis,' he says, motioning to me.

'Pleased to meet you,' I say, shaking hands and smiling perfunctorily, before heading off.

Two days later, the fair is in full swing and packed to the gunnels, mainly with middle-aged men in suits and ID badges hanging on bits of chain with the sponsor's name printed over them. The media centre is a big glass box in the middle of the central concourse. An escalator leads to a separate coffee bar for journos, who can sup filter Java while filing reports from a row of computer terminals, or casually network over one of the corporate wooden tables that are fixed to the floor with a single metal pole like a giant mushroom, or they can while away the time glancing down at the throng below. The fair's organiser wanders over as I chat to Angus.

'Glad to have you here.' He beams professionally. 'Hope you're not going to kidnap anyone this year.' His entourage and colleagues laugh along with him, presumably in reference to the BAE Systems bus escapade.

'I hardly think I kidnapped anyone,' I meekly reply.

His booming voice blusters back: 'What else could you call it?' and he disappears into the bosom of the hubbub.

For some bizarre reason, which I still have not yet deduced,

Angus and I get talking about the miners' strike over a cup of coffee. Turning to me with the utmost sincerity he says: 'I don't know too much about working-class life.' He muses on as he holds his cup and saucer: 'Nor indeed life up north generally.' Has my jaw dropped, because I am tasting carpet? 'But I will tell you this,' he continues, as I wait with an anticipation that is not disappointed. He voice almost takes on an emotional quiver as he declares, as if pledging an allegiance: '*Brassed Off*! Bloody good film!' He cocks his head and sips his coffee. 'Bloody good film.'

And to my utter amazement I find myself actually enjoying his company.

'You probably think I'm posh and thick,' he says, catching me unawares with an honesty that was without rancour.

'No, not at all,' I lie.

'It is true I don't know much of working-class life. But,' he continues, 'many of the soldiers who served under me came from that sort of background and there's not many men can boast that they have shared their sleeping bag with a miner's son from Durham.' This leaves me with a strange feeling of amiability towards Angus, and it is time to start perusing the fair.

Arms dealers have little love for the press. Though it is fair to say their critical analysis is not from a Noam Chomsky perspective. No, they don't like the press because the press has a tendency to write about what they get up to. The fair's organisers, Reed Exhibitions Ltd, are not too keen on critical press either. They are keen to point up the legitimate nature of the event: there are no electro-shock weapons being sold, no cluster bombs are on offer. 'Not because they [the cluster bombs] are illegal,' I am told. 'It is a matter of being aware of sensibilities.' This is the 'high-tech end of the market', the organisers' mantra runs; this is all legitimate. So it all goes a bit Tessa Jowell when Denel, the South African arms company, gets a visit from an undercover reporter, who asks them if they can supply cluster bombs, gets a positive reply and then writes about it in the

Independent. I visited their stall later that day to ask them about the article only to encounter a furious Boer, gutturally denouncing the media in general. 'What I find disgusting is that he lied to me!' he says in an accent that I am more used to hearing denouncing the black right to vote. 'He said he was from the Pakistan military. He hid his journalist pass from me!'

'Were you offering cluster bombs?'

'Anti-vehicle cluster bombs! Anti-vehicle!' As if this distinction between anti-vehicle and anti-personnel is of great importance. 'And he lied to me!' continues the large, red-faced Afrikaner.

'Well, your marketing director just told me that whereas most cluster bombs have a failure rate of 10–15 per cent, turning the unexploded munitions into de facto mines, Denel's cluster bombs have a 100 per cent explosion rate. None of your munitions fails to explode. Is that true or is that a lie?'

'That is just marketing! Marketing! This was …' He trails off and tells me to 'sort out your own problems; who is it that is dropping cluster bombs, aye?', referring to Tony Blair and the British military in Afghanistan.

So it is safe to say that arms dealers do not like people walking around filming them, and the DSEI organisers are not too keen on random TV folk pointing cameras at missiles the size of bungalows either. Up in the press centre I casually ask Angus if it is all right if I film with my camcorder.

'What for?' he snaps, peering at me in the wonderful way that military types do, in the belief that if they stare long enough into the windows of your soul the truth will reveal itself to them.

'Well, it is for the book.'

'What do you mean?'

'It is so I can record everything and when I come to writing the descriptions for the book I can make sure I am pinpoint accurate, with no room for error and 100 per cent on target,' I burble, hoping that the vaguely forces jargon will resonate with him.

He peers into my eyes, waiting for the truth to rise from the depths and make itself known to him, then suddenly smiles and bluffly says: 'Bloody good idea.' Then changes his tone to work mode. 'Now, what do you want to do? How long do you think you'll need because there is something I would like to attend at two o'clock if I can.'

'I don't know, but look, if you want to go off later and do something, you can leave me and I will behave myself. It's not as if I am going to let off a smoke grenade.'

Without the slightest hesitation Angus snaps back: 'I'd knock you out if you did!'

'Er … have you been in PR long?'

'I'm just telling you what the situation is.'

China, Pakistan and a free grenade

'There's the Chinese delegation,' he nods as I film away. Angus fantastically either assumes I know nothing, which is reasonable enough, or has just gone into autopilot mode and believes he is giving me a guided tour rather than minding me. The half-dozen or so officials all in their military finery are being led around by a British Honour Guard, one of those chaps with a highly polished stick with tasselled cord wrapped round it and a shiny metal knob, probably with a motto in Latin meaning *Who Dares Wins* or *Fuck This For A Game of Soldiers*. It is a little odd seeing the undemocratic, Tibet-occupying, human-rights-abusing, torturing state that is the People's Republic of China being led around an arms fair in Britain, especially when the UK observes a European arms embargo on this particular dictatorship of the proletariat. The message here seems to be: 'We won't sell you guns, but let me introduce you to a man who will.'

Angus continues in tour-guide mode as we approach the display area of the Pakistan Ordnance Factory (POF), the people who offered me a chance to become their agent in Zimbabwe back in Chapter Three. Their company logo has the 'O' in POF with a set of crosshairs through it, like sniper sights.

The POF stall is a bunch of revolving tables at varying heights from the floor, set with display models of machine guns, sub-machine guns, pistols, bombs, rockets and ammunition. As I watch this silent array of weapons revolving under the lamplight, I have the violent urge to play 'The Girl From Ipanema' on a Casio organ.

'Hi.' I grin at the salesman, who looks distressed at the sight of the camcorder. He points to it and says, 'Excuse me.'

'Hello there, no trouble, Angus Taverner.' Angus has jumped in with clipped staccato delivery. 'MoD pass, official escort, this is Mark Thomas, writing a book, permission to film!'

'Ah … ah … welcome, hello,' stammers the sales chap.

'What are these?' I ask, pointing the camera at the salesman and at a set of display hand grenades, mortars and smoke canisters, all done in cut-away-model style to show the inner workings.

'Hand grenades,' he says sheepishly, trying to avoid the camera.

Angus jumps straight in with schoolboy enthusiasm. 'But if you look here you can see the ball bearings this thing throws out,' he says, pointing to them in the model. 'It can do some incredible damage.'

'How far does it kill people, you know, what range has it got?'

'Er …' The salesman from POF is unsure how to answer – after all, how do you politely describe the killing ability of one of your grenades – but Angus is in full flow: 'Generally accepted it's got a lethal range of about ten metres.' Angus gushes facts and statistics like a fan. 'This RPG [rocket-propelled grenade launcher] basically fires a grenade,' he continues, moving to another table. 'This one is AP, anti-personnel, so it fires the grenade into people. Again you can see the ball bearings. The yellow bit – ' he points to the inside of the model – 'is the explosive charge. This other one is anti-tank.' Then he steps back with a huge smile on his face, like he has just completed a task with aplomb in front of a superior officer.

As we tour the corridors and booths, the large displays and

TV screens, Angus is marvellously helpful, introducing me to people and explaining the workings of guns. In the middle of the fair, when both of us have been trekking around it for hours and are burdened down with brochures, he turns to me with a serious face and says, 'Smoothie?'

'What?'

'Smoothie. Mango. Pineapple. Crushed ice. On me?' And then disappears to find juiced fruit to quench our thirsts.

Angus's friendliness only serves to punctuate the surreal quality of the fair. We pace the blue carpets, the stalls forming alleyways like a bazaar. Heckler & Koch, the German company, have their guns mounted on boards as if they were display tools in a DIY shop. In the middle of their stall is a bar. Surrounded by guns, a group of four middle-aged businessmen, who are greying or balding or both, sit quaffing lagers from tall glasses. The Germanic message of 'Get pissed and buy guns', like the Pakistanis' anti-personnel grenade launcher, seems at odds with the organisers' message that this is 'high tech'.

I pop in for a chat with the folk from FN Herstal, the Belgian company whose P90 state-of-the-art Gucci sub-machine guns, which are sold only to security forces like the US presidential guard, ended up in the coke dealer's hands back in Chapter One.

'What can we do?' says the salesman in by far the nicest suit in the place. 'We do try to control it [the guns] but no one can have complete control.'

'How much would it cost on the black market?'

'It retails at about 1,000 US dollars.'

'So?'

'So ... wait a minute while I work this out.' He starts to do the sums in his head, muttering occasionally before he arrives at the conclusion. 'On the black market about £4,000. But this is really a show-gun for the criminals.'

On we tour, trekking through the landscape. Everything in this weird world is for sale, from Cruise missiles to a Camelback water container. We go past Mick Ranger's stall for Imperial Defence Services Ltd, displaying an AK47 and some pistols. Past a laser-gun company who run simulators. They show a street of white houses, low power cables and telephone wires slung between them, badly built slums dotted with palm trees, while huge computer-generated armoured cars traverse the scene. In front of this stand grown men in corporate fleeces that don't quite hide the years of business lunches, blasting away with laser rifles. They could be in a Butlin's arcade rather than an arms fair. We go past the female models wearing short skirts, proffering bowls of sweets while leaning in the vicinity of machine-gun mountings. Past the missiles, past the tanks, Humvees, computer graphics and illuminated signs, we trek on, Angus and I, sampling the mints and chocolates that are placed in bowls on the dealers' front desks.

'We're running a competition,' says Angus to one stallholder, 'to see who has got the best sweets.' Few would contemplate such a competition but, bless him, Angus has. In the middle of a display for the infinite capacity to harm, Angus looks for the best chocolate. I succumb to the free gift experiences of the fair, the winner being a Canadian company called General Kinetics Engineering Corp who make hydro-pneumatic suspensions and shock absorbers.

'What is that?' I gasp at their stall.

'It's free.'

'Can I take one?'

'Of course.'

'But what is it?'

'It is for stress relief. An executive stress-relief toy.'

It is a squeezy hand grenade made of foam. Some high-powered executive has this on his desk and when the pressure mounts he reaches for the green-foam hand grenade and squeezes until the tension goes away. If only Peter Sutcliffe had had one of these.

'Can I take a few of them for the kids?'

'Of course,' say the nice Canadians, who then very politely inform me that I might like to listen to a short pitch about their products. I can't remember a thing about it but I still have the squeezy hand grenade.

Suspect H

Unknown to me at the time, the police had included my photograph in their 'spotter cards'. These laminated cards are about half A5 size and contain mini passport photos of twenty-four anti-arms-trade activists. We are meant to be the real hardcore troublemakers and the cards enable the police to make quick checks to see if any of us are about the place so they can take the appropriate action. The top of the card reads: '13/09/2005 DSEI … CO11 PUBLIC ORDER INTELLIGENCE UNIT … THIS CARD MUST BE DESTROYED AS CONFIDENTIAL WASTE AT THE CONCLUSION OF THIS EVENT'. Underneath the photos it has the words: 'Police eyes only – do not copy'. Friends of mine also featured called them cop bingo cards; they thought the cops might cross us off and get a prize.

The people on the cards are lettered from A to X. I am Suspect H. I phoned my agent and friend Ed to tell him. He was furious. 'Next year I'll get you top billing. You'll be suspect A!'

One of these cards was found by a friend, passed to me and now is framed on my study wall. At the time, however, I knew nothing of this, though it might help explain one incident.

On the press day, as Angus and I had taken a stroll along the dock, we passed some wire fencing there to keep protestors out, and a police officer had shouted from behind it.

'Oy!'

I ignored it. Angus's head was swivelling in every direction.

'Mr Thomas!'

'I think that's for you,' said my minder.

I ambled over to the fence. 'Hi there, what can I do for you, officer?'

'What are you doing in here?' The question was asked with a big smile and a degree of astonishment.

'You shouldn't be in there,' said another officer, holding onto the fence from its other side. I had the feeling I was about to be interrogated and possibly kicked out, when I heard: 'Angus Taverner, official pass, I'm Mr Thomas's escort.'

'Everything seems to be under control,' smiled the officer, raising his hands in a gesture that indicated he had no more to say. 'He's all yours.'

'What did he mean by that?' said Angus as we turned our backs on the police and walked away. I was about to say I have no idea, when an officer called out, 'Be gentle on him, Mark.'

FINDING TORTURE EQUIPMENT AT THE HIGH-TECH ARMS FAIR – STUN GUNS

A stun baton is basically a battery-operated plastic stick that has a handle at one end and discharges high voltages of electricity at the other. A stun gun is a smaller, more compact version. You can even get ones that look like mobile phones. After the craze of Happy Slappy, where young thugs hit complete strangers while their friends filmed the event on their mobile phones, we should all be grateful that stun weapons are banned in the UK. Few would relish the prospect of Funny Stunny, where Nike-clad oiks randomly electrocute members of the public with a weapon looking like a phone, while their mates film it with a camera looking like a phone. These images would eventually find their way onto a website somewhere, which in turn would find their way into the pages of lads mags, like *Zoo*, *Nuts*, *Twatz*, *City Whizz Wank Lad* or whatever.

The good and fine folk of our kingdom have a relatively benign perception of electro-shock weapons. Part of the reason for this might be that UK police forces use the taser: a gun that fires a dart attached to two wires. The dart hits the victim/ suspect and the electric charge goes down the wires, incapacitating and temporarily paralysing the person on the other end of it. There is a reasonable argument for the use of tasers, as an alternative to shooting someone.

However, there is a world of difference between that scenario and an interrogation room in an Egyptian jail or police station, where the use of electro-shock is routine and systematic. This fact is recognised by the UK government and the European Union. Electro-shock batons, guns, tasers and belts are classified by the UK government as weapons and are included on Robin Cook's torture list and therefore 'restricted'. Illegally selling electro-shock weapons carries the same jail sentence as illegally flogging rocket-propelled grenade launchers.

Amnesty International describes the stun baton as 'the universal tool of the torturer'. It is cheap, relatively easy to purchase and highly effective at inducing extreme amounts of pain. The batons tend to turn up in prison cells and have a habit of discharging in the vicinity of the softer parts of a prisoner's body.

Shake your law-maker

Many in the UK still do not know that it is illegal to possess a stun gun or baton in Britain without a Section Five Firearms Licence. I have met taxi drivers who have 'mates' who have one in the cab, 'in case it gets a bit lively, kno' worra mean?' A very liberal friend was shocked when I explained that the stun guns her parents had recently thrown out should have been handed in at a police station. 'Illegal! You're shitting me!' was her North London Jewish reaction. 'Oh, thank God she threw them out. Originally my mum was going to take them down to the Help the Aged shop with a load of old books and videos. Shit. She didn't know they were illegal. She called her stun gun Frank … after the American musician.'

'What?'

'Zappa.'

To be fair, the UK police haven't led the way in awareness either. This is how seriously the authorities took the brand-new export controls on torture equipment and brokerage. The very first person to break this law was an ex-cop who sells tasers to the UK police and he did it at the Association of Chief of Police Officers' conference. Peter Boatman is that former police officer, and director of Pro-Tect Systems, the company that sells the M26 taser. He says the tasers are safe if used correctly and to prove a point he claims to have given a five-second burst from a taser to his wife. That's got to be a wedding anniversary she'll not forget in a hurry. Mr Boatman was quoted as saying, 'My wife works for the company ... She volunteered to do it because she felt she needed to do it for the good of the company.' A valuable lesson that everyone should learn: this is what happens when you sleep with the boss.

However, Boatman was exhibiting at the Association of Chief of Police Officers' show, called the International Police Conference and Exhibition, from 11 to 13 May 2004 in Birmingham, just after the new laws came into force (May 2004). He should have been one of the first people in Britain to get a trade licence to promote electro-shock weapons. In answer to a Parliamentary question though, the DTI said 'no licence applications were received for the ACPO exhibition in May 2004 so none were issued'. Mr Boatman chatted to me from his car by phone and confirmed he had not got a licence but he explained, 'You have to apply for and book the show and make all the arrangements six months prior to the show, don't you?'

'I don't know – if you tell me it's true, that's fine,' I had replied.

'Well, it is between three and six months that you apply for it. At that stage there was no legislation that said you have to have a licence to go to that show.'

Being stupid and untrustworthy I asked the DTI if this was true; they said that Mr Boatman was talking utter bollocks and should know better for a former police officer ... all right, they didn't exactly say that. What they said: 'That Boatman is a ropey fucker and no mistake.' ... Oh all right, they didn't say that either. What they really, truly and actually said was: 'No company exhibiting restricted products [tasers] or advertising to promote the supply of such goods is exempt on the grounds that they had organised their presence at an event prior to 1 May 2004. This is irrelevant.' The DTI kindly explained further that there is in fact an 'implementation period of six months (from October 2003) so, effectively, this is a six months' notice period.' Which would be about the time Mr Boatman arranged to exhibit at the Association of Chief of Police Officers. So they sort of did say he was talking bollocks.

This leaves us with the government's vaunted new export control laws broken within eleven days of them becoming law, at a police conference, by an ex-cop.

Under the counter at the fair

The DSEI organisers were keen to stress how above board and high tech their arms fair was and their PR offensive appeared to have paid off in at least one paper, the *Daily Telegraph*, which ran a piece about the fair's PR makeover. Considering the *Telegraph*'s readership legendarily consists of retired colonels, it would be a strange day when an arms fair couldn't count on them to give them a good review. 'It is all very different from the bad old days when electric-shock batons were quietly flogged to men in sunglasses from repressive Third World regimes,' it wrote. Unfortunately, the *Telegraph* didn't try that old journalistic technique of actually looking for them because, lo and behold, they were there. Offered by three companies directly. The 'torturer's tool of choice', as Amnesty describes them, are cheap, easy to use and cause a lot of pain, and are available at a British arms fair.

Firstly, Imperial Armour, a South African company, whom I contacted before the fair asking for a quote for stun batons. They were happy to oblige. A riot stun baton would cost 77.09 euros plus freight. Imperial Armour were keen to meet to discuss a deal at the fair, offering to set up meetings with the managing director. The company might not have advertised electro-shock weapons at the fair, but the torture equipment was available under the counter.

The second company was TAR Ideal Concepts. Wandering past their stall with Angus, Suspect H – the comedian on the police's spotter card – stopped to pick up a brochure. In the middle of the fair, TAR Ideal were offering stun batons and leg irons, both classified as torture equipment and 'restricted goods'. You cannot even advertise the stuff without a licence. Suspect H picked up the brochure entitled *Riot Control – equipment and training*, opened it and uttered the phrase, 'Fucking hell.'

'What's up?' says Angus.

'That is very fucking naughty, that should not be there.'

'What?

'Torture equipment, electro-shock batons.'

'It's not illegal, is it?'

'It most definitely is.'

'Right then, I better take a brochure and report this to the organisers.'

Angus reminds me of those brown and white retrievers you see charging around the Cotswolds, forever returning sticks to women in Barbour jackets and headscarves. He is virtually impossible to dislike and I imagine him standing proudly to attention under a regimental motto carved into a wooden shield: *Always Loyal*. We sit next to each other and share a final juice in the concourse by a massive inflatable tank. It looks like it is to scale, too. 'It's a decoy,' he explains seriously, as if all that kept the Commie hordes from pouring through Germany were inflatable tanks blown up and dotted around the countryside.

As we walk out of the ExCeL Centre to say goodbye, a chant of 'Murderers!' goes up from the other side of the docks, where protestors, probably people I know, people named after cartoon characters and animals, have got on the megaphone. 'Murdering scum!' someone shouts and then the chant goes: 'Scum! Scum! Scum! Scum!'

'This is a first for me,' I tell Angus. 'I've never been protested at before.'

'Well, they have a perfect right to protest,' he formally announces.

'Scum! Scum! Scum! Scum!' But Angus is not scum. He was a soldier, and if being a soldier in the British army makes someone 'scum', then why do we mourn each soldier's death in Iraq? There are differences and they matter. They matter enormously. If Angus has beaten Iraqi prisoners, would he be scum? Probably. If he had been killed in Sierra Leone, where he served, would he be scum? Probably not. There are people in the arms fair I would not hesitate to call scum, but Angus isn't one of them.

Arms dealers are not ethical beings. At best they stay within the law and at best that law is half baked. 'Isn't it right, though,' they will say in their defence, 'that countries like Liberia have armed police forces to bring stability after years of war and warlords?' To which the answer has to be yes. It would be immoral to ask countries to achieve stability in those situations and not arm them. What do we think the authorities should use to control bandits and rampaging armies? Peer pressure and the naughty step? I think not. However, the very dealers who would arm a police force seeking to establish order and calm in post-conflict situations would also arm a hundred other people who would create conflict. Arms dealers would arm murderous thugs and barbarians in an instant. It is what they do. Would this make them 'scum'? Equally, the answer has to be yes.

We shake hands, I board the train, carrying brochures and pamphlets and free pens and bags. My eyes sting with tiredness as I dangle from the hand rail and I can barely smile when an announcer informs us that we should change trains due to protestors preventing the smooth running of the service. Then someone, possibly an arms dealer or a delegate to the fair, leans over to me and says, 'Best take your ID and chain off.' He is alluding to the possibility that the DSEI ID will identify me to protestors on the train, who may have a go at me. Whether this threat is real or imagined, it is a friendly gesture.

It is a relief to get back on the more familiar territory of the London Underground, surrounded by iPods and discarded copies of the free paper, *Metro*. In my slightly exhausted state I bump into some family friends. Standing at the end of the carriage by the open window, Sal asks me: 'Where have you been in your suit?'

'Arms fair,' I half shout over the clatter.

'Is that where you got all this clobber?' she asks.

'Yeah – you'll never guess what they were giving away as a free gift.'

'Surprise me,' she says, and I pull the squeezy grenade out of the bag and hold it up in the carriage.

'Put that away right now!' she hisses urgently.

Innocently I begin to explain: 'It is an anti-stress toy—'

'Not on the London Underground it fucking isn't.'

'It's just foam.'

'We've just left Stockwell station, the police shot people round here, put it away, Mark. Thank you.'

SPRAY 'N' STUN

The foam hand grenade sat on my desk ready for some stress-relief work when Suspect H phoned TAR Ideal Concepts the next day. The Israeli company offered stun guns, batons and leg irons at the fair, which in terms of torture equipment and UK law is pretty much a royal flush. Suspect H doubted it could get much worse, but one thing H has learnt from the arms industry is never underestimate the depths to which human endeavours can sink. Indeed, Suspect H remains convinced that some of these people were not raised on Dr Seuss but a kind of pre-school Hieronymus Bosch. A is for Amputee, B is for Boiling lead, C is for Cadaver …

I spoke to Mr Michael Simon (he was running the stall at DSEI), posing yet again as a potential client. 'We are also developing a new stun gun that may be very interesting for you to know about,' he said, before telling me that if I nipped into the stall the next day we could discuss a deal for stun weapons and he would show me a CD-Rom of a new stun.

'How is it different? Is it a baton?' I queried.

'It is not a baton,' he said proudly. 'It is a gun that shoots a kind of liquid, so it allows you to keep your distance between you and, er, the person you are shooting and treat a large number of persons at the same time.'

'That's fantastic. So this is like a multi-person taser?'

'Yes.'

'So you can hit them with the liquid, then with the charge, and they all get the shock.'

'Yes, that is correct. We are working [on it].'

I can almost hear the voiceover for the commercial: 'Why electrocute individually when you can Spray 'n' Stun?' said in that same slightly incredulous voice that says: 'Take shampoo and conditioner into the shower?' It's like Shake 'n' Vac for torturers. It's convenience torture for those with an 'on-the-go 24/7 life'.

Michael Simon continues. TAR Ideal are showing the liquid stun gun to 'all the units in Israel, to the police, to the army; we are getting a lot of people interested in that product'.

There is already far too much testimony from places like Egypt and Turkey, where entire families are tortured together, to make the prospects of TAR Ideal's new weapon anything but grim. The Israeli state actively pursues a policy of collective punishment, so showing them a weapon that brings the economies of scale to the world of torture is depressing. More often than not, those involved with what the arms trade calls 'research and development' do display considerable imagination. A more pedestrian mind would not venture to dream of a liquid electro-shock weapon.

Company number three

The more alert among you may feel some disquiet at the absence of the third company offering electro-shock at the fair. Imperial Armour and TAR Ideal Concepts Ltd being only two entities. Company number three is Global Armour, also from South Africa. This is how they were found ...

On Friday morning, the last day of the arms fair, the *Guardian* published my story of the torture equipment on offer. The *Guardian* named TAR Ideal but not the other company, and only mentioned a 'South African company' being involved. The fair organisers rush round to the South African stalls, searching for evidence of a company offering electro-shock, and find yet another company – Global Armour, who offer stun batons. The organisers promptly throw TAR Ideal and Global Armour out of the fair, shut their stalls down and Her Majesty's Revenue and Customs take immediate and swift action ... they write a warning letter.*

---

* HMRC gave evidence in May 2006 at the Quadripartite Select Committee, pointing out that their investigations are intelligence led and that their major focus at the fair was monitoring the armoury itself, as well as ensuring the correct paperwork for UAV and long-range missiles was in place.

14

MR LEE AND THE LAW

CHAPTER FOURTEEN

A chapter in which there are more tales
of adventures in the world of electro-shockery.

THE PLAYBILL OF PLAYERS

❏ **Mr Tony Lee** Merchant in electro-shockery
❏ **A founder member of Genesis** As himself
❏ **Mr Mark Thomas** Humble narrator and egotist
❏ **Mr Osman Kilic** Kurdish journalist/alter ego of Mark
  Thomas
❏ **Mr Robert Mugabe** Dictator and homophobe
❏ **Men In Black (MIB)** A better acronym than film; also the
  name given to anonymous informants on the arms industry
❏ **Assorted stun batons** Weapons and walk-on cast

THE BEAUTIFUL SOUTH

It was in December 2004 when one of the founding members of
super-group Genesis helped me finalise a transhipment of electro-
shock batons to Zimbabwe before I headed off to the local
primary-school winter fair. Frankly, after that opening line the
second sentence was always bound to be a bit of a disappointment, but it does contain the important point that the above
facts are true. This is the convoluted story of how a prog-rock
hero, not content with creating late-1960s guitar licks that
shaped the plinth upon which Peter Gabriel stood, also helped
expose a British arms dealer in electro-shock batons.

'Which member of Genesis was it?'

Aha, my pretties, you must wait for that jewel. For the time being content yourself in the knowledge that the Genesis founder in question is not Phil Collins. All Phil can do is look on with shame in his heart, knowing that his glories are but transient baubles given by fools. Knowing that his only contribution to the arms trade debate is to provide a reasonable excuse for gun control to be liberalised. By which I mean, whenever I have heard a Phil Collins song played in a public place I have also heard numerous people say: 'Wouldn't you love to shoot that bastard?' Especially when 'In The Air Tonight' was riding the charts like a tuppenny harlot.

Before I tell what happened, let me point out exactly where it happened. None of this occurred in London. I do not live in London, I live in South London. South London is different, a warm melting pot where anyone can become a bona fide South Londoner by virtue of two things. One: living in South London, and two: having no aspiration to live in the Cotswolds. Anyone who is waiting for their husband's wallet-busting bonus to come through from a deal in the City before heading out and converting a barn, can just load their jeep with Labradors and leave now. Everyone else is welcome to experience the thrill of crossing the Thames on a summer's day when the bright light slaps the water and the glare makes your eyes squint with joy, knowing you're back home in the deepest south of London. For some of us, the Ealing comedy *Passport to Pimlico*, filmed in Stockwell, where a London community tries to claim statehood and cede from London, isn't a story, it's a documentary.

The phone rings on a winter afternoon in South London. It is one of the Men In Black. This particular MIB sounds like ex-PM John Major recovering from a cold.

'You near a 'puter?'

'Yeah.'

'Get on the web and have a look at this cheeky bastard.

WWW dot TLT international dot com forward slash stun under-score gun dot HTM. Found it?'

'Blimey.'

'Oh yes.'

The Man In Black is online too, so we can look at the same information and tut simultaneously. In front of us is the sales site for one type of stun baton and four types of stun guns. And this site is run from Britain; more than that, the company TLT International is based in South London, in Brockley, a few miles from where I live. I am shocked into silence.

'Mark? ... Mark ... you still there?'

'I ... I ... I mean North London you expect this kind of thing, but not Brockley ...'

'Arms-dealers-work-in-South-London shock. Get over yourself.'

The electro-shock equipment sits on the same page as some incongruous advertising for aviation headsets. It could be a pilot's catalogue but with stun batons. It's like Stelios had gone mad and invented EasyTorture. 'No waiting around for check-ins, just turn up and torture.'

My MIB cuts in. 'The weapons look like they are made in Korea.'

'The same place they make the American flags.'

'Same country, different factory.'

'It says at the top of the page: "This is a manufacturer's outlet, please make enquiries Only [sic] by Bulk [sic] purchasing."'

'The company seems to be run by Tony Lee.'

'But he is openly doing this on the web. Anyone can see it. A cop could see it, a journo, a peacenik, anyone with a pilot's licence browsing for a new set of aviation earphones. Why is he so stupid?'

'Dropped on the head at birth? I don't know.'

Mr Lee's first order

I intended to write in the *New Statesman* about Mr Lee advertising the stun batons. As the law says no person shall do any act calculated to promote the supply and delivery of stun batons without a licence, it looked like Mr Lee was breaking the law just by advertising them. After all, what is the intention of advertising if not to promote a sale?

It was a guess that a man operating out of Brockley flogging stun batons on the net wouldn't have a licence to broker a restricted weapon. (A guess that proved to be accurate.) But between writing the article and its publication, it struck me that Mr Lee had a small section on his website, as most do, with the words 'contact us'. It suddenly seemed rude not to. So together with a Kurdish friend and colleague, Osman Kilic, who lives and works in Belgium, we set up yet another front company, and posing as potential clients emailed Mr Lee from Belgium. We asked if he could provide a quote to ship to East Africa. He replied:

December 2004

I thank you for your above-referenced enquiry and have pleasure in submitting our offer as follows:

❑ Stun Baton 18' w/ring belt clip.300KV
❑ Power Source: Two 9 Volt Alkaline Battery or N.c. Rechargeable Battery
❑ Power Emit: 300,000 Volt Output
❑ Electrodes distance: 20mm
❑ DIMENSION: 18' x 1.57'
❑ OPTION: HOLSTER
❑ Packing: Per Unit in a carton box. 30pcs G.W 15.60 kgs
❑ Price term: Fob S. Korea US$29.10 each Q'ty 500 Total Fob S.Korea US$14,550.00
❑ Warranty: 1 year
❑ Delivery: within 2 weeks after receipt of payment

❏ Payment terms: T/T advanced [sic] 30 per cent with order, the balance just before shipment

I would very much like to secure your order. Should you have any questions regarding price, delivery or anything else, please do not hesiate [sic] to contact me.

Best regards

Tony Lee

So Mr Lee quoted US$29.10 for a stun baton, under £20, which seems very cheap. It's the kind of price that you see for X-ray specs at the back of *Marvel* comics. The batons can come with a holster, which must be for the torturer's image. After all, an interrogator doesn't want to start work by pulling an electro-shock baton out of a Lidl supermarket bag – it just looks unpro-fessional, some might even say tacky. Importantly, the batons come with a year's warranty, and unlike Curry's Mr Lee doesn't try to sell me three years' worth of insurance as well. We later find out the batons come with a CE mark, the European Economic Area's kite-mark, so should the batons short-circuit or electro-cute the user, the torturer can sue the company for compensation.

As far as business integrity was concerned, Mr Lee was a real gent. Though I should point out that it was only after four and a half weeks of negotiations that Mr Lee sent over an email with the classic line: 'Forget to mention batteries are not included in all sales.' Well, pity the poor torturer on Christmas Day amid the strewn wrapping paper with nary a spark in his stun, all because someone forgot the batteries.

The man from Genesis

The *New Statesman* magazine has a discerning readership, which is a polite way of interpreting its circulation figures. As it tran-spired, Mr Lee was not an avid reader. Fortunately he was one of fifty-seven million seven hundred and twenty-five thousand non-*New Statesman* readers in Britain, and thus remained oblivious to the fact that he was being written about in public by the man posing as his client.

My neighbour Anthony Phillips is not a *New Statesman* reader either, so I have to explain the story to him when he answers his doorbell. Anthony was one of the founding members of Genesis. He went to Charterhouse School in Surrey, along with the other members of the band, writing and performing on the first two albums before leaving Genesis in 1970.

And so on a winter Saturday afternoon, the very day I need to attend my children's primary-school fair and record a phone conversation with Mr Lee the electro-shock salesman, I discover that every tape recorder and mini disc in my house is broken. Anthony kindly stirs from his *Times* crossword and answers his door.

'This is a bit embarrassing,' I say, looking at my shoes, which are now gently kicking his doorstep in distraction.

'Go on.'

'I need to record a phone call with an arms dealer and all my tape recorders are broken and I wondered if you had anything I could record a phone call on. Always best to have proof.'

'An arms dealer.' His eyes widen at the same time as his brow furrows.

'He is selling torture equipment.'

'Really!'

'From Brockley.'

'That's just over that way, isn't it,' he says, pointing east. 'But of course you can, come in, come in. This sounds dreadful. An arms dealer, you say – ' he wanders through the hall – 'and you want to record him and presumably catch him doing all this dreadful stuff. Gosh. Right then, let's see what we can do … come in, come in.'

The pair of us kneel facing each other on the rug in front of his cast-iron fireplace hood. Between us, in the centre of the room, sits Anthony's 1980s white telephone with speaker, over which Anthony holds the mic.

'Before we start, erm, I should explain that because the emails to Mr Lee have been sent from Belgium, Mr Lee doesn't think I am British.'

'Oh right, I see, you're going to put on an accent.'

'Yes.'

'How's your Flemish?'

'Well, Mr Lee thinks I am a man called Osman Kilic, a Kurd from Turkey, living in Belgium.'

'OK, right. A Kurdish-Turkish-Flemish accent. I won't laugh. I promise … Are you ready? Right, off you go, Osman, we're recording.'

Me, Mr Lee and Mr Mugabe

Mr Lee is in when we phone. As a Korean national living in Britain, his English is good though not perfect, but frankly neither is mine. And my Kurdish accent would cause most mammals to flinch with embarrassment. My vowels strain like a buckling ship's engine. If it were possible to mix the accents of Janet Street-Porter and Omar Sharif in a food blender, you could not produce a worse result. Between Mr Lee and myself we sound like a bad 1970s sitcom on funny foreigners.

'I should warn you the client is from Zimbabwe,' I say to him. Suggesting a destination that is not only marked for its human rights abuse but to which it is also illegal to export weapons, as there is an EU arms embargo on it enforced in law by the Trade in Controlled Goods (Embargoed Destinations) Order 2004.

'Clearly,' I intone, 'there is some problem in Britain with Zimbabwe – that should be no problem, though?'

'No problem,' says Mr Lee.

'You are happy for the goods to go there?'

'Yes, I will sort it out, you know.'

I look at Anthony, whose face is shocked and indignant.

'No, is no problem. We will ship directly from Korea, anyway.'

After finishing our pleasantries and goodbyes, I put the phone down. With that, Anthony packs away the recorder, hands me a recorded CD and says, 'Well done, it's great, you've got him recorded saying that. Outrageous really. Well done, you,' in the way a cricket captain might congratulate a really good innings. I put my finger through the hole in the CD and twirl it like a six-shooter.

'The next step,' I say, 'is to see if he will meet up.'

'What, like a real sting operation?' says one of the founders of Genesis. 'Well, I hope you get him.'

'I don't care what you do with it. I don't want to know.'
Mr Lee agrees to meet in a London hotel. He believes he is going to discuss the sale of 20,000 electro-shock batons with the chief of Zimbabwe's secret police, Mr Thachiveyi. 'They have an election coming up,' I tell Mr Lee over the phone. 'They need to make sure that these people are under control. There are thousands of police stations and secret service agents who will use these batons and need them for protection and for interrogation.'

In fact, Mr Lee is going to meet Patson Muzuwa, a Zimbabwean exile and member of the opposition group, the MDC. Patson is an average-looking man. Average height, average build, average clothes, but his face is lived in. Before he came to Britain, Patson was tortured in Zimbabwe. Part of the torture Patson received at the hands of Mugabe's henchmen was electrocution. It seems fitting that he should play the part of a Zimbabwean security chief out to buy stun batons. While Patson chats to Mr Lee, I am in another part of the hotel listening in on headphones.

Lee and Patson are in a spacious room that has all the charm of a Jasper Conran-designed industrial estate. From the low IKEA-style coffee table and dried poppy heads in a vase, the design is business-class and corporate. Over a buffet lunch of pre-packed sandwiches, Mr Lee explains how no paperwork will appear in Britain for the stun weapons. He says he can 'ship to anywhere you want ... it won't show in any accounts here'.

'How will that be done?' Patson asks.

'It won't show any transaction here. Everything goes through Korea,' says Lee. The money, some US$580,000, is to be paid into his personal bank account in Korea, and he will pay the manufacturer, Hanseung Electronics Inc. The electro-shock in this brokered deal will not even touch British soil, moving from Korea to Zimbabwe. Were this a real deal there is little chance it would have been detected by the authorities, despite the new laws covering brokerage and sanctions.

Mr Lee produces sales brochures, detailing where the batons have been sold to in the past, including Egypt, the Philippines, Indonesia and Thailand. He hits his stride with his sales patter. 'The stun baton speaks for itself. You'll love it, you know!'

It is an odd moment hearing a grown man enthusing like this, talking of love and stun batons in the same sentence.

Patson plays the part of Zimbabwe's head of security with a cold authority. The time he spent being tortured gave him ample chance to gain an insight into the mindset of a security man. Bizarrely though, Mr Lee is not comfortable talking about what the batons will be used for. Patson's constant reference to the batons being used for interrogations unnerves him. He shuffles uneasily and suddenly blurts out, 'I don't care what you do with it. I don't want to know.'

'What I am talking about is interrogation,' says Patson.

'That's your business, I don't want to know.' He splutters out the words, as anxious as he is polite. 'It is your business. Say you bought a PC, yeah? Computer. It is up to you if you use it for a game, sending emails, letters, it is up to you ...'

A silence descends. Lee is genuinely disturbed by what he is hearing. And in a quiet part of the hotel, over a set of head-phones, I hear the sound of a human being struggling with an attempt to be human. What sane person would want to help inflict torture on people they had never even met?

In the short silence I wonder if Lee might get up and leave and walk away from the deal. This could be a Jimmy Stewart moment.

But Lee doesn't push his chair back in disgust. He doesn't leave without a further word. He stays and chats. He talks of the deal. He is still chasing the deal and the money. His objection to torture is instinctive. His pursuit of money is persistent. Money it seems was always going to win in this battle. Yet despite this, and the fact that weeks after the meeting with Patson he was still trying to chase the deal, I feel sorry for Lee. He is a small-time cowboy, not a full-time arms dealer; he has been doing IT work in banks recently, so he can't be earning enough from TLT International.

I'm forty-two, too old to be discovering ambiguity. I like my arms dealers to be evil through and through. I want black hearts, grasping hands and cheap shirts. Mr Lee just about covers 50 per cent of that requirement. Perhaps I recognise something in Mr Lee that is in me. Just as he doesn't want to think about the consequences of his sale, I don't really want to think about the consequences of informing the authorities about him.

Mr Lee has two daughters; one of them is fourteen. No age is a good age to see your father humiliated or worse still jailed, but fourteen seems a particularly bad age, nearly adult but still painfully childish. Perhaps it was Mr Lee's daughter that I heard in the background of one conversation with him. When I first mentioned Zimbabwe (as Osman) to Mr Lee, a young voice reacted in the background. I didn't catch it at first, during the conversation in Anthony's living room, but when I played the tape back I heard it quite clearly. The sound of a girl's voice, which utters one solitary shocked word, a long low disbelieving 'No'. Perhaps Lee was on a speaker-phone or the two of them were listening at the earpiece. I don't know. What I do know is someone at Lee's end of the phone knew Zimbabwe was wrong and that someone had the voice of a girl. I played the tape back, trying to find another clue as to who it might be saying 'no'. A real and genuine chill spread across me as I played it back time and time again, hearing that long solitary word, 'no'. I tried to work out how far the voice was from Mr Lee. The voice can't have been standing more than three metres from him, maybe even next to him. I tried to picture the face of the voice, playing back that 'no' and seeing if an image would come into my mind. Eyes shut and searching. It is a young voice; it could be Mr Lee's daughter. If I reported Mr Lee to the authorities, how much damage would I inflict on the owner of that voice?

When I later emailed Lee, asking for his response to the allegations that were about to be published in the *New Statesman* magazine, Lee's reply was far from conventional. He asked me to help him. 'I was truly not aware of any legislation or licensing on this product,' wrote Mr Lee. He continued, 'Please let me know what to do if you can, as I have never come across this situation.' I didn't reply to him, but part of me wanted to. I wanted to help him. But I can't.

Lee provided new quotes and business advice a week after meeting Patson, a man he thought was in charge of Zimbabwe's security. A week after he was told of the batons' intended use. Lee might be unaware of the law, he might be unhappy at the thought of what use the batons would be put to, but he was content to go ahead with the deal. In fact, during this time Lee expanded his product range, offering a stun pen. This is a small electro-shock device less than 5 inches long, emitting 100,000 volts, available in a gift box and can be cunningly hidden in a row of pens in a top pocket of a sports jacket. Who on earth would want a stun pen?

Once again adopting another front company, I wrote from Ireland posing as a different potential client. I sent Mr Lee an email claiming to represent an Irish educational establishment that was experiencing difficulties with discipline in school ...

Some of you might already guess where this is going ... Might, I wrote, the stun pen be suitable for instilling good behaviour in the school? Could it work, bearing in mind that some of the people using the stun pen would be elderly nuns? Mr Lee quoted a price of US$16 per stun pen. Yes folks, we were on the verge of Irish Stun Nuns! Not only were nuns brokering stun weapons, in my twisted world they were ready to use them.

For the more astute psychoanalysts among you, the answer is yes. I am probably painting a picture of Mr Lee as someone who cares little for the harm of others, especially children, in an attempt to distance myself from the harm I may cause his family when I report him.

NICKED

The penalty for brokering arms on the Military List without a licence ranges from a fine of unlimited amount to ten years in prison. It all depends on the gravity of the offence. Had our stun jockey Mr Lee been subject to an investigation from Her Majesty's Revenue and Customs for brokering torture equipment to an embargoed destination, one would have thought he was due for a bit of angry wig-wobbling from the judge's bench.

After calling Her Majesty's Revenue and Customs, expressing my desire to be an active citizen engaged in the prevention of crime, I finally got to chat to some serious-looking officials. Armed with a file full of transcripts of recorded phone conversations and copies of email correspondence, I went down to their offices by the Thames near Tower Bridge.

Old brick and wrought-iron railings sit on the sunless side of the street from the nondescript entrance, and I wait for a while in reception until two officers come down to walk me through the high-ceilinged corridors that seem to typify the British Establishment. We make small talk until we get to the door of the interview room. God bless Customs, they do not disappoint my preconceptions. One is dressed in a Ted Baker T-shirt and the other in a crumpled shirt that a J-cloth sales rep wouldn't have worn. In the room they drink from Styrofoam cups, and one of the officers had a packet of Benson & Hedges on his person. I didn't see the packet but I just know he had them. He had to have Bennies on him; I was in late 1970s *Sweeney* heaven; it couldn't have been any other way. If they had produced a bottle of Scotch from an official-looking filing cabinet drawer I would have clapped with joy like a pampered dandy.

'Firstly, thank you for bringing this to us, and could you sign this form, which is a receipt for the materials you have brought to us. There are a couple of things we need to go through,' said the one in the suit, while his colleague sat opposite looking at me, all splayed legs, leaning hunched shoulders and noncommittal stares.

'Firstly, just because you have brought this to us does not mean that you work for Customs.'

I was a bit surprised at this, as I have never thought that claiming to work for Customs could in anyway enhance my appearance or desirability. Even in my most desperate teenage years it never crossed my mind to sidle up to a woman in a club and say, 'Bet you don't know how much the Treasury loses in revenue from VAT fraud.' Or, 'Stick with me, sweetheart, and I can get you Chinese fake fags from the warehouse.'

'Secondly,' continued the chap I was mentally referring to as guv'nor, 'secondly, you will now be registered on our database as a human informant.'

I nod my head nonchalantly like I am used to this kind of talk and behaviour, but inside I am thinking like a ten-year-old and my thoughts are: *cool.*

'We will look at the documents you have brought in, and if we think there is a case we will pass them on to our legal team, who will make a decision on whether to prosecute or not. Are you prepared to be a witness if it does come to court?'

'Yes.'

Cooperating with the authorities, this was a new experience for me. I felt a new sense of civic responsibility creep into my being, a feeling that at any moment I might lean over a garden fence and strike up a conversation with a neighbour about Crime Watch or the increase in dog mess near the swings. I phoned Sam, a crusty friend approaching forty with no children or mortgage, a finely tuned sense of irresponsibility and an encyclopaedic working knowledge of Special Brew. 'I need to discuss civic participation.'

'You wha'?' croaked the voice at the other end.

'Being involved in your community.'

'You are involved with your community.'

'I mean officially involved.'

'What have you done?' quizzes Sam, sensing something.

'You know the stun-baton bloke?'

'Matey down your way?'

'Yeah, well, I took all the information I had on him down to Customs and handed it over to them. I have given them the tape recordings, the emails, the lot. And I have volunteered to be a witness if it comes to trial. I am now regarded as humint.'

'Do wha'?'

'Humint. I am a human informant registered on the Customs database.'

Silence descends on the phone line; nothing is heard, not even static. Seconds pass, probably twenty, maybe thirty. Not a long period of time to endure a silence if you're a student with a bong and a moment's break during an evening of PlayStation. In normal conversation, though, thirty seconds of quiet is a pause of Pinter-sized proportions. A cough and a sniff signals Sam is still there, followed by a long inhalation of smoke.

'Does that mean you're a fucking grass, then?'

Wheels of justice

Despite Sam's cackling references to the Witness Protection Programme and relocating to a place where no one would think of looking for me (North London), I felt a sense of civic pride. A strange serenity came over me after the trip to Customs, a sense that I had done my bit. Not much, admittedly; hardly Victoria Cross-winning behaviour, but a campaign medal, I reckon. All I had to do is sit back and wait for the authorities to go through the evidence, do the dawn raid and call me to the Old Bailey. I am ready, I am willing, I am waiting.

I am still ready, willing and waiting. Whoever it was who originally said the wheels of justice turn slowly was making a hasty exaggeration. How long does this wheel of justice take to go round? Halley's comet goes round quicker. Entire species evolve faster than the pace of British justice. Whole generations of Fen families produce children with just the five fingers on each hand quicker. I have seen militant lesbians turn to men faster than the scales of justice can be got out of the packing cases. How long does it take for the British authorities to get their arse into gear? Multinationals recall life-threatening faulty products quicker. Sloths masturbate faster. The only thing slower than the turning wheels of British justice is the appeal against British justice's wrongful conviction.

Her Majesty's Revenue and Customs, as it is now known, is the organisation responsible for investigating shenanigans in the arms export world. In response to a Freedom of Information request, Customs admitted that they had never prosecuted anyone for any offences relating to torture equipment, neither electro-shock nor leg irons. In light of the amount of information on British arms dealers caught flogging electro-shock that has been dug up by journalists and campaigners over the years, the HMRC prosecution rate of zero has to be seen as fantastically bad. You can look at this statistic from any angle and it still looks like a naught. A big fat naught. Nothing. Nada. Nicht. Nil per cent. Zilch. Fuck all.

When information has been routinely presented to investigators by journalists and yet Customs have not brought one single prosecution, you start to conclude that not only can Customs not do their job, but they can't even do it when it is done for them. How shit is that? This is like Milli Vanilli not being able to mime.

The fact that HMRC has prosecuted precisely no one to date is a fact that disturbs Roger Berry MP, chairman of the Quadripartite Committee. He says, 'Look, we have TV licences and we have detector vans to check that those people with a TV have got a TV licence. Now I would suggest that arms are considerably more important to check up on than TV licences, but we don't seem to have any enforcement.'

Now Mr Lee isn't exactly Mr Big. Hand on heart I can testify that his home in Brockley is not in the base of an extinct volcano, nor does he have any assistants with killer bowler hats or knives in their shoes. Lee was clearly willing to flog electro-shock to Zimbabwe and was actively involved in other deals with genuine buyers, but in the world of the arms trade he is pretty much a bottom feeder. The important fact here, though, is that he is easy to spot. Anyone could see the pictures of the stun batons on his company website, under the banner 'Stun Batons' just in case you were confused, and the website conveniently gave out his address with it. So why didn't Customs or the police notice it? It should take a cop with a bit of common sense thirty seconds to see that Mr Lee was breaking the law. Yet no one noticed Mr Lee, and if no one noticed him, we have to ask: is anyone looking out for dodgy arms merchants?

If a law is only as strong as the enforcement of it, then British law on brokerage and torture equipment is not out there fighting wrongdoers, it is sitting in a darkened room with a nosebleed.

When new laws are introduced, the government departments that have to enforce them are asked to estimate how much the new laws will cost to enforce. The DTI wrote that it would have an annual cost of £200,000 to £300,000. Which doesn't sound a lot to enforce a set of laws designed to stop the brokering of guns, the sale anywhere by UK citizens of torture equipment, WMD and long-range missiles, and the enforcement of UN and EU arms embargoes. Compare that money to the sum of money the New Labour government found to fight drug- and people-trafficking the following year – that sum was £90,000,000, or ninety million in old money. According to the government, in order to stop gunrunning you need 0.25 per cent of the money you need to stop drug- and people-running.

Little time or effort seems to have gone into making these laws work. Possibly because HMRC don't appear to have the resources to do so. According to a source close to HMRC, the number of full-time staff in their 'restrictions and prohibitions unit', the unit that deals with everything from child pornography to stun weapons, is six. Six full-time staff for the whole of Britain. When questions were asked in Parliament as to how many staff there were, the reply came back: 'Precise figures are not available.'

Dawn Primarolo MP is the Paymaster General. She is also the only MP to be named after a magazine and a piece of confectionery. It was Dawn Primarolo who was charged with answering the question: How many HMRC are there working on controlled goods (military equipment)? She insists that HMRC 'front-line staff are multi-functional and deployed flexibly', which essentially means 'this is not a priority'. However, 'they are supported by two central investigation and intelligence teams'. So I double-checked with my source.

'There are two teams working on restrictions and prohibitions, right?' I said.

'Yes. That's right. Two teams. With three people in each team. That makes six.'

'Six investigators covering everything from child porn to stun guns across the UK ...'

'Six.'

'Fuck.'

'Fuck indeed.'

It has taken forty-two years to get there, but I have finally joined the chorus of people shouting, 'We need more cops!'

But just a very tiny part of me, a really really tiny part, is relieved that the voice that said 'no', the girl's voice I heard on the recording, has not seen her dad, if indeed she was his daughter, in court …*

---

* In May 2006 HMRC gave evidence at the Quadripartite Select Committee that the number of staff working as Strategic Experts (everything on the military and dual-use list) is calculated at between 60–100. The figure is wide because the staff are multi-functional. This is the total number of staff needed to regulate the export of all military goods (ie licenses, paperwork and customs checks at export points). It is a separate calculation from the number of staff in the 'restrictions and prohibitions unit' which is concerned with *investigating* wrongdoing.

15

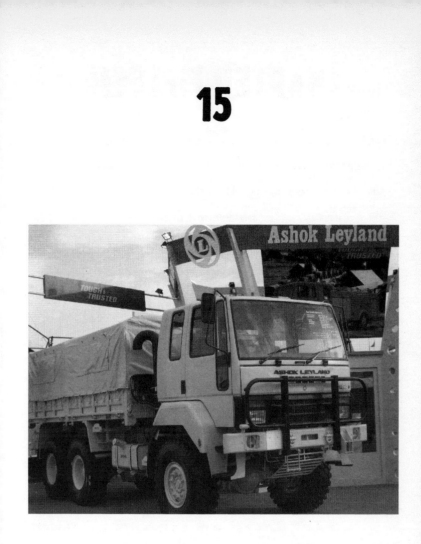

TRUCKS, RUCKS AND MINISTERS

CHAPTER FIFTEEN

A chapter in which the author discovers just how powerful the powerful can be, and paradoxically how the powerless can be very irritating. Members of Parliament behave decently. The author manages to behave.

THE MEMORANDUM WHAT I WROTE

Outside and waiting, that's where I am and that's what I am doing. Booted and suited, I'm outside the committee rooms in Parliament, waiting to give evidence to the Quadripartite Select Committee on the arms trade. Pacing the long corridor where the walls are lined with wooden panels and dark green leather seats like pews. The carpet is a long affair of blues and greens interlaced with knotted red lines. Each doorway has a carved wooden frame with a shield and weird fleur-de-lys; the rooms are numbered in camp gothic paint on scrolls above the large doors hinged with ornate brass. The place is filled with cops, campaigners, arms industry lobbyists and MPs' researchers, and me. I'm the chump in the sentencing suit, who is sweating like a parole prisoner on a first date. As a stand-up comic I've done plenty of weird gigs in my time. I have performed in soup kitchens during the miners' strike. I have done a Jewish stag night. I have had sniffer dogs in the dressing rooms in Belfast and Provos in the audience. I have been threatened by a man with a knife, dressed only in swimming trunks at the Glastonbury Festival. But being questioned by a group of politicians for an hour on the arms trade is the weirdest so far and I'm as nervous as a squeamish rabbi at his first circumcision.

There are three of us giving evidence on this session, Ollie Sprague, Roy Isbister and me. Ollie Sprague works for Oxfam on their Control Arms campaign; he's five foot ten and uses the same workout videos and fitness programme that I do. Ollie sports a stoner's gait and a ponytail, which he'll have to lose when he hits his fortieth birthday. He has brushed his ponytail specially for today and it hangs neatly in a straight line over his suit collar. He also knows the issues of arms control better than any MP in the committee room. Roy works for Saferworld, doing fact-finding, research and lobbying. Roy is balding, trim and a New Zealander who meets the mistaken assumption that he is Australian with calm but persistent correction. He co-wrote the research on the public subsidising of the arms trade that I so obviously ripped off in Chapter Six. All of us are over-cheery, with stuck-on smiles. I'm kicking the caps of my shoes on the floor and chewing gum too loudly.

'Last time we appeared before the committee they really went for us,' says Roy, in an understated *Neighbours* kind of way.

'What did they do?' I ask, not really wanting to know.

'A group of MPs from Trade and Industry and the MoD just decided to really hammer us,' adds Ollie. 'Said we didn't know what we were talking about and had no evidence. It was really shit.'

'Really shit,' Roy chimes.

'So,' smiles Ollie optimistically, 'it is their turn to be nice to us.'

'This year they are going to like the NGOs,' Roy agrees, more in hope than certainty.

Between the pair of them Roy and Ollie possess a huge amount of knowledge on the arms trade, and if they are worried I'm doomed. I'm the mental lightweight of the team, I do smiling, nodding and the odd funny; and on this note of realisation I suddenly empathise with Jamie Theakston's entire career.

Ollie has two things on his agenda for the MPs: an international arms trade treaty and some Land-Rovers. It was Ollie and a Man In Black who spotted some British-supplied kit in a place that it shouldn't be. In this case the kit was a Land-Rover. Land-Rovers always seem to be found in inappropriate places, namely Fulham, driven by folk wearing Alice bands and stuffed with baby seats and black Labradors. All of which seems fairly wrong to me. Ollie and the MIB, though, saw a Land-Rover in Andijan on 13 May 2005, the day and place the Uzbek authorities massacred over 500 men, women and children. From a photograph of some Uzbek troops taking up position by army Land-Rovers training guns on unarmed civilians, Ollie and the MIB worked out that the Land-Rover had been supplied by the Turkish company, Otakar. They have a licensed production deal with Land-Rover. About 70 per cent of the parts for the military Land-Rover came from the UK; they are considered 'civilian' parts and so are exported without an arms licence. Otakar assembles a military vehicle using the UK-supplied civilian parts and its own components, and presto, a military Land-Rover ends up in Uzbekistan at the heart of a massacre.

'Could I have those giving evidence first, then press, then members of the public, please,' booms a world-weary security guard holding the big wooden door open. A hush spreads along the corridor like a shock wave and we prepare to file into the committee room.

The Export Group for Aerospace and Defence, the arms industry's lobbyists on export law, is questioned before us. We sit behind them, too wrapped up in preparing for our turn even to muster a sneer. They do an hour of questions before we hit the hotspot, and so the MPs are not at their freshest when we face the horseshoe ring of tables behind which they sit. We take our place on the brass-studded green leather seats, each bearing a portcullis printed in gold. Our nameplates are in front of us on the light wood table. I go to pick up a bottle of water to pour myself a glass, but my hands are shaking like the loser in a pickpocket contest. I grip the bottle harder hoping this will somehow stop the quivering. The art is not to let other people see you are nervous. At the moment I haven't mastered it. I've modelled my gaze on some classic Johnny Cash stoicism but my hands are George Best. A large cheerful chap with the jowls of the well dined is the nearest MP to me. He is within touching distance and his name is Robert Key, the MP for Salisbury. Fuck – that's the place the army train at. Fuck. He hates me. He is flicking through some of the memorandums I have submitted to the committee, swathes of pages detailing facts, figures and recommendations. As I try to pour some water, he smiles and says, 'So, the famous Mark Thomas.'

'Hello,' I manage to say through the desert that has taken occupancy of my mouth.

Looking straight ahead and almost to no one in particular he continues in pleasant, posh and clipped tones: 'The NGOs have done all the work. They have got all the examples,' he says tilting his head admiringly.

'Thank you,' I say.

'The NGOs have come up with the goods,' he says, stacking his papers before the session formally begins.

I find myself being praised and, in turn, liking, a Tory MP. Oh fuck fuck fuck. Oh please don't let the Parliamentary TV unit be filming us chatting before the session starts … Please. A Tory, for God's sake. I have started to like a Tory. Bollocks. My hand is still shaking as I reach for the glass again and his face is still smiling. I panic. I have never liked a Tory in my life. Oh God, what if I am one, what if I'm a repressed Tory and haven't realised it? I'll have to tell my parents I've been living a lie.

'Here you go, Mark.' Roy calmly passes me a glass of water, dispelling my paranoid fantasies.

'Welcome, good afternoon,' calls the voice of Roger Berry, the committee chairman, across the room to bring the session to order. He sits at the central point of the horseshoe of tables, in the middle of the room a stenographer takes notes of everything that is said. Behind us are the public gallery and the Parliamentary

TV unit, discreetly operating the cameras placed round the room. On the tables in front of some of the MPs are copies of the memorandum I submitted to the committee. This memorandum is due to be printed and made public in the Quadripartite Select Committee's annual report 2006; it is subject to Parliamentary privilege and can be found in full via the QSC (http://www. parliament.uk/parliamentary_committees/quad.cfm). It tells the story of an investigation I did with BBC 2 *Newsnight* into companies belonging to the Hinduja Group, posing the question: did individuals within these companies break the EU arms embargo to Sudan?

SPONSORING FAITH

The Hinduja brothers set up their home and business base in London in 1979 and are well known to watchers of political scandal in Britain. They are the four Indian brothers whose attempts to get British passports ended the ministerial career of Peter Mandelson. In that respect we owe them a thank-you. The Hinduja brothers have an extended family as well as an extended business empire and they are rich. Extremely rich. Their fortune is estimated at about £2.1 billion. They run their own Swiss bank and numerous companies involved in the defence industry. They are neighbours to the Queen, whose Buckingham Palace is some 600 yards down the road from the Hindujas' family home, a luxury block of flats just off The Mall.

The Hinduja Foundation (the brothers' charitable entity – which listed Labour MP and one-time Cabinet enforcer Jack Cunningham and former Prime Minister Ted Heath as trustees of the Hinduja Cambridge Trust) even sponsored the Faith Zone in the Millennium Dome to the tune of £1m. The unique failure of the Dome will forever symbolise Blair's love of all things corporate and his Achilles heel – a belief in his own infallibility.

Only Blair could be oblivious to the incongruity of a family linked to arms scandals sponsoring the Faith Zone. Perhaps he was impressed by the family's spiritual qualities when he and his wife attended the Hindujas' lavish Diwali party.

In 2001 Srichand, Gopichand and Prakash Hinduja appeared in court in India accused of criminal conspiracy and bribery in connection with the purchase of field guns by India from the Swedish company Bofors. In 2005 the case against them collapsed and their name was cleared, but not before it had been dragged around the globe linked to an arms scandal. When it comes to negative publicity, the Hindujas have quite a track record.

Ozzy's cocaine breastmilk*

Ashok Leyland is a Hinduja Group company based in India – it is 51 per cent owned by LRLIH, another Hinduja Group company based in the UK. In February 2005 Ashok Leyland announced on its company website a deal to supply 100 Stallion 4x4 army trucks to the Sudan Defence Ministry. The EU arms embargo on Sudan does not apply to an Indian company. *But* four members of the Ashok Leyland board were UK citizens or residents, including the vice-chairman Dheeraj Hinduja, son of GP Hinduja, the president of the family company. The EU arms embargo on Sudan is extraterritorial, meaning it applies to any UK citizen anywhere in the world. The UK law states that no citizen or person in the UK should do 'any act calculated to promote the supply and delivery' of military goods to embargoed destinations. This means that if any UK-based board members of Ashok Leyland were involved in a deal to supply army trucks to Sudan they would have broken the law (unless they had a licence from the UK government). I worked on a BBC 2 *Newsnight* investigation that found evidence that Ashok Leyland directors

---

* For those who didn't read it, the reference to this title can be found in the note to the skim reader on page iv.

Dheeraj Hinduja and Anders Spare, who were both based in the UK, were involved in a deal potentially in breach on the UN embargo (albeit perhaps unwittingly).

The Sudanese refugee's story

'So why the fuss?' you may ask. 'These are trucks, big deal.' If the Hinduja trucks destined for Sudan are army trucks it matters, and it matters for two reasons. Remember the refugee from Sudan who met and talked to me – on condition he would remain anonymous for fear of reprisals on his family back home. 'You must hide my face and change my voice on the television screen,' he had said. 'You must not name my home, where I am now or where we met.' I can't tell you where he lived, except to say that refugees, contrary to anything the *Daily Express* says, do not live like kings. I cannot tell you of the place where we met, except that the bench we sat on was wooden. But I can tell you that like many refugees' his clothes are decent but months away from threadbare and he carried an optimism borne out of necessity.

The nameless refugee had an answer to the question why the fuss about army trucks. 'These vehicles are a source of power and flexibility. They enable the Janjaweed to attack anywhere in Darfur,' he said. 'Whenever a villager sees a lorry or a military vehicle coming in, it is a sign there will be an attack.'

There is no allegation that the Hinduja Group were involved in a conscious decision to export army trucks to assist in this genocide. Indeed they have said to *Newsnight* that the Sudan contract was meant to be a humanitarian contract. However, if the army trucks described in the Ashok Leyland press release reached the Sudanese military, then those trucks could end up in the hands of the Janjaweed.

The second reason a deal to supply army trucks to Sudan matters is because the law says it matters. If the law on embargoed destinations says it matters for the self-employed Mr Lee in the previous chapter, then it must surely matter for someone in the employ of a company that owns a Swiss bank.

In the *Newsnight* investigation I set up yet another front company and posed as a potential client for Stallion 4x4 army trucks for Sudan. In order for that claim to be believable, I had to come up with a reason to need the trucks. This was tricky. As Ashok Leyland were working with the Sudanese government they would know a great deal about the market for army trucks in that region. So the producer, Jonathan Patterson, and I invented a fictitious charity, claiming it was starting aid work in the Sudan region and therefore needed Stallion 4x4 trucks to deliver supplies. For those of you who believe in an omnipotent deity running an afterlife, yes of course I will burn in the fires of hell for pretending to work for an aid charity... and guess what? I've sworn at newborn puppies too. Bad to the bone, that's me. It was, however, a successful ploy. The *Newsnight* investigation found that Anders Spare demonstrated a detailed knowledge of the deal, from its history to its current financial status. He also talked of being 'involved behind the scenes' in the deal and being able to strategise with the company. Dheeraj Hinduja said, 'Initially whenever we develop new markets and new customers we try to identify those for Ashok Leyland and we were very closely involved in how the deal was structured.' On the basis that the directors weren't lying to the *Newsnight* team and the Stallions were army trucks going to the Sudanese military, then there would certainly be room for the HMRC to investigate. *Newsnight* were happy enough with our report. All we had to do was get the Hindujas' formal right of reply to the story and we would be ready to broadcast.

Familiarity has bred an inability to appreciate the mental images that accompany our most well-used phrases. So consider for a moment a quantity of excrement hurled into the rapidly revolving blades of a device meant to produce cooling currents of air ... Events took a turn for the worse in the *Newsnight* office.

The Hindujas issued pre-emptive media briefings and threatened legal action. 'Hindujas seek to gag BBC over "military sales" sting' thundered a full page in the *Sunday Times*. The Hindujas' lawyers repeatedly threatened high-court injunctions that would stop our report from being broadcast. They threatened libel action if it was broadcast. 'If the BBC chooses to ignore the truth of this matter,' said their lawyers, 'it could very well end as the BBC's most expensive mistake ever.' The two most important men in the BBC, Mark Thompson and Michael Grade, received a letter from the Labour peer Lord Temple Morris (who is paid £20,000 a year as an advisor to the Hinduja Group-owned AMAS Investment and Project Services Ltd). In his letter Lord Temple Morris warned that the story was wrong, repeating the line that the Hindujas wouldn't hesitate to take the BBC to court.

So the BBC allowed the Hindujas and their lawyers a preview of the report on the day it was due to be broadcast. GP Hinduja (the president) arrived with a legal team – those present remember at least five lawyers. After the viewing, the Hinduja team consulted for a while and then met with the *Newsnight* team (excluding me). One of the Hinduja's team of lawyers shouted obscenities and pointed at each of the *Newsnight* team in turn, informing them he would put every one of them in the dock if the report was aired. He said if it was broadcast the BBC would have to put up the licence fee to cover the libel damages the Hindujas were going to win.

However, the BBC is the most respected and well-known broadcaster in the world. It has stood up to legal threats before them and will no doubt stand up to them again. It didn't this time, though. Less than two hours before broadcast, the *Newsnight* editor Peter Barron pulled the broadcast. The BBC had been legally bitch-slapped from broadcasting an investigation into potential breaches of the EU arms embargo on Sudan, one of the most wretched and conflict-ridden countries in the world.

MILITARY TRUCK OR NOT?

So had the BBC and I got it wrong? The central argument the Hindujas put forward was that the trucks for Sudan were not military equipment. Therefore the BBC had no story.

Initially the Hindujas said the vehicles were not armour-plated and were therefore not of a military specification. However, the UK government classifies military vehicles as 'ground "vehicles" or components therefor, specially designed or modified for military use'. So this Hinduja argument is irrelevant.

The Hindujas said the agreement they had to supply 100 Stallion 4x4s (in kit form to be assembled in Sudan) didn't refer to supplies to the army/Defence Ministry of Sudan. However, the company press release of 16 February 2005, which was up on their website for nearly six months, has the headline 'Ashok Leyland to export defence vehicles to Sudan'. It goes on to say, 'The Hinduja Group flagship Ashok Leyland has signed an agreement for an initial supply of Stallion 4x4 army trucks and Falcon buses to the **Sudan Defence Ministry** [my bold]. This was announced at the sidelines of the IDEX [an arms fair] 2005 in Dubai.'

The Hindujas said the Ashok Leyland press release was 'wholly inaccurate'. They said: 'The BBC's error is in supposing that the trucks are "military specification" vehicles. They are not.' *Newsnight* noted that Ashok describe the Stallion as an 'army truck'. The company designed the Stallion 4x4 to 'address their [the Indian armed forces] special needs' and the company would promote the Stallions at defence trade fairs.

The Hindujas said: 'You say our clients market these Stallion trucks as a military vehicle. So they do. That is not the point. It is simply a commercial truck which can well be used for military use.' However, it is the UK government who decide if it is a military truck or not. The Minister Malcolm Wicks said: 'From the information available on the company website, it appears these vehicles are specially designed for military use and therefore potentially require an export or trade licence.'

The Hindujas said the trucks (in kit form) to be supplied to Sudan had been stripped of all military features. When asked by *Newsnight* if the BBC could see the specifications for these stripped-down kit-form trucks, the Hindujas said: 'No specifications were attached to the cooperation agreement nor were any specifications prepared or exchanged.' In addition, during the *Newsnight* charity aid ruse, Anders Spare, one of the UK-based Ashok Leyland directors, expressed the view that the specification for military and humanitarian production would be more or less the same.

The BBC decided not to broadcast. The *Newsnight* editor Peter Barron (a slim fellow with a likeably brusque manner and a Northern Irish accent) had shown intelligence, persistence and support throughout the investigation. Unfortunately, it was his decision to spike the report. Unfortunately, it's my decision that he acted like a coward.

In March 2006 the Trade and Industry Select Committee went on a fact-finding trip to India. By chance they visited Ashok Leyland's Chennai headquarters for a trade briefing. The chairman of the Quadripartite Committee, Roger Berry, to whom I submitted the memorandum on Ashok Leyland, was also by chance on the trip.

On 13 March 2006 at a select committee evidence session in Parliament, Berry recalled meeting Ashok Leyland, who he says were quite open about the fact that the trucks intended for export to Sudan were indeed military vehicles.

Chairman: … there was no question that they were not military vehicles. It was perfectly clear that they were hoping to export military vehicles. It was the military vehicles director who was providing the committee with this information, was it not, Peter? [speaking to MP Peter Luff, who also met Ashok in India.]

Peter Luff: That is correct, from India.

Chairman: From India to Sudan, so there is no question that we are talking about military vehicles here. They were quite open about that.

Perhaps the Hindujas' lawyers might like to tell Roger Berry MP and Peter Luff MP that their 'military vehicles director' was 'wholly inaccurate'.

WHITE MAN IN WESTMINSTER PALAIS

Inside and sweating, that's where I am and what I am doing. I'm in the Houses of Parliament about to give evidence to the select committee, sitting at a desk in front of a room full of inquisitive politicians. The MPs half surround us, and as if that wasn't enough, portraits of dead politicians line the walls staring down in what feels like contempt. So even when the real live ones doze off, the other bastards are eyeballing you. Taking a second to look round the room, I clock the MPs properly for the first time. Fourteen middle-aged MPs, twelve men, two women, and between them enough head of hair for seven. Look at their suits closely and you could be pleasantly surprised at just how many shades of grey there are in the world. I find myself gazing at the MPs' clothes. Lost for a moment in the hues of monochrome, it's like an acid trip for the colour blind.

Ollie Sprague from Oxfam and Roy Isbister from Saferworld are sharing the evidence session. Along with Amnesty, their organisations have worked for the past two and a half years calling for an international arms trade treaty, and their work appears to be moving in the right direction, as the campaign grows internationally. Between the two of them they can quote endless facts and figures on the globalisation of the arms industry and international precedents in law. Me, I'm so nervous I couldn't quote a Clash lyric.

If I was a Monty Python cartoon, the top of my head would pop open and a scroll of gothic script would emerge from my skull with the words, 'What the fuck am I doing here?' This would be quickly followed by a burst from a brass instrument and a farting noise. But my feeling of isolation is just misplaced jitters. I have to be in this room, as the fact is no one else would listen to me rant about the Hindujas and army trucks to Sudan without running for their lawyers.

I breathe out heavily and give myself a minute more to soak

in the MPs, and it occurs to me I have misjudged them. They do not look all the same; there are differences. What unifies them for a split second is not the elite club of Parliament or political parties, it is that they all look like misfits. They genuinely do. They are all slightly odd. One is charmingly Bunteresque, one looks like a mad drama teacher, another is like a young Spitfire pilot, one in a certain light looks like a trade-union shop steward for the Oompa-Loompas. On one side of the room an MP looks like a nightwatchman, on the other like a 1950s clerk for a menswear department in Regent Street. One frankly looks like he could do with a weekend in the Welsh mountains with close male friends and lots of naked swimming in glacial lakes. All of them look like misfits. Which for a moment I find incredibly endearing.

Like a kid at a wedding service I twist my neck in my shirt collar, trying to find some breathing space. The eyes of the room, both real and oil-based, are on Ollie from Oxfam, who has been invited to outline the progress of the international arms trade treaty. The arms trade is globalised, therefore it needs a global law to control it, though an old friend and trade unionist put the argument more succinctly when he said, 'If the arms dealers keep going on about how if they didn't do it someone else would, then let's clobber the other fucker as well.' And while we're on the subject of argument, half a million dead people a year make a pretty compelling case too.

'I spoke to the committee last year,' says Ollie in a soft voice. 'We were up to twenty governments which had given support; we are now up to forty-three governments which have said they support an [international] arms trade treaty.'

Forty-three governments around the world who support an international arms trade treaty isn't enough, but it isn't bad either.

'Obviously,' Ollie continues, 'we have an awful lot of work to do to get that forty-three up to nearer a hundred governments.' But it is achievable; even the arms trade lobby groups support the idea. Only half an hour ago we had all put our heads up when Brinley Salzman, one of the arms industry's experts on arms export law, said: 'I would like to reiterate our support for the principle behind an arms trade treaty which should establish a much greater degree of transparency.'

The arms industry supports an international arms trade treaty! The MPs support the idea of an international arms trade treaty. Tony Blair supports it … but I think we can overcome that drawback.

'Mr Thomas,' says a voice that belongs to the committee chairman. Just time for a quick slurp of water as he thanks me for submitting the memorandum. 'Can we deal first with the one in relation to Ashok Leyland? It would be very helpful if you could briefly summarise that case,' he says.

WATERLOO SUNSET

Nick Hildyard from the Corner House perches on a lightweight metal frame that the café has the audacity to call a chair. He hunches over his cup, held in the palms of his hands, like a sacred rite. We're at Waterloo again. The low throb of the stationary engines provides a background diesel hum against the clatter of trolleys, shouts and scrambles on the concourse. So we lean in across the table to hear each other properly, more out of necessity than conspiracy.

'You're near the end of the book,' Nick says, with a grin on his thin posh face.

'How do you know?' I half slurp through a mouthful of milky foam that sticks chocolate powder onto my lips.

'I know everything, man,' he laughs, with the air of a bankrupt lord. 'You said on the phone you wanted to talk about finding conclusions.' He halts to cough. 'Excuse me.' He rasps, barks and then playfully bangs his bony fist on his chest, unconsciously drawing attention to the fruitcake-coloured jumper that was fashionable in Norwegian ecologist circles about two decades ago. His face is slightly reddened from the coughing. 'From your tone on the phone you've either had too much coffee or have had some good news – which one is it?'

'The deal to export Stallions to Sudan collapsed.'

'Brilliant. That's great news.' Nick is delighted and spends the next two minutes hugging me and repeating, 'Well done, man!'

When he stops hugging me, we sip coffee, smiling stupidly at each other.

'Well …' Nick says, waiting, knowing there are more questions.

'Well, I don't know if the deal collapsed because the Sudanese didn't get the money together, or if we had any part in its collapse.'

'Doesn't matter.' He is surprisingly stern on this point. 'What matters is the trucks didn't get there.'

'It would just be nice to know, I suppose.'

'What, so you can put it on your CV? Mark has worked with Jonathan Ross and Robert Newman and has stopped arms deals in Sudan. For commercial voiceover work, contact his agent on 020—'

'Fuck off.' I laugh. 'There is something else.'

'Yes …' he says slowly.

'The Quadripartite Committee has written to the government demanding an investigation into the whole saga. And Oxfam has.'

'Oxfam?'

'Has demanded an investigation too.'

'Oxfam? Woolly hats and second-hand-clothes Oxfam?'

'Don't knock your tailor, Nick.'

'I'm glad I made you pay for the coffee.'

'Thing is …' I sigh. 'The thing is this, Ollie at Oxfam and the Men In Black are always there. But it was Roger Berry, an MP, who encouraged me to bring this stuff to Parliament to try to make it work there.' I look round conspiratorially. 'There was even a guy in the arms industry who dug out some handy information. So the bad guys came up trumps. And the good guys ...'

'*Newsnight* and the liberal media generally?'

'Yes.'

'Bunch of shits,' he says this matter-of-factly as he fishes out a blob of milky foam with a teaspoon. 'What was the official reason the BBC gave for not running the report?'

'They said the story had become too complicated to tell in a meaningful way.'

Nick bursts out laughing. 'Tell me, was it too complicated two hours before it was scheduled to be broadcast? No. Of course not.' Then he stops and smiles in realisation, fixes me with a questioning look and asks, 'You're not upset because some of the good guys weren't goodies and some of the baddies helped you out, are you?'

'In a way, yes. I just feel uneasy about working with ... well ... with ...'

'The "man"?' suggests Nick helpfully, giving me his hippy look.

'For want of a better phrase, yes.'

'Look, if you have some chaps in the arms trade agreeing with you on the international arms trade treaty, that's good. The more people that want it, the better. They don't have to be your new best friends, trust me. There will come a time to fall out with them later. As long as you don't undermine what other activists are doing, it's fine. But don't assume that because they are agreeing with you on this that they are going to be with you on struggles for wider change.'

'Right, and the arms trade lobbyists don't mind talking to us lot because then they look reasonable. They are trying to prove they are not all profiteering yahoos; they want to draw a big line between themselves and the "illegal" arms trade. Between the good arms dealers and the bad arms dealers.' I take Nick's tobacco from him and begin to roll a cigarette for him, not smoking but keeping my hand in. 'I'm not too sure about working closely with the DMA and MPs, being drawn into the lobbying process. I worry that I am going to end up as a lobbyist.'

Nick sprays the remains of his cappuccino foam skyward. 'You! A lobbyist! Oh bless ...' Though he quickly adds, 'Lobbyists are people who don't offend anyone. Your skill is ... well, on occasion your skill is offending people.'

'Yes, I suppose so.'

'And, anyway, working with MPs doesn't preclude direct action or chaining yourself to a bus every now and again.'

I remember a conversation I had with Roger Berry. When I asked him what the chances were of getting the government to change the law on the simple matter of including new items on the torture list or introducing a catch-all clause for torture equipment, he grinned and said, 'I don't see why not – it's not as if we are talking about BAE Systems here, is it?' I tell the story to Nick.

'He's right. In that sense, that particular law change won't directly affect BAE and so there is more chance of it happening. BAE are one of the most protected companies in Britain. The government would rather shoot half the Cabinet than lose a contract for them.'

'BAE Systems are fucking immune to the law,' I say without thinking. Stupidly. Because here is Nick. Sue Hawley and Nick are living proof that even BAE Systems can on occasion be forced to drink from the same trough as everyone else.

He smiles, going all Yoda on me. 'Apparently, the word is BAE Systems hate the Corner House.'

We spend a few minutes grinning and giggling at that, then I have to confess something. 'The Men In Black reckon they have seen a UN report that is yet to be published.'

'Interesting,' he says, in an Alec Guinness sort of a way.

'They reckon someone from the UN saw a shitload of army trucks down at the docks in Sudan. Chinese, they reckon.'

'That's a bugger ... predictable though.'

'So Sudan might have got its trucks, regardless of the Hinduja deal collapsing … Takes the shine off events.'

'Yes … yes, it does. But you're a UK citizen and you stopped the UK involvement. That's the important thing. And as for China, it is not a monolith. Dissent and resistance didn't stop with Tiananmen Square. There are riots and protests every single day. Over land and the state and all sorts of things.'

'Which means?'

'Which means work on the bits you can and other people will work on the bits they can, and we support each other … Look, if the trucks got to Sudan from China it is a fucker, but use that as an argument for an international arms trade treaty.' He shrugs as if this is all obvious, then looks at his watch. He takes the rolled cigarette from me.

I tell him of a conversation I had with George Lear, the teacher who ran the Lord Williams Upper School arms company with the students. 'George Lear and I were chatting about the school project the other day.'

'Oh yes …'

'And he mentioned that by getting the students to come down and meet the minister and lobby and be involved in trying to change the law, that I was encouraging the students to have faith in the system.'

'What did you say to that?' says a genuinely bemused Nick.

'I said if he repeated that in public, I would sue him.'

'Too right, can't have people bad-mouthing you like that.'

'Remember, the arms dealers are right when they say "If I don't do it, someone else will".'

'The same argument they used to justify the slave trade.'

'Which means me farting about catching and embarrassing one or two is fine, but if we get an international arms trade treaty, then we might get some serious work done on this.'

'Something like that … Yes, something like that.'

EPILOGUE – THE NEW BATTLES

In this globalised world, companies find it increasingly profitable to locate the assembly of armaments to areas with a cheap labour force, and bring in the high-tech components. And so it was that components manufactured by a UK company called Radstone, in Towcester, ended up connected to the apparent extrajudicial killings of the CIA.

Radstone exports components for the Predator, an Unmanned Aerial Vehicle (UAV) commonly known as a pilotless drone. The Predator can be controlled hundreds of miles away from its operations by satellite and joystick. Equipped with a Hellfire air-to-ground missile, it is the ultimate PlayStation game. In 2002 in Yemen, the CIA launched a Hellfire missile from a Predator against al Qaeda suspects, killing them. The popular response to this would be: 'Bollocks to 'em, al Qaeda, innit?' However, Amnesty International said, 'To the extent that the US authorities deliberately decided to kill, rather than attempt to arrest these men, their killing would amount to extrajudicial executions.' Extrajudicial killings tend to be frowned upon by Britain, with the exception of Brazilian electricians and blokes carrying chair legs wrapped in paper.

On 13 January 2006, at 3 a.m., the CIA used a Predator once more to launch a Hellfire missile strike. This time the attack was on the Damadola village in Pakistan. There appears to be no evidence that the CIA's target Ayman al-Zawahiri was among the dead. Five women and five children were, though. In total the death toll is reported to be between 17 and 21 people.

What link these killings with a British firm are the components. Radstone exports Single Board Computers to General Atomics Aeronautical Systems, the Predators' maker's, specifically for the pilotless drone. Radstone have described the equipment they export as the 'brains' of the Predator. In fact, the managing director went one stage further, saying, 'The Predator wouldn't fly without Radstone technology.'

Radstone develop and manufacture for the defence industry; they are a defence company. Yet they do not need a licence to export the 'brains' of a pilotless drone that goes round the place firing missiles courtesy of the CIA. This is a tad odd. Britain's main focus of arms control is licensing. Everything from body armour to missiles needs a licence from the UK to be exported. It is more than a tad odd because UAVs are regarded as 'long-range missiles', classified alongside WMD and some torture equipment as 'restricted goods'. As such, *Jane's Defence Weekly* has to get a licence to publish adverts for UAVs. That's right, folks: an advert for an Unmanned Aerial Vehicle needs a licence, but the computer 'brains' for it do not.

Controlling the widgets of barbarity will be the battle of the coming decades.

THE END

APPENDIX

Mark Thomas submitted a memorandum to the Quadripartite Select Committee on Ashok Leyland and Sudan. This memorandum is to be included in the QSC annual report, published some two weeks after *As Used On the Famous Nelson Mandela* in July 2006. The QSC gave Mark Thomas permission to publish the memorandum prior to the committee's own report. On legal advice Ebury has decided not to publish the memorandum. The report can be found in full via the Quadripartite Select Committee (http://www.parliament.uk/parliamentary_committees /quad.cfm).

THANKS TO THE FOLLOWING:

Geoff Atkinson, Susan Foulis and the Baby, Cree Jones, Henry, Katherine, Urszula, Kelly, Will, Sally Freeman, Tom Bower, Fisheye, Peekay, Plucker, Rochelle Harris and Kerim Yildiz at the Kurdish Human Rights Project, Baggy, Bobby Kool, Winja, Brinley Salzmann, Steve, Kim, Alice and Kate at Amnesty, Campaign Against the Arms Trade and Ann Feltham, DISARM DSEI, Rob Evans, Peter Wilby, Anthony Phillips, techies at Warwick Art Centre, Krysta in Glasgow, techies at Cheltenham Arts Centre, Noel McHale, Jo Moon and Paul Jackson, Amber and Carrie at Vera, Em, Richard Norton Taylor, Roger Berry, Jonathan Paterson, Wendy and Gina, TAPOL and Paul Barber and Kev Mullin, John Kampfner, Collin Jennings, Doug Nunn, Antonio Tricario and Luca Mann at the *Campagna per la riforma della Banca Mondiale*, Dr Sue Hawley and Larry and Sarah at the Corner House, Ross Denton, Roy Isbister and Archana Patel at Saferworld, Chris Martin, Jack Cheshire, Katherine Strauss, Martin Herring, Joe at AFRI, Amnesty Ireland and Jim, Neil Pepin, Kevin Sutcliffe, BASIC and Paul Ingrams. Dayna Winer, David Wilson, Steve Wright and Dave Webb. Seize the Day and Theo especially, Clive Stafford Smith. Peter Hirst. GRIP and Holger Anders, Geoff Leopard. Kate and Robert, Olwyn and Steve from Just ... Martin Hussein and Andrew Katzen.

Lord William Upper School: Jess, George, Maddie, Anna, Simon, Charlie, Paul, Ellie Mykayla, Tim, Chris, Ed, Sam, Robin, James, Kris, Phil, Eilise and Mel. Presentation School: Portlaoise, Barbara, Maeve, Margaret, Mary, Alison, Laura and Claire. Elisabeth Carter at Import Export Solutions. Alan Shiers. Tam and the Scottish Fire Brigade Union. Tess Kingham. Polisario: Breica and Brahim. Richard Stanforth.

Ruth Sheldon, the book's researcher, deserves a massive thank you for being patient as well as diligent.

Ollie at Oxfam – 'You the man' as the young folks say.

Extra special thanks to Bobby Trowman.

And to Nick Hildyard from Corner House – respect and awe to my beautiful skinny friend.

To the Men In Black (and women too) ... salute! ... without whom ...

Phew! And thanks to Hannah, Sarah and Ken at Ebury, and Mari. All of whom have done more than their fair share ...

Jenny, Izzy, Charlie: we can go on holiday now.